American Tensions

American Tensions

Literature of Identity and the Search for Social Justice

Stories, poems, and essays addressing
the most pressing issues of our time

Edited by William Reichard

Foreword by Ted Kooser,
United States Poet Laureate, 2004–2006

NEW VILLAGE PRESS
OAKLAND, CA

Published in the United States by
New Village Press
P.O. Box 3049
Oakland, CA 94609
(510) 420-1361
bookorders@newvillagepress.net
www.newvillagepress.net

New Village Press is a public-benefit, not-for-profit publishing venture of Architects/Designers/Planners for Social Responsibility.

Grateful acknowledgment is made to The Nathan Cummings Foundation, a funder of this publication.

In support of the Greenpress Initiative, New Village Press is committed to the preservation of endangered forests globally and advancing best practices within the book and paper industries. The printing papers used in this book are 80% recycled or recovered fiber, acid-free (Process Chlorine Free), and have been certified with both the Forest Stewardship Council (FSC) and the Sustainable Forestry Initiative (SFI). Printed by Malloy Incorporated of Ann Arbor.

ISBN-13 978-0-9815593-8-4

Publication Date: April 2011

Library of Congress Cataloging-in-Publication Data

American tensions : literature of identity and the search for social
justice : stories, poems, and essays addressing the most pressing issues
of our time / edited by William Reichard ; preface by Ted Kooser.
      p. cm.
   Summary: "American Tensions is an anthology of American poetry, short-fiction, and non-fiction that explores issues of identity, environmental justice, and social change in the United States. Comprised of pieces from 1980 to 2010, the work addresses the shifting perspectives and changing role of writing in the social justice field"—Provided by publisher.
   ISBN 978-0-9815593-8-4 (pbk. : alk. paper)
   1. Social problems—United States—Literary collections. 2. Social justice—United States—Literary collections. 3. Group identity—United States—Literary collections. I. Reichard, William, 1963–
   PS509.S5A64 2011
   810.8'0353–dc22   2011006166

Front cover collage, *Divers*, by Brooklyn artist Erica Harris
Cover design by Lynne Elizabeth
Interior design and composition by Leigh McLellan Design

Also By William Reichard

Sin Eater

This Brightness

How To

To Be Quietly Spoken

An Alchemy in the Bones

NOVELLA

Harmony

EDITED WORK

The Evening Crowd at Kirmser's:
A Gay Life in the 1940s
by Ricardo Brown

For all my teachers and all my students

Contents

SECTION TWO   **That Which Holds Us Together,
That Which Pulls Us Apart**   *111*

Acknowledgments

I'd like to thank the entire staff and board of the Higher Education Consortium for Urban Affairs, who made it possible for me to take a one semester professional leave to work on this anthology. Everyone there has been so supportive of the project since I first conceived of it, and their generosity, of time and thought, made the work possible. I owe a deep debt of gratitude to the three wonderful Teaching Assistants I've had the great pleasure of working with over the last ten years. Molly Van Avery has been my assistant and teaching partner for over three years, almost since the launch of Writing for Social Change. She's helped me develop the course, select and revise the reading list, and shared in the teaching, the successes, and the failures encountered inside and outside the classroom. To Molly, my heartfelt thanks and love. Christa Olson, who worked with me for five years, was my sounding board and advisor. She was there when I first had the notion to design the seminar, and through our shared office space and passion for literature, we spent many months discussing the course and its foundations. I'm forever grateful to her. Melinda Hobbs-Childs worked with me for two years, as the course was first taking shape and passing through the complex web of approvals from HECUA's member campuses. Melinda was there to celebrate with me when things went well, and to offer support when things fell apart. Her energy was invaluable to the development process. I'd also like to thank the students who have enrolled in Writing for Social Change, and in City Arts, the two seminars I teach for HECUA. Their questions and observations are what powered me through this process, and their feedback on various pieces of work has been invaluable. Heartfelt thanks to my partner, James Cihlar, who listened to me as I talked this book into being, and who consoled me when things took unexpected turns. His loving support means everything. Thanks to all of the writers and publishers who gave me permission to use their work, and to my friends and colleagues who gave me feedback and input throughout the editorial process. Finally, I want to thank Lynne Elizabeth, Stefania De Petris, and everyone at New Village Press. When I first sent my proposal to Lynne, she responded by calling it "delicious." What an inspiring word! It kept me going while I selected work, finetuned the project, and brought it to fruition. Without the support of Lynne and New Village Press, this book wouldn't exist.

Foreword

Ted Kooser, United States Poet Laureate, 2004–2006

I discovered the value of anthologies quite early in life. In the little house in Ames, Iowa, in which I spent my childhood were two built-in bookshelves, tucked into either side of the hardwood archway between the living and dining rooms. With the assistance and insistence of The Book of the Month Club, as well as a subscription to the Reader's Digest Condensed Books, my parents had assembled a small library, and in their collection, which contained among other books a collected plays of Shakespeare, a collected stories of Balzac, and the complete works of John Fox, Jr., were two anthologies edited by John Beecroft and Thomas Costain, Stories to Remember and More Stories to Remember.

I can't recall whether as a little boy it had yet occurred to me that life might be full of altogether forgettable stories, but I remember appreciating and being impressed by the fact that these two editors had read through a whole lot of stories—hundreds maybe, maybe thousands—reading all day and long into the night—to pick out the ones that were worth remembering, ones that they wanted to share with me, with my family, the *best* of what they'd found.

From my teachers at Beardshear Elementary I had gathered that there were stories and then there was literature, and that there was an important difference. It seemed that stories were just stories but literature was writing that lasted, writing worth remembering for a long while. A story all by itself, in a book or a magazine, might not qualify as literature, but by being selected for inclusion in an anthology it *became* literature or at least had a pretty good shot at it. And I was glad that somebody else had had to pore over all those other, lesser, duller stories to find the really good ones that might last.

Long ago, my parents' collection of books got shelved in the past, volume by volume, disappearing one at a time, but shortly after my 70th birthday I happened to find, in a Goodwill store, for fifty cents each, nice copies of both volumes, *Stories to Remember* and *More Stories to Remember*, and I have been reading through them again. They were deemed lasting literature when I was a child and I believe they are literature still. It's wonderful to read the books you read as a child, and I heartily recommend it.

The best anthologies, like the one you've got in your hands right now, are full of wise, deeply felt writing that one reads with an intimation of eternity, as if one were looking up into the stars. For a person to come upon something in a magazine or literary journal is one thing, but for a discerning reader like Bill Reichard to discover a story or poem or essay worth setting afloat on eternity, and then, with friendship and generosity and a sense of community to enthusiastically present it to someone else, to hundreds of others, well, that's a very fine and public-spirited thing to do. It isn't just being good writing that makes a work last for years and years, it's being good writing that has found enthusiastic and respected advocates, people like Bill Reichard.

I have collected books all my life, possibly because we owned so few of them when I was small, and always I've wanted more. I have a library of perhaps eight or nine thousand volumes, and have read only a fifth of those. For every five books I buy, I manage to get one read. Yet I keep buying. If I were to read one book a day I couldn't live long enough to get to the end of my library. I need an anthologist, or a team of anthologists, who will read all those books and tell me which of them I ought to remember, to tell me what among them is the very best.

But since I don't have that kind of help, and can't possibly read all those books, I find myself turning to the anthologies among them, *The Best* of this and that, *Stories to Remember, More Stories to Remember, Chief Modern Poets of England and America*, and now, *American Tensions*. Anthologies are the best way for any of us to get to the best. And here in your hands is a generous portion of the best contemporary writing about contemporary issues, about *our* issues, discovered, compiled and presented to us with generosity and enthusiasm. The introduction speaks to its themes and I needn't do that here. I just want to say that this book is a gift made to last. It deserves a place in any fine library, or in a small family library wedged between living and dining rooms.

Introduction

William Reichard

I grew up believing the myth that the United States is a great leveler, a place where every person has the same rights, is treated equitably and fairly, and where opportunity is equally available for everyone—the delightful mix of all our differences thrown together to create a people not separated by differences, but bound by similarities. It's a nice story. For those not born into the mythical state of what an American is *supposed* to be (white, straight, male, financially comfortable, Protestant), however, it's only a story, and one concocted by the very people who believe themselves to be the epitome of this state, the perfect Americans, those who will do anything to preserve their own sense of power and entitlement. In truth, who Americans are is a messy, fractious web of cultures, myths, relationships, and races.

People who read like to untangle knots, to resolve complications. People who read like puzzles that ask them to consider how each piece sits in relation to the next, and how the individual pieces relate to the whole. Over the years, as a student and a teacher, I've encountered anthologies at every turn. Some have been particularly enlightening. I still remember the *Introduction to Literature* anthology required for my first class, my first year of college. That single volume introduced me to authors and works that I still read and often teach today. Sophocles' *Oedipus Cycle*, for instance. Plays that were, in the time of their creation, part of a complex religious ceremony. Stories that resonated with the ancient Greeks because they spoke of characters trapped in a powerful game being played by the gods, characters that could only do what fate had dictated for them from the moment of their birth. When I read or teach these plays now, I explore the urges that drive each of us, the role that notions of sin or guilt play in shaping our lives, and especially the way that every citizen is faced, at one time or another, with a crisis of allegiance, whether to follow the dictates of one's heart, the pull of family ties, or follow the law of the land, even when it flies in the face of what one knows, in one's heart, to be true. Antigone, in a contemporary context, is a perfect example of this struggle, choosing to defy state law and bury her dead brother, and thus forfeit her life, rather than follow a royal dictate that's issued in order to preserve civil peace. All of those years ago, and that anthology, those remarkable plays, still resonate with me.

The same anthology contained a powerful short story about the slow disintegration of a marriage, one partner hanging onto a past that is no longer possible, while the other seeks out a future that will, inevitably, pull her way from her husband and the world she's always known. The story is "Shiloh" by Bobbie Ann Mason. As a freshman from a small town, the first in my family to attend college, the first to choose a life outside of the factories and farms that employed most of my family, I was transformed by this story. There I was, barely eighteen years old, raised in working class poverty, sitting in a classroom at one of the largest research universities in the country. I wasn't in a crumbling marriage, yet "Shiloh" spoke to me about the power of personal choices, changes I knew I would undergo, and the unavoidable truth that my experiences would take me away from the world I'd always known, and, in a sense, pull me forever away from my family. "Shiloh" still affects me deeply, and it's in the anthology you now hold. I pass it on so that you may find its power within the context of your own life.

Some anthologies were built to obscure, whether by purposeful erasure or willful ignorance, the full context of the creative work itself, the racial, ethnic, religious, gender and sexuality-based identity of the authors. One popular school of literary criticism would have us read each work without context, and judge the work on its own merit. This isn't a bad way to approach a piece of writing, but it's only part of the work of reading and fairly judging what we've read. In order to reach a fully informed understanding of a story (or poem, or essay, etc.), the many threads that form the knotted string must teased out into their separate strands. Here is where what many have come to call "multicultural" anthologies come into play. These are collections that strive to present work with the cultural, social, political, sexual, and racial contexts of the authors included. The 1980s and '90s saw an explosion of such collections—African-American fiction, Asian-American plays, queer poetry, working-class narratives—it's an enormous and admirable list.

While in graduate school, I was often assigned to teach sections of a course titled The Literature of American Minorities. At first glance, this seemed like a great course, a chance to expose students to authors they'd never read, authors whose names weren't familiar because they hadn't yet migrated into our national canon. No "dead white guys" in this course! I made full use of the myriad anthologies available. I assembled photocopied packets of work that wasn't anthologized, some that had only seen print in small journals and magazines. The course exposed students to minority writers, teaching them, through the voices of those who knew best, what it meant to be essentially different in the U.S. Still, this didn't seem to take things far enough. While the identity-based anthologies provided a venue through which under-appreciated and relatively unknown authors could speak, they still kept these writers from being understood within the full context of what it means to be an American writer. They relegated such authors to a literary ghetto, thus protecting the traditional canon from infiltration. Although they were a step in the right direction, such books also had the potential to be literary and cultural dead ends, a place where any writer who didn't fit the narrow confines of what had defined writers of "quality" literature could be safely contained, very separate and not very equal.

It's been many years since I believed in such simplified categorization. I still have the books I used in those courses, and I take them out when I'm looking for a particular story or poem or essay that's exquisitely written and address issues related to social justice. I strive to read these works, and teach with them, within the full context of their making. I want to know who wrote them, and when, and where. To ignore this aspect of any work is to engage in a form of injustice, because it strips the work of its history, and reduces the richness and complexity each work possesses. I work to understand the historical framework of their making, those worldly matters that, on the surface, appear to exist beyond the concerns of literature and literary studies. I teach my students to look for the whole story, the bigger picture, and help them to realize that art and literature do not exist in a bubble.

The silos we've constructed to discretely contain each part of our society, our culture, our educational system, are merely concepts. All educational disciplines are related. Science and math can inform our understanding of art and literature; literature can give a more subtle and complex understanding of the raw statistical data gathered in the social sciences. Theatre and its history are inextricably linked to religious studies, to the grand scale of the development of contemporary religious rites. All cultural work carries encoded within it the specific contexts of its maker, and thus provides a very focused picture of one moment in one time, yet this same work also exists and functions within the culture as a whole. Successful work provides any reader a mirror into her own life, a life that might be very different from that of the author, but one linked by the emotions and narratives and constructs of the piece. Sophocles understood human nature, and his writing still accurately shines a light on it. Shakespeare understood longing and love, and his words still powerfully evoke these same emotions for contemporary readers. Zora Neale Hurston knew how to gather stories from an oral tradition, then craft them into masterful narratives, and her work still stands as an example of what great literature can and must convey.

In *Firebird*, Mark Doty's honest and searing memoir about his early years, he tries to come to a better understanding of the "story" he's created of his own life. "We live the stories we tell; the stories we don't tell live us. What you don't allow yourself to know controls and determines; whatever's held to the light 'can be changed'—not the facts, of course, but how we understand them, how we live with them. Everyone will be filled by grief, distorted by sorrow; that's the nature of being a daughter or a son, as our parents are also. What matters is what we learn to make of what happens to us." Each of the authors in this anthology have learned, first simply by living, and then through the constant honing of their craft, how to tell their own stories, how to make something meaningful from experience. What sets their writing apart from the stories we each construct about our own daily lives is the skill and the originality with which they convey lived experiences. Their ability, as writers, is to make their stories about something more than themselves, to bear witness, albeit often on a very personal level, to the making of what we will come to call history, even as this history is unfolding. Writers capture something of the zeitgeist in which they live. Because human nature doesn't seem, on a basic level, to change much over the millennia, they're also capturing stories, experiences, and observations that transcend time.

American Tensions is based on the longstanding tradition of using literature as a tool for social critique, as a means of calling for social change and justice, and as a tool for social transformation. This anthology brings together literature that addresses issues of race, class, gender, sexual identity, and a variety of social inequalities. It uses poetry, short fiction, and essays to delve deeply into these issues, to put a human face on what otherwise can become an abstract set of statistics, names and historical facts.

The anthology's title, *American Tensions*, grew out my search for the perfect word to describe what I wanted to bring together in this volume, and why it makes sense to do so at this time. A friend suggested I look up the word *tensegrity*, an architectural term coined by R. Buckminster Fuller from a contraction of 'tensional integrity.' As Fuller describes it, "a *Tensegrity* provides the ability to yield increasingly without ultimately breaking or coming asunder." "The world is a harmony of tensions," wrote Heraclites of Ephesus, and he might have been describing one of the primary energies that holds the United States together. There are so many competing interests, economic and social philosophies, which constitute this collage of a nation. Sometimes it feels as if Yeats was describing the United States when he wrote, in *The Second Coming*, "...things fall apart, the center will not hold..." Yet, our center does hold. The basic structure of the nation is dynamic and strong. I don't mean to imply that things here are perfect. I've created this anthology because they are *not*, and because I believe that the work included here can teach us about some of the causes of the injustice that is endemic in our society, about all that remains out of balance. *American Tensions* is about that which holds us together, and that which pulls us apart, not a negation, but an acknowledgement of the simultaneously tough yet fragile nature of identity in the United States.

I've created this anthology because it's both timely and timeless. The ideas of social change and social justice have, since the 2008 election of Barak Obama, taken on an almost frenzied presence in American society. They fuel hope to a new generation of voters, and have reenergized the progressive social base. What seemed impossible for the last eight years—the end of a war, universal healthcare, etc.—now seems possible, even in the face of the current economic downturn. The "Millenial Generation" now coming into its own, and the X, Y, and Z's that preceded it, seems to approach life with a confidence and deep-seated belief in the necessity of social justice. Peace and Justice Study programs are growing rapidly on college campuses across the country. There is a renewed interest in what it means to be a citizen in a democracy, and a growing sense that the simple, binary history lessons most of us learned as children are much more complicated than we'd previously thought. A new base of voters, activists, academics, and politicians has been set in motion, and they're hungry for information, ideas, and a means of integrating areas of thought and philosophy that have previously been segregated.

American Tensions challenges the conventional framework used to construct most identity-based anthologies in terms of the work it features, the issues it addresses, and its intention to break down walls that have long separated popular and academic traditions. It would be more accurate to say that this anthology is constructed around a framework of intersections. In some of the writings in this collection, family, class, and race overlap. In others, American identity is seen as a collage of multiple selves—public and private, ethnic and gender-based, homo- and heterosexual. The possible combinations are endless, and so this anthology is built around selected timely issues that unite us and are common across a variety of identity-based lines.

I have assembled here a wide cross-section of American literature written between 1980 and the present, works that address one or more social issues, and varied in the manner in which each addresses issues. All of the work selected has a sense of subtlety, an approach which is not pedantic, but offers readers a sense of discovery, a moment when they feel they've come to understand the author's deeper intention. Work that is too obviously "about" an issue, a work too preachy, doesn't allow the reader to experience personal insight. One of the great rewards of reading is that sense of discovery, of having traveled with the author to some new place in the world and the imagination, that sense of empathy and connection that a good piece of writing will elicit.

Collected in these pages, is the work of some of our greatest living writers, as well as work by mid-career writers, emerging authors, and some only just beginning their careers. In the case of poets, I've included a sampling of each writer's work, to give the reader a sense of the voice and style of each author.

American Tensions is divided into three sections. Section One: The Lives We're Given, The Lives We Make, focuses on economic, social and cultural class in America, on issues of race as they relate to class and family, and on the shifting dynamics and structures in the contemporary American family. It features authors from a wide spectrum of ethnic and socio-economic groups, and sheds light on what *class* and *family* mean at this moment in the U.S. The work here refuses the notion that American society is without class, that democracy alone can level the playing field. Each author offers a unique view of the *idea* of the family, proving that what works for one individual or family unit does not necessarily work for another. These stories, poems, and essays move beyond the concept that a family consisting of a mother, father, and one or more children. They show that "family" is a word with many meanings, and family structures are malleable, and largely self-defined by the individuals within them. There are the families of birth, families created with partners and children, and families built of a community of loved ones. Most inhabit more than one of these family units, and these units often combine in a fluid and dynamic way.

Louise Erdrich's short story, "Future Home of the Living God," for instance, follows a young Native American woman, adopted as an infant by a middle-class white couple, who becomes pregnant and in need of medical information about her birth family. This need sends her on a quest that brings together her seemingly disparate worlds. "Good to Go," a short story by Jonis Agee, follows a working-class family involved with NASCAR racing, and reveals the tensions that threaten to break apart a "traditional" family. J. C. Hallman's "Manikin" examines the effect of a disintegrating marriage on the children in the family, and shows us to what lengths a child will go to find some sense of security when his world begins to collapse. Poet B. H. Fairchild's poems bring to light the beauty and struggle found within the lives of factory workers, while the excerpt from Patricia Hampl's memoir, "The Florist's Daughter," examines what happens when a family tries to shift from working class to middle class status. Nick Flynn's poems delve into the effects of an alcoholic parent on the life of his child. The work here is meant to both challenge the notion of family, and to reveal the beauty and security that can be found when two or more individuals make a conscious decision to share their lives.

Section Two: That Which Holds Us Together, That Which Pulls Us Apart, features work that speaks directly to the *idea* of America, work that explores the oftentimes slippery definitions of what it means to be American, and who gets to define what it means to be *loyal*, to be a *hero*, a *patriot*, or a *traitor*. The work in this section attempts to tease out and overcome the harrowing power of rhetoric in a country that was founded, in part, on notions of democracy, self-determination, freedom, and basic human dignity. In this section is work that examines the idea, or perhaps the *ideal*, of America, as well as the realities, the bare facts that are often obscured by revisionist history and outright myth. Most Americans were taught a somewhat shallow, sometimes cartoon-like version of the country's history. The complications, contradictions, and outright lies that were also a part of that history were left out of most of the K-12 lesson plans. For instance, Americans were taught that Abraham Lincoln freed the slaves, and indeed, he did sign the Emancipation Proclamation. What is less well known is that he also signed an execution order that resulted in the largest mass hanging in United States history. Thirty-eight Native American men were hanged in Mankato, Minnesota, on December 26, 1862—men who were fighting for their own nation's sovereignty and for the rights they were given in a string of broken treaties with the U. S. government.

An excerpt from Diane Wilson's memoir, "Spirit Car: Journey to a Dakota Past," sheds light on this incident, and on the awful impact of white culture and government on the lives and cultures of Native people. Heid Erdrich's poems take on this same culture clash, and employ humor and a sharp wit in examining how white society has appropriated Native traditions and artifacts. Yusef Komunyakaa's long poem, "Autobiography of My Alter Ego," excerpted here, looks at the intersections of African American identity and contemporary American history. Elizabeth Alexander and Philip Bryant use their poetry to reflect on earlier eras, as a means of examining their own contemporary experiences. Adrienne Rich, in an excerpt from "An Atlas of the Difficult World," asks tough questions about what it means to be a loyal American in this era of war. Brian Turner, a poet and a soldier, uses his work to examine similar questions, but from the perspective of the battlefield. Marvin Bell tackles the topics of loyalty and allegiance in his work, while Scott Hightower focuses in on 9/11 as a means of shedding light to that particular tragedy and on contemporary American mores. Other work in this section looks at what it means to be a person of color in the United States, the experiences of LGBT people in a homophobic society, and who and what defines "disability" within the culture at large.

Section Three: Landscape with Figures: Human Experience in the Natural World features work that telescopes out from individual experience, and takes as its focus the place of humans within the larger, natural world. This section also features work that focuses on the contemporary environmental movement, global warming, and green living. My goal, in gathering the work featured here, was to bring multiple perspectives to bear on issues that, in a very real way, are a matter of life and death. Every day, we hear reports on the impact of greenhouse gases on the Polar ice caps. We see images of polar bears and other cold weather animals starving as their environment is destroyed by our human habits. We read about the destruction of the rain forests, those beautiful and enormous oxygen-producing engines. What becomes clear is that we, as a species, are quickly moving every single living thing toward the brink of annihilation.

Many think of "nature writing" as something lovely, lyrical, that speaks poetically about trees and clouds and a peaceable kingdom. The writers featured here do, in fact, speak about trees and clouds and the animal kingdom, and they're not short on the beauty and lyricism, either. However, the work here is complicated. Deborah Keenan's poetry is beautiful, but possesses a sense of gravitas. Bill McKibben's essay, "Designer Genes," is at once witty and terrifying, as it explores the quickly expanding boundaries of genetic manipulation. Linda Hogan's poetry places the human experience squarely within the larger, natural world, and doesn't privilege homo sapiens over other forms of life, and Allison Hawthorne Deming's essay, "Culture, Biology, and Emergence," breaks down the differences between cultural and biological heritage. None of the work here lets anyone off easily. And, all of it celebrates, even in dark times, the potential of our world.

This anthology is full of threads and knots. If you enjoy discovering what connects each of us, the threads of experience and insight that translate across time, place, and culture, then you'll likely enjoy the work you encounter here. It may help to think of the world as a web—each knot in the thread is necessary to the integrity of the whole. The tensions that stretch each thread taut, that constantly threaten to break each connection, are also the tensions that hold our delicate web together and give it resiliency. The push and pull between one power and another, one voice and its opposite, and the freedom to engage in this ongoing process, is part of what defines American culture and identity. The push toward cultural homogeneity is balanced by the pull toward multiculturalism. While one person attempts to tease apart the knotted threads of contemporary America, another is there to tie them back together and create more. We've been engaged in this struggle since the founding of the United States and if we're to remain a free and democratic society, this process must never stop. Debate, dissent, and difference don't weaken us as a nation, they define us, and assure that the complex web of American identity retains its strength and vitality.

The Lives We're Given,
The Lives We Make

WHAT MAKES A "nuclear family"? Is it a husband, a wife, and 2.5 children, preferably a boy and a girl? Is it a solidly middle-class unit, probably white, living in an outer-ring suburb in a house that has at least as many bathrooms as bedrooms and a two (or three) car garage? How many such families do any of us know? Does this describe your family, or does it sound suspiciously like one that might be found in an old sit com or movie? While there's no doubt that such families exist, there's also no doubt that for the majority of Americans, this doesn't accurately describe reality. So what is a family? Perhaps, at the simplest level, a family is a group of people who love you, whom you love. This could be your mother, father, and siblings. It could be your husband or wife or partner. It could be your friends, your companion animals, and your community. The work in this section explores the fluid definition of family, and the ways that class, gender and ethnic identity help to shape this definition. Here you'll find blended families, couples without children, disintegrating marriages, sibling rivalry, and lost parents. You'll find work that delves into the lives of poverty—and working-class families, transgendered children, adopted children, and beloved grandparents. The work in this section explores how individual lives are shaped by cultural and socio-economic forces. It doesn't set out to prove that the middle-class, suburban family is a myth, but rather, to show us the lives of individuals and families who exist in the vast continuum between the real and the ideal.

Future Home of the Living God

Walking down the long sage-green corridor at Fairview Riverside Hospital in Minneapolis, on my way to a Class 2 Diagnostic Ultrasound, I promise you this: I'll be a good mother even though I've fucked up everything so far. I've been keeping track of you in my secondhand edition of the Mayo Clinic Guide to a Healthy Pregnancy, and so I am prepared. You will be ugly, but recognizably human. You've gone from tadpole to vaguely humanoid and lost your embryonic tail. Absorbed the webs between your toes and fingers and developed eyelids, ears, a tiny skeleton. Grown a 250,000-neuron-per-minute brain. I have paged past Spina Bifida, Down Syndrome, Trisomy 13. I know you're fine. You can already squint, frown, smile, hiccup, and perhaps are doing so as I slide my hand along the banisters that line the wall.

"God, they should call the uterus, just...*God*," I tell the slender nurse, who has the body of a ballet dancer and is probably Vietnamese. "Then they could say her *God* was filled with a baby, or her *God* had fibroids, or they had to do a *Goderectomy* on her—don't you think?"

"Excuse me, what did you say?"

"Don't you *think*?"

"Oh, you bet."

The perfect Minnesota Nice accent is surprising, coming from such an exotic and elegant person. She leans over the form with me. There are questions upon questions, all dealing with inherited conditions of the heart and liver, cancers, even addictive behaviors.

"I'm adopted," I say.

"Do ya know your biological parents?'

"My biological mother wrote me a letter about a year ago."

The exquisite nurse waits.

"We correspond," I say faintly, which is a minor fib, though I do still have a letter from her. One page, never answered.

"Wull, I guess you could ask her, anyways," she approves. "This information could really help your baby." She cradles my elbow. "Your name is beautiful. Cedar Hawk Songmaker. Where's you get that, your tribe?"

Most people notice my name. "Songmaker is an old British name."

"What about the Cedar? What about the Hawk?"

"My Indian name is Mary Potts," I tell her. She looks down at the sheet of paper again, musingly; her face has a permanently mysterious smile.

As Mary, I was removed from my Potts mother because of our mutual addiction to a substance she loved more than me. As Cedar, I am the adopted child of Minneapolis liberals, whom I disappoint. As for the letter from my Potts mother, I opened the envelope, read what it contained, said, *Fuck that*, crumpled it up, and threw it, then retrieved it. I know exactly where the letter is—at home.

"I will, I *will* ask her," I say forcefully as the nurse steers me into a darkened room.

"You got nice hair, anyways." She smooths it down my back.

After she helps me up onto the high tablelike bed from a portable stool, I feel exposed and shaky. Other women bring friends, maybe even a husband. But my friends are dead, or in jail. My parents are alienated from me and they don't even know, yet, that I am pregnant. I'm about to lose the job I've faked my credentials to get. Also, five months ago, I forgot to get the name of your father—a man I knew for one night.

I tuck my shirt up underneath my breasts. The doctor, tall and businesslike, unsmiling, shakes my hand. His palm is hard and dry. He sits on a stool next to the swivel chair just at my right thigh, where a technician, a sinewy blond woman, touches a keyboard and adjusts a computer screen.

"Let's get going," says the doctor.

The technician puts a dollop of clear gel on my skin and holds the probe like a fat pencil. I've read all about this thing and know the probe contains traducers that produce and receive sound. The machine is already producing sound waves at frequencies of 1 to 20 million cycles per second. Impossible of course to hear. Propped on my elbows, I watch as the computer interprets the signals bouncing off you.

"This will be cold," says the technician, and she pats my leg. I crane toward the screen. The technician moves the wand carefully, stopping twice. "There you are," she says as she discovers you. She rotates the traducer to one side of my stomach and keeps moving it. At first there is only the gray uterine blur, and then suddenly the screen goes charcoal and out of the murk your hand wavers. It is detailed, three dimensional, and I glimpse tiny wrinkles in your palm and wrinkle bracelets around your wrist before your hand disappears into the screen's fuzz. There is something about your hand, and I am upset for a moment. I want to get off the table. I want to say, *Enough, no more*, but at the same time I want to see you again.

"Can you tell the gender?" I ask. "Can you see me?"

But nobody in the room is listening to me, nobody hears. I see the arch of your spine, a tiny white snake, and again your hand flips open, pressing at the darkness. The technician touches out knee bones, an elbow. Then she goes through the thicket of your ribs. The heart, she says. I see the hollows of the chambers, gray mist, then the valves of your heart slapping up and down like a little man playing a drum. Your whole heart is on the screen and then the technician does something with the machine so that your blood is made of light moving in and out of your heart. The outflow is golden fire and the inflow is blue fire. I see the fire of life flickering all through your body.

I whisper, or sigh, and I want to cry out. The room yawns open. I have the sensation time has shifted, that we are in a directionless flow, as if this one room in the hospital has suddenly opened out into the universe.

"Can you do that again," I murmur, but the doctor is very intent now, pointing and nodding. There, he says, and the technician clicks something.

"Can you tell if I have a boy or a girl?" I ask, louder. But neither one answers. The technician is intent, focused utterly on what she sees. They are inside of your head now, peering up from beneath your jaw and then over into the structure of your brain, which I see as an icy swirl of motion held in a perfect circle of white ash. It looks to me as though your thoughts are arranging and rearranging already, and as I imagine this I also know that there is something wrong, something off. The atmosphere has changed; the doctor is silent. The picture is fixed. They are looking at it, and looking. They will not stop looking.

"Boy or girl?" My throat is suddenly scratchy and dry. I see nothing on the screen, now, just white marks. Then tiny black crosses. Still, they couldn't seem to take their eyes away until I cry out.

"What the fuck do I have?"

They both turn and I see that they are trying to think of what to say to me.

"We can't tell," says the doctor in a very careful voice. His eyes are wide and staring.

A crack opens deep inside, a dark place, and fear seeps into my heart. I am suddenly extremely calm.

"It's Down syndrome."

"No, no, I don't think so. Do you know your genetic..."

"She's adopted," says the nurse.

"What's wrong?" I ask them.

The doctor takes the hand of the frozen-looking technician and gently draws the wand away from my body. He is a kind man, I see now, an ordinary-looking man about my Songmaker father's age, with a square, worn face and gray eyes lighted in the screen's glow.

"I'm not sure," he says gently. "Do you know your biological parents? Can we get some information?"

I jump up while they are consulting, throw my shirt on and reel out of the hospital, wanting in the very worst way to get drunk, pop back a couple Ativans, chill. And when I wake up not be pregnant. My hands shake, rattling the car keys. Before I can even start the car, I have to open the door and bark. *That did not go well*, I say, pulling away from the hospital. *That did not go very well at all*. I suppose it is panic, tears stinging up behind my eyes, the feeling that I am a child again caught in giant trouble. I suppose it is these things that make me grip the wheel and decide I should answer that letter or, first, make that phone call.

My adoptive parents are Sera and Alan Songmaker. We are church mice in a wealthy neighborhood. My parents inherited money, but they made extravagant gestures for causes now defunct, choices they still laugh about over dinner, toasting the large, lost amounts with cheap bag wine. They are, the two of them, descended of those legendary robber barons who scalped the Minnesota earth of ancient forests, who scooped the copper out of Red Cliff mines, ravaged the iron range, and built rails and railroads that still trace the Dakotas like great Frankensteinian stitches. All of that accumulation petered out in Alan and Sera Songmaker. There is nothing left but the carriage house I grew up in, which was divided off from the great, old family mansion. That "perfectly proportioned Georgian beauty"—I've heard about it ad nauseam—was torn down and replaced by a tan brick sixteen-unit apartment building.

Alan's still bitter. When he sold the mansion in the city, it was to become a museum. But the administration changed and that new city government resold the building during the blighted 1970s, when everyone was moving to the suburbs. They stayed on to live near a wide green lake which has of late been invaded by exotic weeds and purple loosestrife and, in 1988, adopted me. During one of Sera's many self-invented ceremonies, which she put together from her eclectic readings on indigenous culture and Rudolf Steiner, we placed sacred tobacco all around our house and then smudged white candles with sage and stuck them in the ground and lighted them too. We ate bread, Jarlsberg cheese, I drank ginger beer, and my parents drank wine. In the shadow of the apartment complex, we curled on blankets in the grass and sang peace march songs until we fell asleep. That was before I fell from grace, before I made them unhappy, before I grew up. It is one of the best memories of my life.

I stop the car in the driveway, and my eyes blur again. Panic tears. It is a mistake to come here, and I know it. As I walk in the back door, I mean to tell my parents about you right away. But they are not home. I use the key they do not know I possess and I go into the kitchen, pour a glass of milk because I am supposed to drink milk. I drink it looking out the back window. In the backyard, Sera has planted the bursts of zinnias, daisies, lythrum, and digitalis. It is an unusually warm September, and a sweet breeze stirs the heavy weight of leaves in the hundred-year-old trees that line our alley.

I drag myself upstairs to my old room, open the suitcase into which I casually threw the letter. There it is, still crumpled in a shoe pocket.

I would like to meet her if possible...I have never forgot...the old lady is still living...me and my daughter Mary own the Superpumper now...hoping to hear

I smooth it out and bring it down to the kitchen. There is a phone number at the bottom, which I dial.

"Boozhoo?"

God, I think, they speak French.

"Bon jour," I say.

"H'lo?"

"Hello."

"Who's this?"

"I'm, ah, Mary Potts, originally. I got this letter from Mary Potts Senior about a year ago; she contacted me about the fact that she is my biological mother. Is this? I mean, you don't sound like Mary Potts Senior, but are you maybe—"

"Whatthefuck?"

"No, I mean, I've got a little sister—"

"MAAAAAHM! Some INSANE BITCH is on the phone who says you're her mom and wrote her last year."

Mumbling. A voice, *Gimme that.* A crackling thump as someone drops the receiver. A quavery voice saying, *Who's that, Sweetie?* Woman's voice. *Nobody!* First voice again. *Getthefuckawayfromme.* A raging scream that fades and ends abruptly in a crash—slamming door?

"Mary Potts Senior?" I ask the hollow breath on the other end.

"Speaking." A whisper. A croak as she clears her throat. "Yeah, it's me. The one that wrote you."

And I suddenly want to cry, my chest hurts, I can't breathe, I'm breaking. The only thing that could possibly overcome what I feel in right that moment is a simultaneous mad crazy anger that bubbles up in me and freezes my voice solid.

"By any chance, will you be in tomorrow?"

"In?"

"Home."

"I'm not doin' nothing."

"I am coming up there. I am going to visit you. I have to speak to you."

"Alright."

Who's that, Sweetie? Old lady voice. *Nobody!* she says again.

I ignore the awful prickling in my throat, the reaction to the second time she has said *nobody*.

"Who's that calling you sweetie?" I say.

"That's my name," says Mary Potts Senior. "They call me Sweetie."

"Oh."

Her voice is so humble, so hushed, so astonished, so afraid. I feel a sweep of something, maybe more rage, that makes me shaky, but it just comes out in cold, weirdly complicated, grammar.

"Well that's very fitting, I am sure, Sweetie. However, I think that I will just call you Mary Potts Senior, if that's all right."

"I'm not senior though. I'm almost senior, not quite. Grandma's still alive."

"Okay, Mary Potts Almost Senior. Now, might I ask for directions to your house?"

"Sure you might," says Mary Potts, or Sweetie, but then she doesn't say anything.

"Well?" I say, ice voice.

Sweetie gets a little sly now.

"You said you *might* ask. You asking?"

Now I feel a stab of what is probably instant hatred, because she is the one who wrote me and she is the one who asked me to contact her and she is the one who originally bore me from her body and then dumped me. But I can handle her petty manipulations.

"Just tell me," I say in a cool, neutral voice. "I'll be coming up from Minneapolis."

Later, I am about to leave the house, but then, my childhood training takes over. Always tell us where you're going to go! I leave a note for my parents. *Dear Sera and Alan, a.k.a. Mom and Dad. I am pregnant. I am driving up to see my biological mother because I need information. Your erstwhile daughter, Cedar.*

I get into my vintage Chevy Cavalier, the car that will not die. It is a dark, classic red with matching red squares set into the centers of the hubcaps. I love my car although it has no airbags and the shoulder belt is a weird rig that would probably strangle me if I stopped too fast. I pull onto the highway, which bears only slightly less traffic than usual, and travel north to my Potts reservation home. Always, on four-lane highways, I have this peculiar sensation, as though I am going backwards and forwards at the same time. The future could be pouring into the past, and it would be like this, my car the connecting bottleneck.

It comforts me to see things pass too swiftly to absorb. Just surface impressions linger. Pines, maples, roadside malls, insurance companies, and tattoo joints. Ditch weeds and the people entering or leaving their houses. Church billboards. ENDTIME AT LAST! GET READY TO RAPTURE! In one enormous, empty field stretching to the sky a sign is planted that reads FUTURE HOME OF THE LIVING GOD.

It's just a bare field, fallow and weedy, stretching to the pale horizon.

My head clears, and a few hours later I am on the reservation. I pass the Potts Superpumper without stopping, though I do slow up a little. *Well, there it is,* I think as it goes by, *my ancestral holding*—a lighted canopy.

I cross a bridge with a trickle of water underneath—qualifies just barely as a river. But no turn for a while. The left turn I do take leads past six houses. Five are neat and tidy, trimmed out and gardened, birdhoused, decorated with black plywood bears and moose or bent-over lady-butts with dotted bloomers. One yard is filled with amazing junk—three upended kid swimming pools of brilliant blue and pink plastic, a wild trampoline sprouting foam noodles, dead cars, stove-in boats getting patched I guess, heaped-up lawn mowers, and little rusted-out lawn tractors and barbecue grills. Dogs pop from the ditches here and there, at random, and pump themselves after the car, snapping harrowingly at the wheels. Finally, I come to a bridge and a big river. A real river. At last, one with moving water. And a left-hand turnoff right after with a promising road I know will end in a yellow house.

And there it is. I turn into the gravel drive out front of my birth family's yellow house—fairly new, three or four bedrooms. There is the inverted bathtub with a plastic statue of the Blessed Virgin, a wheelchair ramp and doghouse out front, the broken-down black van with purple detailing to one side, a brand-new pickup to the other side and the bent wooden, willow frame that must be the sweat lodge. And there, about the appropriate age, Mary Potts Almost Senior. She wields a garden hose, an unattached garden hose, and she is beating the crap out of a dusty couch cushion. She grins a sly, lopsided smile as I drive up, and gives the cushion a few finishing whacks.

Here is the woman who gave me life.

"Holeee...," she puts her arms out and comes over to the car. She is wearing a tight, black muscle shirt that shows pink bra straps, and a pair of flared black capris. Her shapely, bearlike body is all muscular fat, and she has a pretty face with neat features. She's so much prettier, and younger than I imagined. She has all of her teeth and shifty little merry black eyes. Her dark brown hair with red highlights painted in is fastened on top of her head in one of those plastic claw clips, a blue one, and she wears pearl earrings. They look like real pearls. I get out of the car.

We stand facing each other, completely awkward. This is not a hugging moment for me, and I don't know what to do about the tears filling the eyes of my birth mother.

"Pretty," I say, touching my ears. "Pretty earrings."

She sniffs and looks away, blinking.

I notice that she is chewing on a shoelace. She notices that I notice and says that she does that when she's trying to quit smoking. Then she starts smiling at me, a little, but with the shoelaces in her mouth this is very strange.

"You look like...," she says

"Who?"

"Never mind."

"Who? Really?"

"Well, me."

"I do not," I say instantly, without thinking, just a gut reaction. She looks down at her feet. Then she turns with a little shake of her topknot and walks away, which makes me notice that although she is built sort of thickly up and down, she has the perfectly flat hard butt of a much younger woman. As it is packed tightly into those black capri jeans I can't help but wish, for a moment, I'd inherited her ass. I'm so soft and round all over. When I do not follow my birth mother—I am actually just watching her ass move, as lots of people probably do—she looks over her shoulder, jerks her head at the house. I walk behind her, up the wheelchair ramp, through the little porch, in the front door. The house is thickly carpeted inside and smells of wild stuff—bark, maybe, or birdseed, or boiling berries—and cigarette smoke.

"You wanna smoke," she says, "I got a coffee can of sand outside for butts. I don't smoke in here, though."

Well, somebody does, I think.

I put my backpack and my laptop by the door and sit down at the table— speckled Formica. I watch while in silence she makes a strong pot of tea. She gives me a mug of the tea, sugared, and sits down across from me.

"You turned out nice," she says right off, then yells into the next room. "She turned out nice!"

"Who's in there?"

"Oh, your grandma. She's old, she had me when she was fifty-three, no lie, remember that. Use condoms until you're sixty, ha!"

"Hundred and a half," says a reedy little voice from around the corner. A tiny, brown, hunch-up little lady then wheels herself incrementally—she wheeling herself on carpet—around the corner.

"Here," says my birth mother, "Mary Potts the Very Senior."

"Pleazzzzzz," the little woman actually buzzes, or hisses, inching closer. I jump up and push her to the table.

"Mary Ignatia," says the grandma, nodding wisely as I park her. "Hundred and one."

"Everybody's driving me crazy," says my birth mother, to nobody. "And her"—she gestures at me—"she calls me Mary Potts Almost Senior. She thinks that's funny."

"I don't think it's funny," I say, "I just don't know what to call you. You're not Sweetie to me."

"Hehhehheh." The ancient grandma laughs, waving forward a cup of tea that Mary Almost Senior is pushing carefully across the table. I can't bear this and decide to get it over with. I lean forward and address my birth mother.

"Two things. First, why did you give me up? Second thing. I want to know about genetic illnesses."

Both of the women are quiet now, sipping tea and looking at the top of the table. My birth mother studies the freckles in the Formica like she is divining the future from their pattern. At last, she gives one of her sighs— I'm getting to know her sighs—and then she starts to cough. She's getting wound up to speak. After several false starts, she begins.

"It wasn't because I was that young," she says, "obviously." Big sigh again. Restart. "It was because...it was because...I was stupid. Not one day has gone by since then where I haven't thought. Have not thought about how stupid I was."

She just looks at me.

"Stupid," she says again, and nods. She curls and uncurls her fingers from the handle of the cup. "Took drugs. Not while I was pregnant. After. Fucked every jackass in sight. Just dumbass stupid," she whispers. "Not one day has gone by, though, when I have not thought about you."

Not one day? How about not one hour? I think. *I wanted you. I wanted you.*

"Well, you thought about me more than I thought about you," I say, shrugging.

Nobody talks after that. We're kind of deadlocked. Her tears dry up and we sit there in silence.

"You got a good family, yeah, rich as hell," she says, shaking herself up straight. "They sent me pictures for two years. Then I wrote and said no more, I can't take it."

"You couldn't take it?" I feel my eyes narrow, and this thing builds up in me, this thing I know well and which I say mantras and breathe deeply to avoid, this anger. It fizzes up like shook pop. *"You couldn't take it?"*

"I lost...," she begins.

"Lost what?"

But there is the sound of a motor roaring off outside and footsteps, fast clunking footsteps. The door behind me slams and I turn around to witness the dramatic entry of the Princess of the Damned—Little Mary.

"She's a Mary, too?" I can't believe it. "What? Have you no originality?"

I sound exactly like my father, Alan, but I don't care. Mary Potts Almost Senior shrugs at me, her face sad, as her non-adopted-out daughter stalks into the room on three-inch-heeled black boots, in ripped fishnets, too many piercings to list, and long hair with clipped pieces spiked purple. The spikes are comically drooping from the humidity, not bristling except for a wisp of bangs. Her eyes are surrounded neatly with red paint—Magic Marker? Sharpie? The pupils are black and luminous. She sways in the doorway, obviously high.

"Soooo," she says.

"This is your sister," says my birth mother, nodding at me. Her look is gentle. "The one I told you about last night."

"Oh, *nobody?*" Little Mary smiles at us, dreamily vicious. Her teeth look sharpened, could they be? Her incisors are a bit longer than her front cuspids, and very white against the black lipstick, like elegant fangs. She's pretty, like her mom, prettier than me, think, instantly doing that thing girls do. Who's prettier. I suppose sisters compare all of the time and right at this minute I am glad I didn't have a sister, ever before, in my life. I'm glad I didn't have this mother and this family, except maybe the grandma. I think of Alan and Sera and all that we share, and tears now do come into my eyes. I turn to my birth mother and I reach over. I take her fingers off the handle of the tea mug. I hold her fingers and then warmly grasp her whole hand in mine.

"It's all right, Sweetie. Really, it's all right," I say, with absolute sincerity. "Just looking at Little Mary I can tell what a good mother you would have been."

My sister Mary is sixteen and it turns out, after Mary leaves, and we really start to talk, it turns out that my Potts parent believes that, although she isn't doing very well in school, Little Mary has no drug habit —she does not abuse alcohol nor does she smoke. Sweetie actually shakes her head, marveling, and takes her shoelace out of her teeth.

"I know you meant your comment as sarcastic, you know, ironic, what have you. Good mom. I know I'm not the best mom. I know that. But Little Mary's really doing good. She's the only girl who doesn't fuck and do drugs in her whole class. She says that she's about to crack, though."

"And who can blame her." I swallow the urge to fall down on the floor and laugh.

After a while, Sweetie walks into the bathroom. All is silent. She does not come out. Then I hear her quietly talking, as if on a cell phone. Little Mary is sitting in front of the television and she does not acknowledge me. There is an odd smell emanating from her—more than that something wild I smelled the first time I entered the house. This time, it's a powerful feet smell, plus something slowly going rotten. Behind her, I notice, the door to her room is open. Through that doorway, I can see it—the sort of spec-

tacle you can't help gawking at, like a car accident. Only this is a stupefy-
ing dump. I stand there a moment, gaping at the mess, and then see that
Grandma's wheelchair is drawn up to the table and she's snoozing upright.
I walk past Little Mary and sit down to wait for Grandma to surface.

While she's sleeping, I watch her. I've never seen anybody this old.
Grandma Mary Ignatia has the softest skin, silkier than a baby's, and her
hands are little delicate curled claws. Her eyes are covered with thin mem-
branes of skin. I think perhaps she can see right through her lids, they're so
transparent. I do know, from before, that she can stare a long time at you
without blinking. She has not allowed anyone to cut her hair, I see, not for
a very long time. Maybe an entire hundred years. It is braided into one thin
white plait and wound into a bun. Her ears stick out a little as her hair is so
thin. A pair of white shell earrings hang off her earlobes, which are delicate
and soft as flower petals. Most remarkably, I notice when she happens to
yawn, she still seems to have most of her own teeth. Though they are darkened by time, her teeth are still strong.

Suddenly, she's looking at me, those bright eyes tack-sharp. Grandma
Mary Ignatia laughs, soft and breathy, when she sees she's startled me. She
has a very sweet, ancient type of laughter that comes out in panting gusts.
We laugh together and I ask about her teeth. She tells me that she had a
full French grandfather who counseled her on the importance of scrubbing
her teeth with a peeled willow twig. She takes a cracker from the table and
shows me how she chews and bites with the vigor of a young person. The
strength of her teeth, she says, is the key to her longevity.

"I am pregnant." I tell her quietly, so my newfound sister will not hear.
"Are there illnesses in the family? Genetic anomalies? Anything my baby
might inherit?"

At first, her expression does not change. I think perhaps my identity,
our place in time, the muddy river of reality, all of this is bundled in shadow.
But then she puts out her withered little paw and says, "We lose some."

"You lose some? What do you mean?"

Grandma Ignatia drops her head and sinks into a motionless and rigid
sleep. I wheel her into her room and help stand her up beside the little single
bed, then lower her slowly onto the mattress and lift her legs over and set
them gently down. Her little tan moccasins stick straight up. Her arms are
plucked brown chicken wings, soft and limp. I cover her with a bright quilt
made of all different versions of yellow calico—a golden cloud.

When I come back out, my little sister is again sitting in the TV glow. She
has on so much black eyeliner that her eyes smolder demonically into the
changing screen. I count her piercings—her ears have six or seven each—
her earrings look like twisted nails and screws. She has sprayed her bangs
straight up into a black woodpecker's crest. The rest of her long, thin hair—

permanented and bleached and colored with those purple highlights or bleached again and again—hangs down her back in a dead and crinkled curtain. She's made some changes to her outfit, though, added a pink bow to her hair. She's wearing an incongruously sexy baby-doll nightie, ankle socks, and white Mary Janes. The cuteness/evil contrast has an effect even creepier than when she was dressed in full Goth. She's sort of a nightmare kitten.

"Hey." I sit down next to her.

She maintains her stony pose.

"Hey," I say again, "what's up with you?"

"What's it look like?"

"I mean in general, what are you up to in a general way?"

She looks at me with black contempt, her eyes sizzle from their deep mask. Her lips part in a snarl and the pink bow in her hair bobs up and down like a sinister butterfly. She nods as she speaks, agreeing with herself.

"You're just a stinking slut. You suck, you imposter. You're not my sister, you're an STD. You're a piece of syphilis."

Her outfit keeps throwing me—cutie-pie vampire. But her hatred is simple. Predictable. I tear my gaze away and try to hold my own.

"You're suffering from misplaced self-disgust," I tell her. "Your feelings have nothing to do with me. I've never hurt you."

"And I heard you tell Grandma you're pregnant, but I can see it anyway," she sneers. "You're such a whore."

"Oh, really. How do you think my being pregnant makes me a whore?"

My heart is surging but I keep my voice calm. I've always found that the best way to deflect hostility is to ask questions. But Little Mary is like a politician, adept at not answering the question asked but sticking hard to her own agenda. She stays on the attack. There's a frilly white garter on her leg.

"You got adopted out and grew up rich and think you're smart as hell, but you had unprotected sex! Ooh!" She opens her painted eyes wide and screws up her mouth like a wooden doll's.

"You're possessed," I tell her and, embarrassingly, my voice squeaks. "Your brain's all cooked on meth."

"Oh yeah!" She cocks her fists. "Oh yeah! Let's go!"

But then she slumps down and in a typical display of sick emotional liability begins to cry. Fat tears swell from her eyes.

"Don't tell Daddy, don't tell Mom, okay?"

"I think they know. They live around you. They smell your room. I can smell it from here."

"Will you help me clean it, huh?"

I stare at her and my mouth drops open. It is so bizarre that I might be charmed, in a weird way, were it not for the room itself. That unnatural disaster. Still, I stand up and follow her as she makes her way to the open door.

Little Mary's room has the odor of rank socks, dried blood, spoiled cheese, girl sweat, and Secret. The room is knee deep in dirty clothes she's packed down and walked on—sort of a new conglomerate flooring. Within the stratified layers of clothing I can see potato and corn chip bags, cans of pop she hasn't even drunk dry. A tiny haze of baby flies circles one orange Sunkist. Stuff is balled up, pasted together with sparkle glue, thrown on the wall, smearing the windows. Spray-can confetti hangs off the fancy fanlight fixture, and thongs are every place I look. Pink glitter thongs, black ones, gold lamé, sequined, lace spiderweb, and zipper thongs, thongs with little devils on them. She's undressed by kicking them up onto the blades of the ceiling fan. The curtains are balled up around the cock-eyed rods and there's broken glass sifted over one entire corner.

"It's your mother's job to make you clean this," I say, feebly.

"Yeah, maybe," says Little Mary. "She read in a parenting magazine that it is best to pick your battles with teenagers and that a teen's room is her own personal space. But I'm"—her chin trembles and her painted mouth sags—"just don't know how...it's too much."

"I can't face your room," I tell her now, but I try to be kind. Obviously, she's suffering from some heritable mental instability and it's all come out in the feral state of this room. Thongs. Darkness. Chaos. While I'm thinking apocalyptic thoughts, Little Mary takes a deep, sobbing breath, and edges past me, into that ninth circle. I step back as the door to her room gently closes and I reel away and sit down on the couch. I move off the warm spot she's just vacated, thinking of an unseen thong. After a while, watching the nothingness go by on some teen TV channel, where there is a dating show sadly rerunning, I decide that I will leave a note for Sweetie. I get up, lift my bag, take out a pen, and find a scrap of paper on which to compose it. As I am writing the words *It was such a pleasure to finally meet you,* Sweetie comes out of the bathroom with her cell phone pressed up to her ear. She looks out the window and I follow her gaze. I see a vintage Volvo just like Alan and Sera's. Then, astounded, I see my adoptive parents get out of the Volvo. First Alan, then Sera. Without a word to me, Sweetie goes outside to meet them. They approach my birth mother, both with a hand out to shake.

They must have worried about me. They must have always known Sweetie, or been in touch. The explanation doesn't really matter right then, though, just the face that they are *here.*

From the picture window of the house, I can see them in the driveway, all together now, gesturing and talking, a phantasmagoria of parents—I don't understand it, but it's happening. Now they are actually walking toward the house together. I am at the center of some sort of vortex. I go dizzy. I hold the strap of my backpack in one hand, and now I lift my laptop in the other, and I slowly walk backwards, navigating through the living room, somehow, by subterranean memory, not bumping into anything, retreating. I put my hand behind me and there is a doorknob. I turn it, and I back into the room, Little Mary's room. I close the door and stare at it.

The reverse side of the door is pasted over with hand-drawn green Magic Marker hearts, a tragic-eyed Siouxie and the Banshees poster, an Alien Sex Fiend T-shirt, a thong with actual little silver spikes in it, held up by a tack, many German beer coasters, and what all else. Frills, those too. Bucketloads of frills—lots of candy-pink flounces and bows. I turn around. Little Mary is sitting on the mammoth pile of clothing that is probably her bed. We look at each other. Her eyeliner has run down her face in two tracks like the tears of a tragic clown. When she opens her mouth, I think that she might scream, or belt out a high C, anything but use a normal voice and speak to me as a normal person for the first time.

"You changed your mind? Oh, wow! I know it's a lot to ask," she says. "But this is, like, a big statement. Really nice of you. Thanks."

I look down. At my feet there is a box of black Hefty steel sacks, no doubt placed there by Sweetie as a subtle hint. I bend over, put my pack and computer where I hope I'll find them again, and pull the first plastic bag from the box.

Slowly, I stand up straight again. Outside the door, I hear the other door open, shuffling feet, voices.

"Let's put all of the colored dirty clothes in this one," I say, holding up the bag. "And the ones we need to bleach, the white stuff, in this one." I hand Little Mary a second black trash bag. Her pink bow bobs and sways again, sweet and strangely demure.

"Your look's kind of shocking, I like it," I tell her.

"Gothlolita," she says.

"Lolita? You read the book?"

"Wha...it's a look I got off a Web site."

"Huh."

She takes the bag and looks at me with something like grateful awe. I don't have to bend over yet. I can pick up one limp black piece of clothing, another, another, off piles at waist height, off hooks on the wall. I pray that as I do excavate ever deeper there are no used condoms or old puke or large insects in the pile that I see that I will have to peel up from the floor, layer by layer.

I hear them in the kitchen now, the two sets of parents clinking mugs and making tea, together, talking.

At my feet there is a powdering of Asian twelve-spotted lady beetles from last fall's infestation, but they are dead, and crumbled to dust. There are thongs like aggregate rock, glued into patterned bricks. I just heave those into the bag.

"So," says Little Mary, shaking out the quarter-moon cups of a 36A, "you got the name yet?"

"There's something wrong with my baby," I tell her. "They saw it on the ultrasound."

"Yeah?"

I'm all of a sudden light and dizzy. My vision is narrowing. Blackness and shadow are welling all around me.

"Mom lost two babies before she had me," says Little Mary. "That's why I'm spoiled. She told me last night that she thought losing the babies was punishment for giving you up."

"Is there a name for what they had?"

"It has 'thirteen' in it. Bad luck. She said that she promised to name me Mary, after you, if I lived."

"That makes sense." Nothing makes sense, and I sit down in the thickest litter, sensing the numb edge of the beginning of a feeling so powerful it has no name.

"Hey! You're not going to call your baby Mary, are you?"

I am slumping over the stuff on my lap.

"You got the name yet? Say if it's a girl?"

I hold up a swatch of red boy-leg lace and read the label.

"Victoria."

"Wow," says my little sister, "that's beautiful."

She leans over and puts her arms around me. As she holds me, we begin to sway back and forth. My sister is rocking me in her Gothlolita, boy-smelling, strangely comforting live-wire arms. She is wearing tattered gloves with the fingers cut off and frayed. Green chipped fingernail polish on her fingers. The scent of a harrowing musk—sulfurous sweet, distantly volcanic, a perfume that consoles and irritates me all at once so that I begin to cry, not with pity for myself, but with a sense that I have accidentally tampered with and entered some huge place. I do not know what giant lives in this vast and future home. I don't know whether the door opens in or opens out. I hold on to my sister just waiting for the hinge to creak.

B.H. Fairchild

Speaking the Names

When frost first enters the air
in the country of moon and stars,
the world has glass edges, and the hard glint
of crystals seeping over iron
makes even the abandoned tractor seem all night sky and starlight.

On the back porch taking deep breaths like some miracle cure,
breathe, let the spirit move you,
here I am after the long line of cigarettes
that follows grief like a curse, trying to breathe, revive,
in this land of revivals and lost farms...

It is no good to grow up hating the rich.
In spring I would lie down among pale anemone and primrose
and listen to the river's darkening hymn, and soon
the clouds were unraveling like the frayed sleeves of field hands,
and ideology had flown with the sparrows.

The cottonwood that sheltered the hen house is a stump now,
and the hackberries on the north were leveled years ago.
Bluestem hides the cellar, with its sweet gloom of clay walls and bottles.
The silo looms over the barn, whose huge door swallowed daylight,
where a child could enter his own death.

What became of the boy with nine fingers?
The midwife from Yellow Horse who raised geese?
They turned their backs on the hard life,
and from the tree line along the river they seem to rise now,
her plain dress bronze in moonlight, his wheatshock hair in flames.

Behind me is a house without people. And so, for my sake
I bring them back, watching the quick cloud of vapor that blooms
and vanishes with each syllable: *O.T.* and *Nellie Swearingen,*
their children, *Locie, Dorrel, Deanie, Bill,* and the late *Vinna Adams,*
whose name I speak into the bright and final air.

The Machinist, Teaching His Daughter to Play the Piano

The brown wrist and hand with its raw knuckles and blue nails
       packed with dirt and oil, pause in mid-air,
the fingers arched delicately,

and she mimics him, hand held just so, the wrist loose,
       then swooping down to the wrong chord.
She lifts her hand and tries again.

Drill collars rumble, hammering the nubbin-posts.
       The helper lifts one, turning it slowly,
then lugs it into the lathe's chuck.

The bit shears the dull iron into new metal, falling
       into the steady chant of lathe work,
and the machinist lights a cigarette, holding

in his upturned palms the polonaise he learned at ten,
       then later the easiest waltzes,
etudes, impossible counterpoint

like the voice of his daughter he overhears one night
       standing in the backyard. She is speaking
to herself but not herself, as in prayer,

the listener is some version of herself,
       and the names are pronounced carefully,
self-consciously: Chopin, Mozart,

Scarlatti, ... these gestures of voice and hands
       suspended over the keyboard
that move like the lathe in its turning

toward music, the wind dragging the hoist chain, the ring
       of iron on iron in the holding rack.
His daughter speaks to him one night,

but not to him, rather someone created between them,
       a listener, there and not there,
a master of lathes, a student of music.

Work

Work is a transient form of mechanical energy by means
of which certain transformations of other forms of energy
are brought about through the agency of a force acting
through a distance...Work done by lifting a body stores
mechanical potential energy in the system consisting of
the body and the earth. Work done on a body to set it in
motion stores mechanical kinetic energy in the system
of which the body is one part.
　　　　　——HANDBOOK OF ENGINEERING FUNDAMENTALS

1. *Work*

Drill collars lie on racks and howl
in the blunt wind. A winch truck waits
in the shop yard beside an iron block,
hook and cable coiling down, dragging
through dirt that blows in yellow gusts.

East across a field where the slag sky
of morning bends down, a man walks away
from a white frame house and a woman
who shouts and waves from the back porch.
He can hear the shop doors banging open.

Inside, where the gray light lifts dust
in swirls, tools rest like bodies dull
with sleep, lead-heavy. The lathe
starts its dark groan, the chuck's jaw
gripping an iron round, the bit set.

Outside, the man approaches the iron block,
a rotary table, judging its weight,
the jerk and pull on the hoist chain.
A bad sun heaves the shadow of his house
outward. He bends down. A day begins.

II. *The Body*

Looping the chain through the block's eyes,
he makes a knot and pulls the cable hook through.
The winch motor starts up, reeling in cable slowly

until it tightens, then drops to a lower gear
and begins to lift. The motor's whine brings
machinists to the shop windows, sends sparrows

fluttering from high-wired where the plains wind
gives its thin moan and sigh. When the brake
is thrown, the block jerks and sways five feet

above the earth, straining to return, popping
a loose cable thread and making the gin poles
screech in their sockets like grief-stricken women.

From the house the man is lost in the blaze of a sun
gorged to bursting and mirrored in the shop's
tin side. The block hangs, black in the red air.

III. *The Body and the Earth*

Beneath the rotary table the man reaches up
to remove the huge bearings, and oil winds
down his arm like a black rope. He places
each bearing big as a pendulum in the sun

where it shines, swathed in grease.
It is the heart of the day, and he feels
the long breeze cool his face and forearms,
wet now with the good sweat of hard work.

The wind scrapes through stubble, making
a papery sound that reminds him of harvest:
him, his father, the field hands crowded around
a beer keg to celebrate the weeks cut, dirt

drying to mud on their damp faces, leaving
bruises and black masks. Now, kneeling
in the block's cool shadow, he watches clods
soak up the brow pools of oil and sweat.

IV. *The System of Which the Body Is One Part*

On the down side of the work day,
when the wind shifts and heat stuns the ground
like an iron brand, the machinists lean
into the shadow of the shop's eaves
and gulp ice water, watching the yard hand now

as he struggles in his black square
to slip each bearing back in place, each steel ball
that mirrors back his eyes, the stubble field, the shop,
the white frame house, the sun, and everything beyond,
the whole circumference of seen and unseen, the world

stretching away in its one last moment when the chain
makes that odd grunting noise, and sighs *click*, and then *click*,
and sings through the eyes of the block as it slams the ground
and the earth takes the thud and the men freeze
and the woman strolls out to see what has happened now
in the system of which the body is one part.

Keats

I knew him. He ran the lathe next to mine.
Perfectionist, a madman, even on overtime
Saturday night. Hum of the crowd floating
from the ball park, should, slamming doors
from the bar down the street, he would lean
into the lathe and make a little song
with the honing cloth, rubbing the edges,
smiling like a man asleep, dreaming.
A short guy, but fearless. At Margie's
he would take no lip, put the mechanic big
as a Buick through a stack of crates out back
and walked away with a broken thumb
but never said a word. Marge was a loud,
dirty girl with booze breath and bad manners.
He loved her. One night late I saw them in
the kitchen dancing something like a rhumba
to the radio, dishtowels wrapped around
their head like swamis. Their laughter chimed
rich as brass rivets rolling down a tin roof.
But it was the work that kept him out of fights,
and I remember the red hair flaming
beneath the lamp, calipers measuring out
the last cut, his hands flicking iron burrs
like shooting stars through the shadows.
It was the iron, cut to a perfect fit, smooth
as bone china and gleaming under lamplight
that made him stand back, take out a smoke,
and sing. It was the dust that got him, his lungs
collapsed from breathing in a life of work.
Lying there, his hands are what I can't forget.

Shiloh

Leroy Moffitt's wife, Norma Jean, is working on her pectorals. She lifts three-pound dumbbells to warm up, then progresses to a twenty-pound barbell. Standing with her legs apart, she reminds Leroy of Wonder Woman.

"I'd give anything if I could just get these muscles to where they're real hard," says Norma Jean. "Feel this arm. It's not as hard as the other one."

"That's 'cause you're right-handed," says Leroy, dodging as she swings the barbell in an arc.

"Do you think so?"

"Sure."

Leroy is a truck driver. He injured his leg in a highway accident four months ago, and his physical therapy, which involves weights and a pulley, prompted Norma Jean to try building herself up. Now she is attending a body-building class. Leroy has been collecting temporary disability since his tractor-trailer jackknifed in Missouri, badly twisting his left leg in its socket. He has a steel pin in his hip. He will probably not be able to drive his rig again. It sits in the backyard, like a gigantic bird that has flown home to roost. Leroy has been home in Kentucky for three months, and his leg is almost healed, but the accident frightened him and he does not want to drive anymore long hauls. He is not sure what to do next. In the meantime, he makes things from craft kits. He started by building a miniature log cabin from notched Popsicle sticks. He varnished it and placed it on the TV set, where it remains. It reminds him of a rustic Nativity scene. Then he tried string art (sailing ships on black velvet), a macramé owl kit, a snap-together B-17 Flying Fortress, and a lamp made out of a model truck, with a light fixture screwed in the top of the cab. At first the kits were diversions, something to kill time, but now he is thinking about building a full-scale log house from a kit. It would be considerably cheaper than building a regular house, and besides, Leroy has grown to appreciate how things are put together. He has begun to realize that in all the years he was on the road he never took time to examine anything. He was always flying past scenery.

"They won't let you build a log cabin in any of the new subdivisions," Norma Jean tells him.

"They will if I tell them it's for you," he says, teasing her. Ever since they were married, he has promised Norma Jean he would build her a new home one day. They have always rented, and the house they live in is small and nondescript. It does not even feel like a home, Leroy realizes now.

Norma Jean works at the Rexall drugstore, and she has acquired an amazing amount of information about cosmetics. When she explains to Leroy the three stages of complexion care, involving creams, toners, and moisturizers, he thinks happily of other petroleum products—axle grease, diesel fuel. This is a connection between him and Norma Jean. Since he has been home, he has felt unusually tender about his wife and guilty over his long absences. But he can't tell what she feels about him. Norma Jean has never complained about his traveling; she has never made hurt remarks, like calling his truck a "widow-maker." He is reasonably certain she has been faithful to him, but he wishes she would celebrate his permanent homecoming more happily. Norma Jean is often startled to find Leroy at home, and he thinks she seems a little disappointed about it. Perhaps he reminds her too much of the early days of their marriage, before he went on the road. They had a child who died as an infant, years ago. They never speak about their memories of Randy, which have almost faded, but now that Leroy is home all the time, they sometimes feel awkward around each other, and Leroy wonders if one of them should mention the child. He has the feeling that they are waking up out of a dream together—that they must create a new marriage, start afresh. They are lucky they are still married. Leroy has read that for most people losing a child destroys the marriage—or else he heard this on *Donohue*. He can't always remember where he learns things anymore.

At Christmas, Leroy bought an electric organ for Norma Jean. She used to play the piano when she was in high school. "It don't leave you," she told him once. "It's like riding a bicycle."

The new instrument had so many keys and buttons that she was bewildered by it at first. She touched the keys tentatively, pushed some buttons, then pecked out "Chopsticks." It came out in an amplified fox-trot rhythm, with marimba sounds.

"It's an orchestra!" she cried.

The organ had a pecan-look finish and eighteen preset chords, with optional flute, violin, trumpet, clarinet, and banjo accompaniments. Norma Jean mastered the organ almost immediately. At first she played Christmas songs. Then she bought *The Sixties Songbook* and learned every tune in it, adding variations to each with the rows of brightly colored buttons.

"I didn't like these old songs back then," she said. "But I have this crazy feeling I missed something."

"You didn't miss a thing," said Leroy.

Leroy likes to lie on the couch and smoke a joint and listen to Norma Jean play "Can't Take My Eyes Off You" and "I'll Be Back." He is back again. After fifteen years on the road, he is finally settling down with the woman he loves. She is still pretty. Her skin is flawless. Her frosted curls resemble pencil trimmings.

* * *

Now that Leroy has come home to stay, he notices how much the town has changed. Subdivisions are spreading across western Kentucky like an oil slick. The sign at the edge of town says "Pop: 11,500"—only seven hundred more than it said twenty years before. Leroy can't figure out who is living in all the new houses. The farmers who used to gather around the courthouse square on Saturday afternoons to play checkers and spit tobacco juice have gone. It has been years since Leroy has thought about the farmers, and they have disappeared without his noticing.

Leroy meets a kid named Stevie Hamilton in the parking lot at the new shopping center. While they pretend to be strangers meeting over a stalled car, Stevie tosses an ounce of marijuana under the front seat of Leroy's car. Stevie is wearing orange jogging shoes and a T-shirt that says CHATTAHOOCHEE SUPER-RAT. His father is a prominent doctor who lives in one of the expensive subdivisions in a new white-columned brick house that looks like a funeral parlor. In the phone book under his name there is a separate number, with the listing "Teenagers."

"Where do you get this stuff?" asks Leroy. "From your pappy?"

"That's for me to know and you to find out," Stevie says. He is slit-eyed and skinny.

"What else you got?"

"What you interested in?"

"Nothing special. Just wondered."

Leroy used to take speed on the road. Now he has to go slowly. He needs to be mellow. He leans back against the car and says, "I'm aiming to build me a log house, soon as I get time. My wife, though, I don't think she likes the idea."

"Well, let me know when you want me again," Stevie says. He has a cigarette in his cupped palm, as though sheltering it from the wind. He takes a long drag, then stomps it on the asphalt and slouches away.

Stevie's father was two years ahead of Leroy in high school. Leroy is thirty-four. He married Norma Jean when they were both eighteen, and their child Randy was born a few months later, but he died at the age of four months and three days. He would be about Stevie's age now. Norma Jean and Leroy were at the drive-in, watching a double feature (*Dr. Strangelove* and *Lover Come Back*), and the baby was sleeping in the back seat. When the first movie ended, the baby was dead. It was the sudden infant death syndrome. Leroy remembers handing Randy to a nurse at the emergency room, as though he were offering her a large doll as a present. A dead baby feels like a sack of flour. "It just happens sometimes," said the doctor, in what Leroy always recalls as a nonchalant tone. Leroy can hardly remember the child anymore, but he still sees vividly a scene from *Dr. Strangelove* in which the President of the United States was talking in a folksy voice on the hot line to the Soviet premier about the bomber accidentally headed toward Russia. He was in the War Room, and the world map was lit up. Leroy remembers Norma Jean standing catatonically beside him in the hospital and himself thinking: Who is this strange girl? He had forgotten who she was. Now scientists are saying that crib death is caused by a virus. Nobody knows anything, Leroy thinks. The answers are always changing.

When Leroy gets home from the shopping center, Norma Jean's mother, Mabel Beasley, is there. Until this year, Leroy has not realized how much time she spends with Norma Jean. When she visits, she inspects the closets and then the plants, informing Norma Jean when a plant is droopy or yellow. Mabel calls the plants "flowers," although there are never any blooms. She always notices if Norma Jean's laundry is piling up. Mabel is a short, overweight woman whose tight, brown-dyed curls look more like a wig than the actual wig she sometimes wears. Today she has brought Norma Jean an off-white dust ruffle she made for the bed; Mabel works in a custom-upholstery shop.

"This is the tenth one I made this year," Mabel says. "I got started and couldn't stop."

"It's real pretty," says Norma Jean.

"Now we can hide things under the bed," says Leroy, who gets along with his mother-in-law primarily by joking with her. Mabel has never really forgiven him for disgracing her by getting Norma Jean pregnant. When the baby died, she said that fate was mocking her.

"What's that thing?" Mabel says to Leroy in a loud voice, pointing to a tangle of yarn on a piece of canvas.

Leroy holds it up for Mabel to see. "It's my needlepoint," he explains. "This is a *Star Trek* pillow cover."

"That's what a woman would do," says Mabel. "Great day in the morning!"

"All the big football players on TV do it," he says.

"Why, Leroy, you're always trying to fool me. I don't believe you for one minute. You don't know what to do with yourself—that's the whole trouble. Sewing!"

"I'm aiming to build us a log house," says Leroy. "Soon as my plans come."

"Like *heck* you are," says Norma Jean. She takes Leroy's needlepoint and shoves it into a drawer. "You have to find a job first. Nobody can afford to build now anyway."

Mabel straightens her girdle and says, "I still think before you get tied down y'all ought to take a little run to Shiloh."

"One of these days, Mama," Norma Jean says impatiently.

Mabel is talking about Shiloh, Tennessee. For the past few years, she has been urging Leroy and Norma Jean to visit the Civil War battleground there. Mabel went there on her honeymoon—the only real trip she ever took. Her husband died of a perforated ulcer when Norma Jean was ten, but Mabel, who was accepted into the United Daughters of the Confederacy in 1975, is still preoccupied with going back to Shiloh.

"I've been to kingdom come and back in that truck out yonder," Leroy says to Mabel, "but we never yet set foot in that battleground. Ain't that something? How did I miss it?"

"It's not even that far," Mabel says.

After Mabel leaves, Norma Jean reads to Leroy from a list she has made. "Things you could do," she announces. "You could get a job as a guard at Union Carbide, where they'd let you set on a stool. You could get on at the lumberyard. You could do a little carpenter work, if you want to build so bad. You could—"

"I can't do something where I'd have to stand up all day."

"You ought to try standing up all day behind a cosmetics counter. It's amazing that I have strong feet, coming from two parents that never had strong feet at all." At the moment Norma Jean is holding on to the kitchen counter, raising her knees one at a time as she talks. She is wearing two-pound ankle weights.

"Don't worry ," says Leroy. "I'll do something."

"You could truck calves to slaughter for somebody. You wouldn't have to drive any big old truck for that."

"I'm going to build you this house," says Leroy. "I want to make you a real home."

"I don't want to live in any log cabin."

"It's not a cabin. It's a house."

"I don't care. It looks like a cabin."

"You and me together could lift those logs. It's just like lifting weights."

Norma Jean doesn't answer. Under her breath, she is counting. Now she is marching through the kitchen. She is doing goose steps.

* * *

Before his accident, when Leroy came home he used to stay in the house with Norma Jean, watching TV in bed and playing cards. She would cook fried chicken, picnic ham, chocolate pie—all his favorites. Now he is home alone much of the time. In the mornings, Norma Jean disappears, leaving a cooling place in the bed. She eats a cereal called Body Buddies, and she leaves the bowl on the table, with the soggy tan balls floating in a milk puddle. He sees things about Norma Jean that he never realized before. When she chops onions, she stares off into a corner, as if she can't bear to look. She puts on her house slippers almost precisely at nine o'clock every evening and nudges her jogging shoes under the couch. She saves bread heels for the birds. Leroy watches the birds at the feeder. He notices the peculiar way gold-finches fly past the window. They close their wings, then fall, then spread their wings to catch and lift themselves. He wonders if they close their eyes when they fall. Norma Jean closes her eyes when they are in bed. She wants the lights turned out. Even then, he is pretty sure she closes her eyes.

He goes for long drives around town. He tends to drive a car rather care-lessly. Power steering and an automatic shift make a car feel so small and inconsequential that his body is hardly involved in the driving process. His injured leg stretches out comfortably. Once or twice he has almost hit some-thing, but even the prospect of an accident seems minor in a car. He cruises the new subdivisions, feeling like a criminal rehearsing for a robbery, Norma Jean is probably right about a log house being inappropriate here in the new subdivisions. All the houses look grand and complicated. They depress him.

One day when Leroy comes home from a drive he finds Norma Jean in tears. She is in the kitchen making a potato and mushroom-soup casserole, with grated-cheese topping. She is crying because her mother caught her smoking.

"I didn't hear her coming. I was standing here puffing away pretty as you please," Norma Jean says, wiping her eyes.

"I knew it would happen sooner or later," Leroy says, putting his arm around her.

"She don't know the meaning of the word 'knock'," says Norma Jean. "It's a wonder she hadn't caught me years ago."

"Think of it this way," Leroy says. "What if she caught me with a joint?"

"You better not let her!" Norma Jean shrieks. "I'm warning you, Leroy Moffitt!"

"I'm just kidding. Here, play me a tune. That'll help you relax."

Norma Jean puts the casserole in the oven and sets the timer. Then she plays a ragtime tune, with horns and banjo, as Leroy lights up a joint and lies on the couch, laughing to himself about Mabel's catching him at it. He thinks of Stevie Hamilton—a doctor's son pushing grass. Everything is funny. The whole town seems crazy and small. He is reminded of Virgil Mathis, a boastful policeman Leroy used to shoot pool with. Virgil recently led a drug bust in a back room at a bowling alley, where he seized ten thousand dollars' worth of marijuana. The newspaper had a picture of him holding up the bags of grass and grinning widely. Right now, Leroy can imagine Virgil breaking down the door and arresting him with a lungful of smoke. Virgil would prob-ably have been alerted to the scene because of all the racket Norma Jean is making. Now she sounds like a hard-rock band. Norma Jean is terrific. When she switches to a Latin-rhythm version of "Sunshine Superman," Leroy hums along. Norma Jean's foot goes up and down, up and down.

"Well, what do you think?" Leroy says, when Norma Jean pauses to search through her music.

"What do I think about what?"

His mind has gone blank. Then he says, "I'll sell my rig and build us a house." That wasn't what he wanted to say. He wanted to know what she thought—what she *really* thought—about them.

"Don't start in on that again," says Norma Jean. She begins playing "Who'll Be the Next in Line?"

Leroy used to tell hitchhikers his whole life story—about his travels, his hometown, the baby. He would end with a question: "Well, what do you think?" It was just a rhetorical question. In time, he had the feeling that he'd been telling the same story over and over to the same hitchhikers. He quit talking to hitchhikers when he realized how his voice sounded—whining and self-pitying, like some teenage-tragedy song. Now Leroy has the sudden impulse to tell Norma Jean about himself, as if he had just met her. They have known each other so long they have forgotten a lot about each other. They could become reacquainted. But when the oven timer goes off and she runs to the kitchen, he forgets why he wants to do this.

* * *

The next day, Mabel drops by. It is Saturday and Norma Jean is cleaning. Leroy is studying the plans of his log house, which have finally come in the mail. He has them spread out on the table—big sheets of stiff blue paper, with diagrams and numbers printed in white. While Norma Jean runs the vacuum, Mabel drinks coffee. She sets her coffee cup on the blueprint.

"I'm just waiting for time to pass," she says to Leroy, drumming her fingers on the table.

As soon as Norma Jean switches off the vacuum, Mabel says in a loud voice, "Did you hear about the datsun dog that killed the baby?"

Norma Jean says, "The word is 'dachshund.'"

"They put the dog on trial. It chewed the baby's legs off. The mother was in the next room all the time." She raises her voice. "They thought it was neglect."

Norma Jean is holding her ears. Leroy manages to open the refrigerator and get some Diet Pepsi to offer Mabel. Mabel still has some coffee and she waves away the Pepsi.

"Datsuns are like that," Mabel says. "They're jealous dogs. They'll tear a place to pieces if you don't keep an eye on them."

"You better watch out what you're saying, Mabel," says Leroy.

"Well, facts is facts."

Leroy looks out the window at his rig. It is like a huge piece of furniture gathering dust in the backyard. Pretty soon it will be an antique. He hears the vacuum cleaner. Norma Jean seems to be cleaning the living room run again.

Later, she says to Leroy, "She just said that about the baby because she caught me smoking. She's trying to pay me back."

"What are you talking about?" Leroy says, nervously shifting the blueprints.

"You know good and well," Norma Jean says. She is sitting in a kitchen chair with her feet up and her arms wrapped around her knees. She looks small and helpless. She says, "The very idea, her bringing up a subject like that! Saying it was neglect."

"She didn't mean that," Leroy says.

"She might not have *thought* she meant it. She always says things like that. You don't know how she goes on."

"But she didn't really mean it. She was just talking."

Leroy opens a king-sized bottle of beer and pours it into two glasses, dividing it carefully. He hands a glass to Norma Jean and she takes it from him mechanically. For a long time, they sit by the kitchen window watching the birds at the feeder.

* * *

Something is happening. Norma Jean is going to night school. She has graduated from her six-week body-building course and now she is taking an adult-education course in composition at Paducah Community College. She spends her evenings outlining paragraphs.

"First you have a topic sentence," she explains to Leroy. "Then you divide it up. Your secondary topic has to be connected to your primary topic."

To Leroy, this sounds intimidating. "I never was any good in English," he says.

"It makes a lot of sense."

"What are you doing this for, anyhow?"

She shrugs. "It's something to do." She stands up and lifts her dumbbells a few times.

"Driving a rig, nobody cared about my English."

"I'm not criticizing your English."

Norma Jean used to say, "If I lose ten minutes' sleep, I just drag all day." Now she stays up late, writing compositions. She got a B on her first paper— a how-to theme on soup-based casseroles. Recently Norma Jean has been cooking unusual foods—tacos, lasagna, Bombay chicken. She doesn't play the organ anymore, though her second paper was called "Why Music Is Important to Me." She sits at the kitchen table, concentrating on her outlines, while Leroy plays with his log house plans, practicing with a set of Lincoln Logs. The thought of getting a truckload of notched, numbered logs scares him, and he wants to be prepared. As he and Norma Jean work together at the kitchen table, Leroy has the hopeful thought that they are sharing something, but he knows he is a fool to think this. Norma Jean is miles away. He knows he is going to lose her. Like Mabel, he is just waiting for time to pass.

One day, Mabel is there before Norma Jean gets home from work, and Leroy finds himself confiding in her. Mabel, he realizes, must know Norma Jean better than he does.

"I don't know what's got into that girl," Mabel says. "She used to go to bed with the chickens. Now you say she's up all hours. Plus her a-smoking. I like to died."

"I want to make her this beautiful home," Leroy says, indicating the Lincoln Logs. "I don't think she even wants it. Maybe she was happier with me gone."

"She don't know what to make of you, coming home like this."

"Is that it?"

Mabel takes the roof off his Lincoln Log cabin. "You couldn't get *me* in a log cabin," she says. "I was raised in one. It's no picnic, let me tell you."

"They're different now," says Leroy.

"I tell you what," Mabel says, smiling oddly at Leroy.

"What?"

"Take her on down to Shiloh. Y'all need to get out together, stir a little. Her brain's all balled up over them books."

Leroy can see traces of Norma Jean's features in her mother's face. Mabel's worn face has the texture of wrinkled cotton, but suddenly she looks pretty. It occurs to Leroy that Mabel has been hinting all along that she wants them to take her with them to Shiloh.

"Let's all go to Shiloh," he says. "You and me and her. Come Sunday."

Mabel throws her hands up in protest. "Oh, no, not me. Young folks want to be by theirselves."

When Norma Jean comes in with groceries, Leroy says excitedly, "Your mama here's been dying to go to Shiloh for thirty-five years. It's about time we went, don't you think?"

"I'm not going to butt in on anybody's second honeymoon," Mabel says.

"Who's going on a honeymoon, for Christ's sake?" Norma Jean says loudly.

"I never raised no daughter of mine to talk that-a-way," Mabel says.

"You ain't seen nothing yet," says Norma Jean. She starts putting away boxes and cans, slamming cabinet doors.

"There's a log cabin at Shiloh," Mabel says. "It was there during the battle. There's bullet holes in it."

"When are you going to *shut up* about Shiloh, Mama?" asks Norma Jean.

"I always thought Shiloh was the prettiest place, so full of history," Mabel goes on. "I just hoped y'all could see it once before I die, so you could tell me about it." Later she whispers to Leroy, "You do what I said. A little change is what she needs."

* * *

"Your name means 'the king,'" Norma Jean says to Leroy that evening. He is trying to get her to go to Shiloh, and she is reading a book about another century.

"Well, I reckon I ought to be right proud."

"I guess so."

"Am I still king around here?"

Norma Jean flexes her biceps and feels them for hardness. "I'm not fooling around with anybody, if that's what you mean," she says.

"Would you tell me if you were?"

"I don't know."

"What does *your* name mean?"

"It was Marilyn Monroe's real name."

"No kidding!"

"Norma comes from the Normans. They were invaders," she says. She closes her book and looks hard at Leroy. "I'll go to Shiloh with you if you'll stop staring at me."

* * *

On Sunday, Norma Jean packs a picnic and they go to Shiloh. To Leroy's relief, Mabel says she does not want to come with them. Norma Jean drives, and Leroy, sitting beside her, feels like some boring hitchhiker she has picked up. He tries some conversation, but she answers him in monosyllables. At Shiloh, she drives aimlessly through the park, past bluffs and trails and steep ravines. Shiloh is an immense place, and Leroy cannot see it as a battleground. It is not what he expected. He thought it would look like a golf course. Monuments are everywhere, showing through the thick clusters of trees. Norma Jean passes the log cabin Mabel mentioned. It is surrounded by tourists looking for bullet holes.

"That's not the kind of log house I've got in mind," says Leroy apologetically.

"I know *that*."

"This is a pretty place. Your mama was right."

"It's O.K.," says Norma Jean. "Well, we've seen it. I hope she's satisfied." They burst out laughing together.

At the park museum, a movie on Shiloh is shown every half hour, but they decide that they don't want to see it. They buy a souvenir Confederate flag for Mabel, and then they find a picnic spot near the cemetery. Norma Jean has brought a picnic cooler, with pimiento sandwiches, soft drinks, and Yodels. Leroy eats a sandwich and then smokes a joint, hiding it behind the picnic cooler. Norma Jean has quit smoking altogether. She is picking cake crumbs from the cellophane wrapper, like a fussy bird.

Leroy says, "So the boys in the gray ended up in Corinth. The Union soldiers zapped 'em finally. April 7, 1862."

They both know that he doesn't know any history. He is just talking about some of the historical plaques they have read. He feels awkward, like a boy on a date with an older girl. They are still just making conversation.

"Corinth is where Mama eloped to," says Norma Jean.

They sit in silence and stare at the cemetery for the Union Dead and, beyond, at a tall cluster of trees. Campers are parked nearby, bumper to bumper, and small children in bright clothing are cavorting and squealing. Norma Jean wads up the cake wrapper and squeezes it tightly in her hand. Without looking at Leroy, she says, "I want to leave you."

Leroy takes a bottle of Coke out of the cooler and flips off the cap. He holds the bottle poised near his mouth but cannot remember to take a drink. Finally he says, "No, you don't."

"Yes, I do."

"I won't let you."

"You can't stop me."

"Don't do me that way."

Leroy knows Norma Jean will have her own way. "Didn't I promise to be home from now on?" he says.

"In some ways, a woman prefers a man who wanders," says Norma Jean. "That sounds crazy, I know."

"You're not crazy."

Leroy remembers to drink from his Coke. Then he says, "Yes, you *are* crazy. You and me could start all over again. Right back at the beginning."

"We *have* stared all over again," says Norma Jean. "And this is how it turned out."

"What did I do wrong?"

"Nothing."

"Is this one of those women's lib things?" Leroy asks.

"Don't be funny."

The cemetery, a green slope dotted with white markers, looks like a subdivision site. Leroy is trying to comprehend that his marriage is breaking up, but for some reason he is wondering about white slabs in a graveyard.

"Everything was fine till Mama caught me smoking," says Norma Jean, standing up. "That set something off."

"What are you talking about?"

"She won't leave me alone—*you* won't leave me alone." Norma Jean seems to be crying, but she is looking away from him. I feel eighteen again. I can't face that all over again." She starts walking away. "No, it *wasn't* fine. I don't know what I'm saying. Forget it."

Leroy takes a lungful of smoke and closes his eyes as Norma Jean's words sink in. He tries to focus on the fact that thirty-five hundred soldiers died on the grounds around him. He can only think of that war as a board game with plastic soldiers. Leroy almost smiles, as he compares the Confederates' daring attack on the Union camps and Virgil Mathis's raid on the bowling alley. General Grant, drunk and furious, shoved the Southerners back to Corinth, where Mabel and Jet Beasley were married years later, when Mabel was still thin and good-looking. The next day, Mabel and Jet visited the battleground, and then Norma Jean was born, and then she married Leroy and they had a baby, which they lost, and now Leroy and Norma are here at the same battleground. Leroy knows he is leaving out a lot. He is leaving out the insides of history. History was always just names and dates to him. It occurs to him that building a house out of logs is similarly empty—too simple. And the real inner workings of a marriage, like most of history, have escaped him. Now he sees that building a log house is the dumbest idea he could have had. It was clumsy of him to think Norma Jean would want a log house. It was a crazy idea. He'll have to think of something else, quickly. He will wad the blueprints into tight balls and fling them into the lake. Then he'll get moving again. He opens his eyes. Norma Jean has moved away and is walking through the cemetery, following a serpentine brick path.

Leroy gets up to follow his wife, but his good leg is asleep and his bad leg still hurts him. Norma Jean is far away, walking rapidly toward the bluff by the river, and he tries to hobble toward her. Some children run past him, screaming noisily. Norma Jean has reached the bluff, and she is looking out over the Tennessee River. Now she turns toward Leroy and waves her arms. Is she beckoning to him? She seems to be doing an exercise for her chest muscles. The sky is unusually pale—the color of the dust ruffle Mabel made for their bed.

Dorothy Allison

---

an excerpt from
Bastard Out of Carolina

I've been called Bone all my life, but my name's Ruth Anne. I was named for and by my oldest aunt—Aunt Ruth. My mama didn't have much to say about it, since strictly speaking, she wasn't there. Mama and a carful of my aunts and uncles had been going out to the airport to meet one of the cousins who was on his way back from playing soldier. Aunt Alma, Aunt Ruth, and her husband, Travis, were squeezed into the front, and Mama was stretched out in back, sound asleep. Mama hadn't adjusted to pregnant life very happily, and by the time she was eight months gone, she had a lot of trouble sleeping. She said that when she lay on her back it felt like I was crushing her, when she lay on her side it felt like I was climbing up her backbone, and there was no rest on her stomach at all. Her only comfort was the backseat of Uncle Travis's Chevy, which was jacked up so high that it easily cradled little kids or pregnant women. Moments after lying back into that seat, Mama had fallen into her first deep sleep in eight months. She slept so hard, even the accident didn't wake her up.

My aunt Alma insists to this day that what happened was in no way Uncle Travis's fault, but I *know* that the first time I ever saw Uncle Travis sober was when I was seventeen and they had just removed half his stomach along with his liver. I cannot imagine that he hadn't been drinking. There's no question in my mind but that they had *all* been drinking, except Mama, who never could drink, and certainly not when she was pregnant.

No, Mama was just asleep and everyone else was drunk. And what they did was plow headlong into a slow-moving car. The front of Uncle Travis's Chevy accordioned; the back flew up; the aunts and Uncle Travis were squeezed so tight they just bounced a little; and Mama, still asleep with her hands curled under her chin, flew right over their heads, through the windshield, and over the car they hit. Going through the glass, she cut the top of her head, and when she hit the ground she bruised her backside, but other than that she wasn't hurt at all. Of course, she didn't wake up for three days, not till after Granny and Aunt Ruth had signed all the papers and picked out my name.

I am Ruth for my aunt Ruth, and Anne for my mama. I got the nickname Bone shortly after Mama brought me home from the hospital and Uncle Earle announced that I was "no bigger than a knucklebone" and Aunt Ruth's youngest girl, Deedee, pulled the blanket back to see "the bone." It's lucky I'm not Mattie Raylene like Granny wanted. But Mama had always promised to name her first daughter after her oldest sister, and Aunt Ruth thought Mama's child should just naturally carry Mama's name since they had come so close to losing her.

Other than the name, they got just about everything else wrong. Neither Aunt Ruth nor Granny could write very clearly, and they hadn't bothered to discuss how Anne would be spelled, so it wound up spelled three different ways on the form—Ann, Anne, and Anna. As for the name of the father, Granny refused to speak it after she had run him out of town for messing with her daughter, and Aunt Ruth had never been sure of his last name anyway. They tried to get away with just scribbling something down, but if the hospital didn't mind how a baby's middle name was spelled, they were definite about having a father's last name. So Granny gave one and Ruth gave another, the clerk got mad, and there I was—certified a bastard by the state of South Carolina.

Mama always said it would never have happened if she'd been awake. "After all," she told my aunt Alma, "they don't ask for a marriage license before they put you up on the table." She was convinced that she could have bluffed her way through it, *said* she was married firmly enough that no one would have questioned her.

"It's only when you bring it to their attention that they write it down."

Granny said it didn't matter anyhow. Who cared what was written down? Did people read courthouse records? Did they ask to see your birth certificate before they sat themselves on your porch? Everybody who mattered knew and she didn't give a rat's ass about anybody else. She teased Mama about the damn silly paper with the red stamp on the bottom.

"What as it? You intended to frame that thing? You wanted something on your wall to prove you done it right?" Granny could be mean where her pride was involved. "The child is proof enough. An't no stamp on her nobody can see."

If Granny didn't care, Mama did. Mama hated to be called trash, hated the memory of every day she'd ever spent bent over other people's peanuts and strawberry plants while they stool tall and looked at her like she was a rock on the ground. The stamp on that birth certificate burned her like the stamp she knew they'd trued to put on her. *No-good, lazy, shiftless.* She'd work her hands to claws, her back to a shovel shape, her mouth to a bent and awkward smile—anything to deny what Greenville County wanted to name her. Now a soft-talking black-eyed man had done it for them—set a mark on her and hers. It was all she could do to pull herself up eight days after I was born and go back to work waiting tables with a tight mouth and swollen eyes.

Mama waited a year. Four days before my first birthday and a month past her sixteenth, she wrapped me in a blanket and took me to the courthouse. The clerk was polite but bored. He had her fill out a form and pay a two-dollar fee. Mama filled it out in a fine schoolgirl's hand. She hadn't been to school in three years, but she wrote letters for everyone in the family and was proud of her graceful, slightly canted script.

"What happened to the other one?" the clerk asked.

Mama didn't look up from my head on her arm, "It got tore across the bottom."

The clerk looked at her more closely, turned a glance on me. "Is that right?"

He went to the back and was gone a ling time. Mama stood, quiet but stubborn, at the counter. When he came back, he passed her the paper and stayed to watch her face.

It was the same, identical to the other one. Across the bottom in over-sized red-inked block letters it read, "ILLEGITIMATE."

Mama drew breath like an old woman with pleurisy, and flushed pink from her neck to her hairline. "I don't want it like this," she blurted.

"Well, little lady," he said in a long, slow drawl. Behind him she could see some of the women clerks standing in a doorway, their faces almost as flushed as her own but their eyes bright with an entirely different emotion. "This is how it's go to be. The facts have been established." He drew the work out even longer and louder so that it hung in the air between them like a neon reflection of my mama's blush—*established*.

The women in the doorway shook their heads and pursed their lips. One mouthed to the other, "Some people."

Mama made her back straighten, bundled me close to her neck, and turned suddenly for the hall door. "You forgetting your certificate," the man called after her, but she didn't stop. Her hands on my body clamped so tight I let out a high, thin wail. Mama just held on and let me scream.

She waited another year before going back, that time taking my aunt Ruth with her and leaving me with Granny. "I was there," Aunt Ruth promised them, "and it was really my fault. In so much excitement I just got confused, what with Anney here looking like she was dead to the world and everybody shouting and running around. You know, there was a three-car accident brought in just minutes after us." Aunt Ruth gave the clerk a very sincere direct look, awkwardly trying to keep her eyes wide and friendly.

"You know how these things can happen."

"Oh, I do," he said, enjoying it all immensely.

The form her brought out was no different from the others. The look he gave my mama and my aunt was pure righteous justification. *"What'd you expect?"* he seemed to be saying. His face was set and almost gentle, but his eyes laughed at them. My aunt came close to swinging her purse at his head, but Mama caught her arm. That time she took the certificate copy with her.

"Might as well have something for my two dollars," she said. At seventeen, she was a lot older than she had been at sixteen. The next year she went alone, and the year after. That same year she met Lyle Parsons and started thinking more about marrying him than dragging down to the courthouse again. Uncle Earle teased her that if she lived with Lyle for seven years, she could get the same result without paying a courthouse lawyer. "The law never done us no good. Might as well get on without it."

* * *

Mama quit working as a waitress soon after marrying Lyle Parsons, though she wasn't so sure that was a good idea. "We're gonna need things," she told him, but he wouldn't listen. Lyle was one of the sweetest boys the Parsons ever produced, a soft-eyed, soft-spoken, too-pretty boy tired of being his mama's baby. Totally serious about providing well for his family and proving himself a man, he got Mama pregnant almost immediately and didn't want her to go out to work at all. But pumping gas and changing tires in his cousin's Texaco station, he made barely enough to pay the rent. Mama tried working part-time in a grocery store but gave it up when she got so pregnant she couldn't lift boxes. It was easier to sit a stool on the line at the Stevens factory until Reese was born, but Lyle didn't like that at all.

"How's that baby gonna grow my long legs if you always sitting bent over?" he complained. He wanted to borrow money or take a second job, anything to keep his pretty new wife out of the mill. "Honey girl," he called her, "sweet thing."

"Dumpling," she called him back, "sugar tit," and when no one could hear, "manchild." She love him like a baby, whispered to her sisters about the soft blond hairs on his belly, the way he slept with one leg thrown over her hip, the stories he told her about all the places he wanted to take her.

"He loves Bone, he really does," she told Aunt Ruth. "Wants to adopt her when we get some money put by." She loved to take pictures of him. The best of them is one made at the gas station in the bright summer sun with Lyle swinging from the Texaco sign and wearing a jacket that proclaimed "Greenville County Racetrack." He'd taken a job out at the track where they held the stock-car races, working in the pit changing tires at high speed and picking up a little cash in the demolition derby on Sunday afternoon. Mama didn't go out there with him much. She didn't like the noise or the stink, or the way the other men would tease Lyle into drinking warm beer to see if his work slowed down any. As much as she liked taking pictures, she only took one of him out at the track, with a tire hugged against his left hip, grease all over one side of his face, and a grin so wide you could smell the beer.

It was a Sunday when Lyle died, not at the track but on the way home, so easily, so gently, that the peanut pickers who had seen the accident kept insisting that the boy could not be dead. There'd been one of those eerie summer showers where the sun never stopped shining and the rain came down in soft sheets that everybody ignored. Lyle's truck had come around the curve from the train crossing at a clip. He waved at one of the pickers, giving his widest grin. Then the truck was spinning off the highway in a rain-slicked patch of oil, and Lyle was bumped out the side door and onto the pavement.

"That's a handsome boy," one of the pickers kept telling the highway patrolman. "He wasn't doing nothing wrong, just coming along the road in the rain—that's devil's rain, you know. The sun was so bright, and that boy just grinned so." The old man wouldn't stop looking back over to where Lyle lay still on the edge of the road.

Lyle lay uncovered for a good twenty minutes. Everybody kept expecting him to get up. There was not a mark on him, and his face was shining with that lazy smile. But the back of his head flattened into the gravel, and his palms lay open and damp in the spray of the traffic the patrolman diverted around the wreck.

Mama was holding Reese when the sheriff's car pulled up at Aunt Alma's, and she must have known immediately what he had come to tell her, because she put her head back and howled like an old dog in labor, howled and rocked and squeezed her baby girl so tight Aunt Alma had to pinch her to get Reese free.

Mama was nineteen, with two babies and three copies of my birth certificate in her dresser drawer. When she stopped howling, she stopped making any sound at all and would only nod at people when they tried to get her to cry or talk. She took both her girls to the funeral with all her sisters lined up alongside of her. The Parsons barely spoke to her. Lyle's mother told Aunt Alma that if her boy hadn't taken that damn job for Mama's sake, he wouldn't have died in the road. Mama paid no attention. Her blond hair looked dark and limp, her skin gray, and within those few days fine lines had appeared at the corners of her eyes. Aunt Ruth steered her away from the gravesite while Aunt Raylene tucked some of the flowers into her family Bible and stopped to tell Mrs. Parsons what a damn fool she was.

Aunt Ruth was heavily pregnant with her eighth child, and it was hard for her not to take Mama into her arms like another baby. At Uncle Earle's car, she stopped and leaned back against the front door, hanging on to Mama. She brushed Mama's hair back off her face, looking closely into her eyes.

"Nothing else will ever hit you this hard," she promised. She ran her thumbs under Mama's eyes, her fingers resting lightly on either temple. "Now you look like a Boatwright," she said. "Now you got the look. You're as old as you're ever gonna get, girl, This is the way you'll look till you die." Mama just nodded; it didn't matter to her anymore what she looked like.

A year in the mill was all Mama could take after they buried Lyle; the dust in the air got to her too fast. After that there was no choice but to find work in a diner. The tips made all the difference, though she knew she could make more money at the honky-tonks or managing a slot as a cocktail waitress. There was always more money serving people beer and wine, still more in hard liquor, but she'd have had to go outside Greenville County to do that, and she couldn't imagine moving away from her family. She needed her sisters' help with her two girls.

The White Horse Cafe was a good choice anyway, one of the few decent diners downtown. Her work left her tired but not sick to death like the mill, and she liked the people she met there, the tips and the conversation.

"You got a way with a smile," the manager told her.

"Oh, my smile gets me a long way," she laughed, and no one would have known she didn't mean it. Truckers or judges, they all liked Mama. Aunt Ruth was right, her face had settled into itself. Her color had come back after a while, and the lines at the corers of her eyes just made her look ready to smile. When the men at the counter weren't slipping quarters in her pocket they were bringing her things, souvenirs or friendship cards, once or twice a ring. Mama smiles, joked, slapped ass, and firmly passed back anything that looked like a down payment on something she didn't want to sell.

Reese was two years old the next time Mama stopped in at the courthouse. The clerk looked pleased to see her again. She didn't talk to him this time, just picked up the paperwork and took it over to the new business offices near the Sears, Roebuck Auto Outlet. Uncle Earle had given her a share of his settlement from another car accident, and she wanted to use a piece of it to hire his lawyer for a few hours. The man took her money and then smiled at her much like the clerk had when she told him want she wanted. Her face went hard, and he swallowed quick to keep from laughing. No sense making an enemy of Earle Boatwright's sister.

"I'm sorry," he told her, handing half her money back. "The way the law stands there's nothing I could do for you. If I was to put it through, it would come back just like the one you got now. You just wait a few years. Sooner or later they'll get rid of that damn ordinance. Mostly it's not enforced anymore anyway."

"Then why," she asked him, "do they insist on enforcing it on me?"

"Now, honey," he sighed, clearly embarrassed. He wiggled in his seat and passed her the rest of her money across the desk. "You don't need me to tell you the answer to that. You've lived in this county all your life, and you know how things are." He gave a grin that had no humor in it at all. "By now, they look forward to you coming in."

"Small-minded people," he told her, but that grin never left his face.

"Bastard!" Mama hissed, and then caught herself. She hated that word.

Family is family, but even love can't keep people from eating at each other. Mama's pride, Granny's resentment that there should even be anything to consider shameful, my aunts' fear and bitter humor, my uncles' hard-mouthed contempt for anything that could not be handled with a shotgun or a two-by-four—all combined to grow my mama up fast and painfully. There was only one way to fight off the pity and hatefulness. Mama learned to laugh with them, before they could laugh at her, and to do it so well no one could be sure what she really thought or felt. She got a reputation for an easy smile and a sharp tongue, and using one to balance the other, she seemed friendly but distant. No one knew that she cried in the night for Lyle and her lost happiness, that under that biscuit crust exterior she was all butter grief and hunger, that more than anything else in the world she wanted someone strong to love her like she loved her girls.

"Now, you got to watch yourself with my sister," Uncle Earle told Glen Waddell the day he took him over to the diner for lunch. "Say the wrong thing and she'll take the shine off your teeth."

It was a Thursday, and the diner was serving chicken-fried steak and collard greens, which was Earle's excuse for dragging his new workmate halfway across Greenville in the middle of a work day. He'd taken a kind of shine to Glen, though moment to moment he could not tell what that short stubborn boy was thinking behind those dark blue eyes. The Waddells owned the dairy, and the oldest Waddell son was running for district attorney. Skinny, nervous little Glen Waddell didn't seem like he would amount to much, driving a truck for the furnace works, and shaking a little every time he tried to look a man n the eye. But at seventeen, maybe it was enough that Glen tried, Earle told himself, and kept repeating storied about his sister to get the boy to relax.

"Anney makes the best gravy in the county, the sweetest biscuits, and puts just enough vinegar in those greens. Know what I mean?"

Glen nodded, though the truth was he'd never had much of a taste for greens, and his well-educated mama had always told him that gravy was bad for the heart. So he was not ready for the moment when Mama pushed her short blond hair back and set that big hot plate of food down in front of his open hands. Glen took a bite of gristly meat and gravy, and it melted between his teeth. The greens were salt-sweet and fat-rich. His tongue sang to his throat; his neck went loose, and is hair fell across his face. It was like sex, that food, too good to waste on the middle of the day and a roomful of men too tired to taste. He chewed, swallowed, and began to come alive himself. He began to feel for the first time like one of the boys, a grown man accepted by the notorious and dangerous Black Earle Boatwright, staring across the counter at one of the prettiest women he'd ever seen. His face went hot, and he took a big drink of ice tea to cool himself.

"Her?" he stammered to Earle. "That your sister? That pretty little white-headed thing? She an't no bigger than a girl."

Earle grinned. The look on Glen's face was as clear as the sky after spring rain. "Oh, she's a girl," he agreed, and put his big hand on Glen's shoulder. "She's my own sweet mama's baby girl. But you know our mama's a rattle-snake and our daddy was a son of a gun." He laughed loud, only stopping when he saw how Glen was watching Anney walk away, the bow of her apron riding high on her butt. For a moment he went hot-angry and then pulled himself back. The boy was a fool, but a boy. Probably no harm in him. Feel-ing generous and Christian, Earle gave a last hard squeeze to Glen's shoulder and told him again, "You watch yourself, son. Just watch yourself."

Glen Waddell nodded, understanding completely the look on Earle's face. The man was a Boatwright after all, and he and his two brothers had all gone to jail for causing other men serious damage. Rumor told deadly stories about the Boatwright boys, the kind of tales men whispered to each other over whiskey when women were not around. Earle was good with a hammer or a saw, and magical with a pickax. He drove a truck like he was making love to the gears and carried a seven-inch pigsticker in the side pocket of his rein-forced painter's pants. Earle Boatwright was everything Glen had ever wanted to be—specially since his older brothers laughed at him for his hot temper, bad memory, and general uselessness. Moreover, Earle had a gift for charm-ing people—men or women—and he had charmed the black sheep of the Waddell family right out of his terror of the other men on the crew, charmed him as well out of his fear of his family's disapproval. When Earle turned that grin on him, Glen found himself grinning back, enjoying the notion of angering his daddy and outraging his brothers. It was something to work for, that relaxed and disarming grin of Earle's. It made a person want to see it again, to feel Earle's handclasp along with it and know a piece of Earle's admiration. More than anything in the word, Glen Waddell wanted Earle Boatwright to like him. Never mind that pretty little girl, he told himself, and put his manners on hard until Earle settled back down. Glen yes-ma'amed all the waitresses and grabbed Earle's check right out of Anney's hand, though it would take him down to quarters and cigarettes after he paid it.

But when Earle went off to the bathroom, Glen let himself watch her again, that bow on her ass and the way her lips kept pulling back off her teeth when she smiled. Anney looked him once full in the face, and he saw right through her. She had grinned at her brother with an open face and bright sparkling eyes, an easy smile and a soft mouth, a face without fear or guile. The smile she gave Glen and everyone else at the counter was just as easy but not so open. Between her eyes was a fine line that deepened when her smile tightened. A shadow darkened her clear pupils in the moment before her glance moved away. It made her no less pretty but added an aura of sadness.

"You coming over tonight, Earle?" she asked when he came back, in a voice as buttery and sweet as the biscuits. "The girls miss you 'bout as much as I do."

"Might be over," Earle drawled, "if this kid here does his job right and we get through before dark this time." He slapped Glen's shoulder lightly and winked at Anney. "Maybe I'll even bring him with me."

Yes, Glen thought, oh yes, but he kept quiet and took another drink of tea. The gravy in his stomach steadied him, but it was Anney's smile that cooled him down. He felt so strong he wanted to spit. He would have her, he told himself. He would marry Black Earle's baby sister, marry the whole Boatwright legend, shame his daddy and shock his brothers. He would carry a knife in his pocket and kill any man who dared to touch her. Yes, he thought to himself, oh yes.

Mama looked over at the boy standing by the cash register, with his dark blue eyes and bushy brown hair. Time was she would have blushed at the way he was watching her, but for that moment she just looked back into his eyes. He'd make a good daddy, she imagined, a steady man. He smiled and his smile was crooked. His eyes bored into her and got darker still. She flushed then, and smelled her own sweat, nervously unable to tell if it came from fear or lust.

I need a husband, she thought, turned her back, and wiped her face. Yeah, and a car and a home and a hundred thousand dollars. She shook her head and waved Earle out the door, not looking again at the boy with him.

"Sister Anney, why don't you come over here and stand by my coffee cup," one of her regulars teased. "It'll take heat just being next to your heart."

Mama gave her careful laugh and pulled up the coffeepot. "An't got time to charm coffee when I can pour you a warm-up with one hand," she teased him back. Never mind no silly friends of Earle's, she told herself, and filled coffee cups one at a time until she could get off the line and go take herself a break.

"Where you keep that paper, Ruth Anne's birth certificate, huh?" they'd tease Mama down at the diner.

"Under the sink with all the other trash," she'd shoot back, giving them a glance so sharp they'd think twice before trying to tease her again.

"Put it away," Granny kept telling her. "If you stopped thinking about it, people would too. As long as it's something that'll get a rise out of you, people're gonna keep on using it."

The preacher agreed, "Your shame is between you and God, Sister Anne. No need to let it mark the child."

My mama went as pale as the underside of an unpeeled cotton boll. "I got no shame," she told him, "and I don't need no man to tell me jackshit about my child."

"*Jackshit*," my aunt Ruth boasted. "She said 'jackshit' to the preacher. An't nobody says nothing to my little sister, an't nobody can touch that girl or what's hers. You just better watch yourself around her.

You better. You better. You just better watch yourself around her.

Watch her in the diner, laughing, pouring coffee, palming tips, and frying eggs. Watch her push her hair back, tug her apron higher, refuse dates, pinches, suggestions. Watch her eyes and how they sink into her face, the lines that grow out from that tight stubborn mouth, the easy banter that rises from the deepest place inside her.

"An't it about time you tried the courthouse again, Sister Anney?"

"An't it time you zipped your britches, Brother Calvin?"

An't it time the Lord did something, rained fire and retribution on Greenville County? An't there sin enough, grief enough, inch by inch of pain enough? An't the measure made yet? Anney never said what she was thinking, but her mind was working all the time.

* * *

Glen Waddell stayed on at the furnace works with Earle for one whole year, and drove all the way downtown for lunch at the diner almost every workday and even some Saturdays. "I'd like to see your little girls," he told Anney once every few weeks until she started to believe him. "Got to be pretty little girls with such a beautiful mama." She stared at him, took his quarter tips, and admitted it. Yes, she had two beautiful little girls. Yes, he might as well come over, meet her girls, sit on her porch and talk a little. She wiped sweaty palms on her apron before she let him take her hand. His shoulders were tanned dark, and he looked bigger all over from the work he had been doing with Earle. The muscles bulging through his worn white T-shirt reminded her of Lyle, though he had none of Lyle's sweet demeanor. His grip when he reached to take her arm was as firm as Earle's, but his smile was his own, like no one else's she had ever known. She took a careful deep breath and let herself really smile back at him. Maybe, she kept telling herself, maybe he'd make a good daddy.

Nickole Brown

The Root Woman

A black woman worked for pay on Friday
to feed you mush pears and mush peas
and to teach me how indigo paint and colanders
keep out haints, how uncut hair and unshaven legs
retain strength, how a red ribbon, a brass key and fire
brought love.

With her, the growling ghost of my childhood
did not return, and your daddy disappeared for good
into the basement, building model airplanes
and bluing himself with late night flickerings
of television to put him to sleep. She protected me,

lioness she was jumping down
barefoot to crack clams off the canal wall and eat
them with hot sauce right where she stood, red running
to her elbows. She flushed chitlins for dinner,
a garden hose running the dark flecks out to settle
soft into grass. And fried chicken, marrow
sucked straight from the leg bone.

I held hot rags to my breasts when she said
it would make them grow, imagined
a red bra, a fast blue motorcycle, a boy's fast black hair
flying back into my mouth. Two years later she left
and they came, early enough and barely there—tender
swells with airbrush-pink nipples. It was then I stole
mama's cigarettes, the ones she wasn't supposed to be smoking,
and smoked them out the bathroom window, my lips pressed
to the grain of the flyspecked screen. I changed

my wardrobe with a handful of rubber bands
and a gallon of bleach. It was a poor girl's tie-dye, sister,
because we were poor: all of the rings
a faded version of the cloth's original,
purple on blue, red on orange, a stained glass shirt fit
for my own make-believe stained glass father, worn tight

to sneak out to the asphalt black, crushed glass
twinkling under street lights. I met one with blue eyes there,
watched him spit tobacco in the air
then catch it on his tongue.

The Smell of Snake

Few memories, those years
besides the smell of dead
kittens under the car and the cucumber
of copperheads crisping
the creek where I waded
with a net from our above-ground pool
to scoop up black tadpoles and crawdads,
the adrenaline flash of minnows silvering
an orange bucket. Few memories
of you, nothing to say about

you learning to roll over or sit up
or crawl, and by the time you toddled
down the hall to reach my door
it was locked, shut with a finger-
smashing slam and a sign barred
with exclamation points that read
Private Get Out. I was hoarding

a stash of precious, breakable things,
things you weren't allowed to touch—a boy's
speed skate laces and his sister's stolen
champagne flute of Mardi Gras beads,
a wind-up ceramic ballerina balancing
on one chipped toe, raspberry-flavored
lip gloss and soft plastic bracelets worn to look
like a slut. In two summers,

I had gone from the creek to the all-night
seven-to-seven skate, I had gone
from the freckled giggle pop kiss to the tongue
down the throat, I had learned what acid-
washed jeans can do for a girl, especially
when she learns to skate

backwards, the smooth-footed eight curve
side-to-side sway of her hips.

The kids I knew, like me, all came
straight from the mud, and with legs still
mosquito-pocked and the smell of snake
in our hair, we struck our father's
lighter in one hand and held out
our mother's aerosol in the other,
sprayed *fuck-you* balls
of fire into the air. We wrote *ozzy rulz*
across our eight punch
knuckles, carved our desires
into wooden desks; we passed
notes and played hooky and told stories
of schoolyard rape done
with broken bottles and broom
sticks. We were

afraid, and like a pack of hungry
dogs, we marked
each other—safety pins and blood,
scratched things like *best friends
forever* then vomited
bile into the mud.

Trestle

I gave the best of my body's
new beauty to boys
in basement bedrooms, the walls
sweating groundwater behind posters
that turned electric green under black
lights. Upstairs, always some lump
of a mother clicking overhead who
sold makeup to earn a pink
Cadillac, and a father, usually
drinking but always pissed, who
dropped the coin of his heart into
the red envelope of Tet and threw it

away with everything else
from Vietnam. We clung

to each other—the boy and
I—first trying the gentle hippie
daze watching spirits rise
from the tips of incense sticks
then sick of being underground
with a wild barnyard kitten
that shit the couch, we shrouded
ourselves in black from head to toe and
snuck out to spray paint anarchy
signs on clean, white walls.
We clomped our combat

boots through the old tuberculosis hospital
and screamed out of broken windows
through ivy vines and spider webs, and
finding what we thought were body
chutes, we pretended dead and
jumped down. We walked train tracks
smashing pennies, spoons, keys,
we dangled our tired feet high above
from the rusty bridge and did not hold
hands in a parasuicide skydive

but simply looked out
on suburbs and strip malls
under humid white sky, the black
woods' edge sometimes flashing
with deer at the littered shore
of two ribbons of light, one coming
towards us and another
already gone.

In Winter

Helplessness
crouches
next to the orange glow
of a space
heater
from January til May.
Look
through the window
all you want,
but all you'll see
is a square of steel,
the nerve-ending trees
feeling little
through days
long and brown.

The seasons,
either mosquito
lush or dead
wood, are like
the architecture here—
Victorian or prefab, not much else
in between, the valley brought
to its knees
by drive-thrus and strip
malls, car lots of primary-
colored triangles
flapping in endless dinge.

The mud
is thick, like a mix of dog
shit and deer blood,
construction sites so deep
in suck earth
that the men throw down
two-by-fours just
to walk across. Your daddy brings
that clay

home on his boots
so bad

you can scrape it
with a spoon.

You can hear him
coming a mile down,
gurgling sound of diesel,
the silver silhouette
of two big-tittied girls
flashing on his mud
flaps, and in his immaculate king
cab, an ashtray full of change and one
empty coffee can
for cigarette ash.

In winter, it is all
fried bologna: there is no
work, and when there is,
he works
so hard he can pop
open the skin of his knuckles
by making a fist. It's then
he slathers his hands
in Vasoline and sleeps
wearing kitchen gloves.
Full of endless spring,

he talks about
enough money
for red bicycles, toy poodles, hot tubs.
Full of endless spring, he buys
mama things
he can't afford,
some things she doesn't even
like—that mink stole
round her pretty shoulders,
a tacky grandma
glam she only wore to church, the tiny
bead eyes in its dog face
glinting at me as I pretended
to pray. *Well,* she said, petting
the little dead muzzle,
least he tries.

Straddling Fences

Sister, I've tried it all.
Gardening, yoga, therapy, you name it—
I've smoked my house out
with incense, taped prayers to the inside
of my fridge, worn my fingernails
clipped and bare, neglected

the bottle of pink polish
gumming on the windowsill.
I've tried pills and red wine;
I've thought of the sawed-off
shotgun under mama's bed, of the slow
release of red into a tub, of twisting the white
tulle scallops of my canopy
into a rope to hang myself there.

I've traveled, trying to leave it
behind—heels squeaking on ancient marble,
dolphins chasing my boat on a flat sea,
boys with eyes that spun like bicycle wheels
in rain. I left my first husband, my one
true home, then moved into an empty house
comforted by the nothing

of waxed hardwood floors. I have eaten
turnip greens sautéed with virgin
oil, simple food we never heard of growing up
like sushi, basmati, butternut squash.
But I still drink soda every morning,
and when I'm sick, it's straight
to the fried comfort,
a bottle of hot sauce nearby.

How can I make all this fit? How did I
make it through? Our mama in
therapy makes about as much sense
as putting Buddha in the seat of that car
we used to go to in the woods, that rusted-out Ford
of creeping charlie vine and bullet holes,
the base of a bottle all the kids said

was broken off in somebody.
Sitting there on that dry-rot

driver's seat, our hands on the crusted
wheel, was a terror so beautiful
we never thought of going anywhere.
I had to try something, had to leave
you behind, had to try to be thankful
for the chance to boss my way
through the city gates, switching all the time
between *isn't* and *ain't*, my feet
in designer red heels
with creek mud still between my toes.

Straddling a fence, I think mama would say.
On one side,
rusting barbwire, a tree swing, the green smell
of cow patties in the sun.
On the other,
another me,
pressed,
dressed,
right as fucking rain.

Tony Hoagland
─────────────

At the Galleria

Just past the bin of pastel baby socks and underwear,
there are some 49-dollar Chinese-made TVs;

one of them singing news about a far-off war,
one comparing the breast size of an actress

from Hollywood to the breast size
of an actress from Bollywood.

And here is my niece Lucinda,
who is nine and a daughter of Texas,

who has developed the flounce of a pedigreed blonde
and declares that her favorite sport is shopping.

Today is the day she embarks upon her journey,
swinging a credit card like a scythe

through the meadows of golden merchandise.
Today is the day she stops looking at faces,

and starts assessing the price of purses;
So let it begin. Let her be dipped in the dazzling bounty

and raised and wrung out again and again.
And let us watch.

As the gods in olden stories
turned mortals into laurel trees and crows
      to teach them some kind of lesson,

so we were turned into Americans
to learn something about loneliness.

Dialectical Materialism

I was thinking about dialectical materialism at the supermarket,
strolling among the Chilean tomatoes and the Filipino pineapples,

admiring the Washington-state apples stacked in perfect pyramid displays
by the ebony man from Zimbabwe wearing the Chicago Bulls t-shirt.

I was seeing the whole produce section
                    as a system of cross-referenced signifiers
in a textbook of historical economics

and the fine spray that misted the vegetables
was like the cool mist of style imposed on meaning.

It was one of those days
when interpretation is brushing its varnish over everything

when even the birds are speaking in complete sentences

and the sun is a brassy blonde novelist of immense accomplishment
                    dictating her new blockbuster
to a stenographer who types at the speed of light
and publishes each page as fast as it is written.

There was cornbread rising in the bakery department
and in its warm aroma I believed that I could smell
                    the exhaled breath of vanished Iroquois,
their journey west and
                    delicate withdrawal into the forests,

whereas by comparison
the coarse-grained wheat baguettes
seemed to irrepressibly exude
        the sturdy sweat and labor of eighteenth-century Europe.

My god there is so much sorrow in the grocery store!
You would have to be high
on the fumes of the piped-in pan flutes
                    of commodified Peruvian folk music

not to be driven practically crazy
with awe and shame,
not to weep at the scale of subjugated matter:

the ripped-up etymologies of kiwi fruit and bratwurst,
the roads paved with dead languages,
the jungles digested by foreign money.
It's the owners, I said to myself;
it's the horrible juggernaut of progress;

but the cilantro in my hand
opened up its bitter minty ampoule underneath my nose

and the bossa nova muzak charmed me like a hypnotist
and the pretty cashier with the shaved head and nose ring
                    said, *Have a nice day,*

as I burst with my groceries through the automatic doors
into the open air,

where I found myself in a giant parking lot
at a mega-mall outside of Minneapolis,
                    where in row E 87
a Ford Escort from Mankato
          had just had a fender-bender with a Honda from Miami;

and these personified portions of my heart, the drivers,
were standing there
in the gathering midwestern granular descending dusk

waiting for the trooper to fill out the accident report,

with the rotating red light of the squad car
                    whipping in circles above them,
splashing their shopped-out middle-aged faces
                    with war paint the hue of cherry Gatorade

and each of them was thinking
how with dialectical materialism, accidents happen:

how at any minute,
convenience can turn
          into a kind of trouble you never wanted.

An excerpt from
The Florist's Daughter

He should never have bought the business. I think we all knew that. Eventually even he admitted it ("I should have been ten years younger..."). But to pass up the chance of making it his own would have been like not marrying the girl of your youthful dreams even if she came to you too late, broken-down and haggard. You girl's your girl. Another Scott Fitzgerald sentiment.

The company had been established in the robber-baron days of the late nineteenth century by two Swedish immigrants who had strayed from Minneapolis over to St. Paul. The second and third generations of these family owners were in charge of the business during my girlhood. This was a lengthy pedigree in the Midwest—a company with its centenary within sight.

This heritage meant that my father, as manager of both the greenhouse and the downtown store, was part of *history*, the third aspect of the Trinity I held sacred—beauty, the idea of elsewhere, and the holy ghost of history. Even my mother, house historian who held no brief for the flower trade, grudgingly allowed that the firm was indeed "historical." It had always been *the* florist to the carriage trade, she said. We used that term—carriage trade—as if it still meant something. In old St. Paul it did. Not until the freeways cut their gashes across St. Paul and Minneapolis in the late sixties was the stiff back of the little provincial city broken. And maybe not even then. Maybe not now.

The greenhouse strayed over a city block in the Czech neighborhood where I was born and where some of the growers lived. The small houses of the neighborhood were etched at the narrow sides and cubed backyards with fastidious gardens. All summer long there was much pickling and "putting up" of vegetables and fruits. In the fall, when it was time to change from screens to storm windows, people laid a screen or two on bricks on the back porch to dry the mushrooms they had gathered in the woods by the river. These were people who really would have felt better if they could keep their own chickens.

The greenhouse was cut up into dozens of linked houses. There was, as well, a separate barn where Christmas trees were stacked, and during the unfortunate fifties and sixties, were flocked pink or blue. A bulb cellar was cut into the earth below the cement walkway connecting the houses. A dim lightbulb on a string at the top of narrow stairs led the way down, down to this netherworld. When I read of the catacombs in school, the bulb cellar sprang so powerfully to mind that I felt an eerie shiver of time travel. I had experienced the licking fires of hell at the open door of the boiler room, and my nostrils quivered with the dank molder of martyrs amid the buried tulips.

Each house was dedicated for parts of the year to a different range of plants, a broad array of indoor and outdoor varieties. The geranium house in spring became, by December, the first poinsettia house. The poinsettias were secretly growing much of the summer, unnoticed and unwanted, in a back house, the same house that took in the geranium cuttings in their off-season.

There was even a house for special customers to leave their plants to "winter over" while they themselves were wintering over in Florida or Arizona. Shaggy aspidistras and leggy geraniums, woody tree roses with name tags—Mrs. Ordway, Mrs. Schultz—were lined up like elderly boarders in the first greenhouse, near the design tables where cut-flower arrangements and corsages were made up.

The palm house, with an especially high glass roof, had big dusty palms that lived for decades like old circus elephants, rented out for weddings and charity balls and the theater and opera productions that came through town from New York and Chicago. The orchids were kept in harem seclusion behind a trellis with passion vines trained up one side in little-visited house 11, up the steep hillside.

Charity balls, weddings, debutante parties, the private conservatories that became a sudden fashion in the seventies—there was much of set design to the business. One Easter Saturday my father worked through the night, jamming cut lilies into chicken wire formed in the shape of a massive cross fastened to the soaring wall of Gloria Dei Lutheran Church. On Easter morning the astonished Lutherans were greeted by this unearthly *oeuvre*, the gigantic risen cross of blossoms floating before them, bearing the overpowering scent of ripe lilies. The *Pioneer Press* put it on the front page.

The greenhouse itself may have encouraged my father's Cecil B. DeMille tendencies. It was the kind of glass greenhouse rarely found anymore, not stocked with a single crop like the massive cost-efficient warehouses now in favor, but spilling over in many glass rooms with a little of this, a little of that, a single row of pineapple geraniums, a flat of mixed freesias, a low trailing bundle of damp mosses and maidenhair fern for shade gardens, a sudden riot of rock garden moss roses.

During "spring rush," when everyone was garden-crazed, this house was crowded with celery-and-white and port-streaked caladium, expensive annuals favored for shade gardens of Crocus Hill. For several years, a canny robin made its nest in the house just off the design room. The growers moved around gingerly in this area. They finally transferred all the plants to another house, so the mother wouldn't be nervous. During this period the greenhouse cats were sequestered in the lunchroom, howling at the injustice. But the growers kept the door firmly shut. Even in paradise the peaceable kingdom needed policing.

In the end—or too near the end—he bought the company. It was not what is called a wise business decision. The company had been skidding along on its antique carriage-trade reputation for decades, and for a long time hadn't been a healthy venture. Before the first generation had passed, feuding had become a company tradition. Complicated buyouts of distant family members weighted the annual balance sheets, and there was much bad blood.

The best years for the business, my father said, had been the war years, before my time. All the GIs sending flowers to their girls—their girls and their mothers. Nothing else to spend money on.

The first owners, known by their initials—A.B. and O.L.—had adjoining desks in the greenhouse office, and managed for something over thirty years never to speak to each other. They wrote notes or used their sons or employees for communication purposes. *This is to note that half a gross of roses from Florida...I hope someone will convey to O.L. the information that the Holland tulip market...*

Their picture was on the wall of the greenhouse showroom, two portly men dressed in pre-Great War fussbudget attire, uncannily alike, a Tweedledee and Tweedledum of floristry, one on either side of a horse that was tethered to a boxy wagon with the company logo scrolled across it, big wicker baskets of flowers wedged between great cubes of ice flecked with sawdust. The two men stared ahead. The horse too stared ahead, a diplomatic beast keeping the peace. During the Depression, after my father came to work in the greenhouse just out of high school, A.B. began "doctoring." He even went to the Mayo Clinic in Rochester. He came back from Mayo, briefly, and went through the greenhouse, shaking hands with every grower and worker, including my father who was then low in the pecking order, mixing manure into soil in the back garage area.

A.B. was going back to Mayo, he said, for an operation, something called a lobotomy. He'd come to say good-bye. "When it's over, I won't be myself anymore," he said.

When he came back from the operation, he wandered through the greenhouse, my father said, and it was true he wasn't himself. He wasn't anybody at all.

The middle generation, ten or fifteen years older than my father, carried on the chilly partnership during my girlhood. These were the owners I knew, the one I saw as a playboy, the other a cold fish, both of them having the wary looks of Mafia dons who watch their backs.

With his unerring weakness for a gallant Fitzgerald hero, my father sided with the playboy with the heart of gold who came from the weaker side of the partnership. I would have picked him, too. Rolf wasn't blond—he was golden. He gleamed with good spirit.

Unlike my father, Rolf's association with the Summit Avenue world was not wholly one of service: he belonged to the same clubs, was seen at the same restaurants, owned a cabin on the right lake, lived in a big house a block off Summit.

His blue eyes widened with gladness to see you. He would say, "Ice cream?" as a greeting, and rush to the freezer where he kept his stash. He shared my father's joie de vivre, except for him it was a birthright, easy and natural, not the responsibility of a faithful servant assigned to be master of revels.

He treated my father well. He was the first person, my father said, to treat him "like a gentleman." Whatever that meant. But it did mean something to him; it was the gold standard of his measure of a man. Rolf was his beau ideal. He would do anything for Rolf.

Leo the Lion shook her head: *a drinker* was her verdict, speaking from her Irish authority, though Rolf could charm her too, given a chance—*Mary, darlin', aren't you something tonight!*

My father covered up any number of Rolf's high junks and troubles, his late appearance, his complete absence. He even tried to take over his bookwork, going back to the greenhouse late at night to see if he could get things on track. "What does Rolf *do* down there, anyway?" my mother asked. She claimed he was walking around with gin in his coffee mug at ten in the morning.

I never told them what Rolf's daughter said. Celeste, a string bean with a fall of golden hair that looked like a stream of honey from a jar. We were together at their lake place, the two of us contentedly pouring salt from a Morton's box over leeches we'd caught and laid on the dock, one of those contemplative cruelties of childhood, the inky bloodsuckers writhing without a sound. "My father owns your car," she said out of nowhere. "And your house. My father owns everything you have."

This was not the remark of a gentleman. I knew that. I kept pouring salt, the shiny black creatures curling and withering under the blizzard I hurled from on high. *What are you doing?* my father said, frowning, reaching to take the Morton's box.

Nothing, Rolf's daughter said sulkily, and grabbed the salt away before he could take it. She went on pouring.

Eventually it was impossible to protect Rolf. He cried when he called my father into his knotty-pine office off the main showroom. He had to sell his share of the business to "the other side," he said. The big house a block off Summit—gone. He was moving to Florida where he was getting a job with a big rose-growing outfit. "These wholesale places are the future, Stan."

Rolf with a *job?* Rolf wasn't an ordinary person who got a job—he had a *place.* And of course there was the matter of Florida—Florida was Siberia with high temps, Mars, another universe. Even for me, always sniffing for the escape hatch, it sounded grim. Wholesale was dark, forbidding, all business. We were in retail where the people were, the sparkling spenders.

Rolf was gone forever.

A lot of the fun went out of the greenhouse when Rolf left, taking his glamour, blue eyes, and his afternoon ice cream to the Gulf Coast where he did not prosper. My father continued to worry about him, and years later he covertly sent him a check now and again "just to tide him over."

Leo the Lion shrugged.

My father was left in the employ of Harold, son of the other founding family, who seemed a soul-soured bottom-liner with no apparent love of flowers. This troubled my father, but Harold let him run the greenhouse and the shop. Let him. That was how we saw it—my father was allowed to run the show, keep things going in the downtown showroom and the Banfil Street greenhouse, maintaining the ever changing storefront window displays, keeping the customers charmed and cosseted.

We didn't think of this arrangement, where Harold didn't "interfere" and where my father did all the real work, as a matter of exploitation, so persuaded were we by his own love affair with the greenhouse. Harold rolled in at eleven, in time for lunch downtown at the Athletic Club, then turned up again around three to check the day's receipt, and then it was out for drinks at the Lowry before five. He had a desk somewhere, and sometimes sat at it, calling his broker, speaking low into the receiver. He always seemed distracted. You got the feeling he was a little startled to see all these flowers around, as if he leapt over the irritating intermediate steps of the business to the essential point of it all: the money.

Also a drinker, according to my mother. He seemed narrow, without curiosity, and you didn't really know if he was pickled much of the time. He started talking about moving to California. The business was changing— grocery stores were selling bunches of flowers in plastic pails for a couple of bucks! And people were buying them!

He wanted out. The company was bleeding. They offered it to my father, the aged and broken beauty he had loved all his life.

He didn't hesitate. They left to him, along with the old greenhouse and the shop downtown, various ancient encumbrances, and rumors of financial irregularities.

Then, finally in possession of his beloved, my father turned the other cheek, and several years later was embroiled all over again in problems with his new business partner. The taxman came to the door, that boogeyman of imperiled small businesses. The heart attacks started.

When it became patently evident that his youngest partner preferred investing in more profitable land outside of town rather than tending the greenhouse and store as my father thought he should, and my father lay in United Hospital, wheezing while the cardiologist managed, once again and for a while longer, to drain fluid from his congested heart, his only fury—a brief but bitter rage—was at my brother and me when he discovered we had hired a lawyer to pursue his rights. *A guy has to do the right thing, no matter what the other guy is doing...*

It turned out we weren't living in a Fitzgerald novel after all. This was Dickens, complete with threatening letters on legal letterhead, the gallant dying hero betrayed by advantage-taking villains, generations of cynical venality twisting the plot, and even our very own Uriah Heap who, after all, was a good guy. Nice smile, same Catholic schools, brought up the hard way. This was the sort of reasoning our father had given us as business acumen.

The heart attacks made retirement necessary not long after, and at first it seemed everything was going to be all right. No, more second mortgages on the house to cover the winter heating bill at the greenhouse, no more tax inspectors coming to the house, and a regular check from Uriah Heap every month plus Social Security. Not bad. For a while.

Then we learned (from Leo the Lion) that our father, supposedly retired and out of the company, was taking out a second mortgage on their house and loaning the money to tide the business over, explaining that this made sense, that his partner needed a little boost. This seemed to work for a while, every winter a loan, and then as the spring planting season kicked in, he was repaid. But then, one winter, my father's voice on the telephone, low and embarrassed—their checking account was down to eleven dollars.

His partner wasn't able to keep up. He meant no harm—his point, the point my father urged on me too. The partner felt it needed to be explained to me. *Patricia, if you only knew what the flower business is like now. It's not like it used to be...* I stood in the greenhouse and stared at him with the dead eyes of Leo the Lion.

There were ingrates and phonies, wrongs to be righted, money owed that should be decently paid, and so forth. My brother and I—naturally— were on the side of the good, the true, the beautiful. Our father.

Who wanted no part of our crusade. "You don't *do* this," he wheezed from his hospital bed, trailing his oxygen, horrified that his partner had received a letter from a lawyer, thanks to us. He acted as if we were endangering peace on earth. I suppose we were.

His allegiance was not to the truth, not even to fair play, not even to Justice when it came to his own just claims. His loyalty went to the invisible silken net of human relations webbed with let-it-go shrugs that, every day, keeps the universe from clawing itself to death.

You behave a certain way, no matter what the other guy does, as all his life he mildly called those who did not abide by his form of rectitude. From his lard-eating, we-had-nothing boyhood on the wrong side of the tracks, from his half century of winters stoking the eternal springtime of the green-house, he had somehow fashioned an ethic befitting the Dalai Lama. No blame, no blame.

But you're being cheated, my all-business oral-surgeon brother said, to which I, bully with poetic righteousness, chimed along. My mother, her Irish heart always glad of a fight, encouraged us to pursue our *Bleak House* plots.

But in the end, I suppose it is accurate to say our father got his way: the lawyers said that there wasn't enough money to pursue the matter. He died with the balance of the money owed him never paid back, the ingrates and phonies gone their merry or regretful ways, thinking Stan was a good man with a vicious wife and unkind children. Poor Stan, they could say.

And poor us—they could say that, too. Here was a decent working man, trying to meet a payroll, misunderstood by his greedy, overeducated kids. They didn't understand anything. Just goes to show you.

Nick Flynn

Other Meaning

Coming home from the drive-in, asleep under
blankets in the vast backseat,

my mother full of attention to the road
& we're all wrapped in darkness & steel. Somewhere

lost in the heart of the engine

small fires burn, pushing us away
from where we've been—

the 100-foot-high movie screen
& the airplane that passed through

Steve McQueen's head. My feet stab

at my brother's, wandering his own walled city
of sleep, suspended in an endless present,

endless protection & the low hum of static.
I remember a chair, a maroon &

velvet throne,
I fell asleep in once

under a glacier of coats
as a party raged around me. Only later do I learn

the other meaning of *maroon*—

of sailors, whole families, put out to sea
in inadequate lifeboats, left to drink their own piss

& pull gulls from the sky. I open one eye
but cannot identify the tops of passing trees.

How far to home? Once

she left me on the side of the road & drove off
into the rare green earth, her taillights

fading sparks. Once she cast me out
onto the porch, naked in the snow, merely because

I said she wouldn't dare.

Seven Fragments (found inside my father)

Fragment #1

      birds sing above my bench while the city
sleeps   their chatter
wakes me

Fragment #2

      one doctor asks if I hear things
other people don't
                  one said *frostbite* said
all your toes said *amputate*

but I walked

Fragment #3

before my eyes shut I see the dog-star
crawl across absolute zero

Fragment #4

words come to me in my sleep but they don't
      sound like me   I write
we are put on this earth to help other people...

      why don't you answer?

Fragment #5

          shelters
      shitsville

Fragment #6

> *gentlemen, it's that time again*

    & we rise as one
line the stairwell in our white
                johnnies, a number

tied to our wrists

Fragment #7

    yes I hear things

Father Outside

A black river flows down the center
of each page

& on either side the banks
are wrapped in snow. My father is ink falling

in tiny blossoms, a bottle
wrapped in a paperbag. I want to believe
that if I get the story right

we will rise, newly formed,

that I will stand over him again
as he sleeps outside under the church halogen
only this time I will know

what to say. It is night &
it's snowing & starlings
fill the trees above us, so many it seems

the leaves sing. I can't see them
until they rise together at some hidden signal

& hold the shape of a tree for a moment
before scattering. I wait for his breath
to lift his blanket

so I know he's alive, letting the story settle

into the shape of this city. Three girls in the park
begin to sing something holy, a song
with a lost room inside it

as their prayerbook comes unglued

& scatters. I'll bend
each finger back, until the bottle

falls, until the bone snaps, save him

by destroying his hands. With the thaw
the river will rise & he will be forced
to higher ground. No one

will have to tell him. From my roof I can see
the East River, it looks blackened with oil

but it's only the light. Even now
my father is asleep somewhere. If I followed

the river north I could still
reach him.

Good to Go

Well, we'd mortgaged everything but the baby, and Donnie tore the rear
spoiler half off, lost his downforce, and that was about it. Track came up
and smacked him silly. That was the last time we had any money to speak
of. Since then it's been working at Wal-Mart and a 78 Olds with a hole in
the floor big enough for J.R to lose a sneaker through. Last time it rained I
was ankle-deep in water floating down the blacktop to Cedar Rapids. Donnie's too busy welding other people's cars back together to put that piece
permanent over the floor. He's the nice guy the neighbors call at suppertime
to come fix their mower or disposal. We're making love and somebody needs
a spark plug. Same thing when he was racing. Bob there needed to finish
high enough to keep his sponsor. Frankie Jr. had the wife's medical bills,
and then there was the night Spanus came to look over Owen Brach for the
Craftsman Truck Series. Donnie, I said, Donnie we got bills and babies too.

You pay for your mistakes in racing, my stepdad Walter says. You miss
the setup and you take the wall. Walter has his own garage and Donnie was
working there when we met. It's funny, that's where Mom met Walter too.
She'd driven me and a car full of stuff through one whole night to get away
from her boyfriend and Versailles, Missouri. Needed gas and an answer for
the terrible thumping in the rear end. Walter's Friendly Service squatted
on the outskirts of town in possession of twenty acres of abandoned cars
and a fairly new, pink and white double-wide mobile home that sat in its
own pavilion surrounded by a fence of half-buried tractor trailer tires painted
white. Mom always loved their half-moon scallops, and admired a man who
would take the time, she said. She's gone, of course. Hers was a restless heart,
and even Walter understands how she came to leave with the UPS man right
after Donnie showed up. She'd been going away for a while, her eyes shiny
with longing of an impossible kind whenever she watched those long legged
country singers on cmt. Dwight Yoakam, Alan Jackson, you know the ones.
She loved us, Walter and me, with as much as was free inside her, but the rest
of her, well, it was always going someplace else, and she was just the wagging
tail to its dog.

The UPS man was half-Indian too. That's what she told me the night
she left. Walter and Donnie were at the fairgrounds, watching the Demolition Derby that was our town's annual contribution to the Fourth of July.
The fireworks would follow and I was getting ready to go out and climb
on the roof of the garage to watch. It was my general policy to avoid men

wrecking cars on purpose whenever possible. You see, I had that whole twenty acres of torn sheet metal and smashed windows to grow up in. It didn't take a genius to figure out the evolution. That particular family tree don't branch, I'd tell Donnie later.

Mom always seemed to leave places at night. She wasn't a Monday morning, new start kind of person. She waited and waited for her time, and it always came somewhere between eight and ten at night. She'd make all her decisions then, like one of those nocturnal animals whose brain clicked awake as soon as the sun set. I used to wonder what kept her with us as long as she did stay. I helped her pack that night. Maybe that was wrong of me, but I personally wrapped the pressed-glass swan vase she got from her Ozarks grandmother. I was afraid she'd be in such a hurry she'd forget it or not take enough care packing it, and I couldn't bear the picture of her standing there later with the pieces in her hands, knowing she'd lost something precious forever, something she could never ever make up or come back to. She was that kind of person. You wished her well. She had enough desire and longing for all of us, and I was just glad it was her having to drive away from places in the middle of the night, not me. My desire does not have geographical dimensions, I tell Donnie when he suggests we move to the other side of town.

I miss her. Miss how she could make Walter smile and shake his head and turn fast as a pony on a dime and try to chase her down when she teased him in the middle of work. She never minded the grease prints on her blouse and white-blonde hair or the burn his red stubble made around her mouth when they got to the house. Walter's not too sad now, you understand, he's just lost a little bit of air. He's skinnier somehow, like Mom took the fat out of his life. Now he has to live on lean and while that's good in some ways, it's really less than before and neither of us can forget that. I know he wishes I was more like her, that I'd treat Donnie the same way so he could get that lift out of watching us. But like I said, I'm not that kind of person. I leave Donnie to his work, and he leaves me to mine. Mine being J.R, working part-time at Wal-Mart, and keeping track of the salvage business.

It's funny how those twenty acres of cars became my responsibility. As a kid I wanted a horse, begged and pleaded, tried to win one in contests, prayed for some old man to leave me his money anonymously. I knew no woman would do anything that foolish, but I still believed in the crazy goodness of men then. One night at supper Walter put his fork down, finished chewing his Salisbury steak, swallowed, and announced that he too had been thinking hard about my problem, and he thought he'd found a solution. I could have a horse as soon as I cleared enough of those cars away for a pasture. He figured ten acres would be a good start. It was the kind of announcement filled a kid with despair and hope both, tangled impossibly, leaving you sleepless with frantic planning. I was twelve so it still seemed fairly simple to sell or move enough cars for my horse. First, I decided, I'd have to catalog the cars and make a list I could send around. Someone would want those good parts. Later when I came up with the plan to have them hauled away to a place that crushed and recycled metal, Mom gave a gentle shake of her head. Honey, she said, Walter loves those cars, no matter what he said.

And so it was that I came to see that I would have to defeat Walter's love for one of my own, and the unfairness of it struck me for the first time as what it meant to be helpless in the face of your own desire. It had been a year since our bargain, and while I had increased the salvage business by a good amount with my little catalog, the cars never seemed to do more than grow more hollow, piece by piece, until their skeletons rested mossy and black among the weeds that grew higher and higher, and as much as anything they came to resemble untended graves.

What I had ignored was the fact that new cars would be added as out in the world they grew old and died, got wrecked or totaled, and people in them escaped or died. It came to me after a while to look suspiciously at some cars: the black Trans Am that took Buddy Holden's legs, the green and white Chevy pickup that developed a fatal attraction for the Burlington Northern train taking the whole Smithen family with it. By the time I was fourteen, I began to dread spring nights when the high school seniors would scatter their lives like dandelion seeds to the wind in cars that the next day would be hauled through our gates and deposited, sometimes with blood stains still visible on the upholstery and the jagged glass of the windshield.

I avoided those cars on my walks then, hated to see the cats tiptoeing across the hoods, leaving dusty little prints, then pausing at the smashed windshield, sniffing the air, and pumping their tails slowly up and down before springing inside. Mice and field rats seemed to like those cars best. It took me a while to get on any sort of basis with those cars. Sometimes it never happened. I'd try to sell their parts fast, cheap, get their lethal hearts out of there. Still do.

There is one car I don't ever advertise though. One I'd never sell a piece of. I'd as soon bury it, but for Walter. Kids come around wanting a rocker panel, a header, a camshaft. I tell them take anything but leave that one up by the fence alone. I keep it close, you see.

Donnie and I might never have gotten together if it hadn't been for Mom's car, the one that drove us into Walter's heart. It was an old Chevy Malibu with the paint worn off to gray and rust eating its way up the doors and down through the roof and hood. The trunk lock was gone from the time we'd lost the key, and the lid was held down by a bungee cord. Walter always threatened to do something about that car, but the best thing he could manage was to keep the engine strong after he'd dropped in a new one when it became clear that we were staying on more or less permanently in the double-wide. The motor came from an old Buick Roadmaster and was really too big for the Malibu, which made it a spicy little car that spun its wheels at every stop sign and lifted its front end if you stepped on the gas too hard. When the muffler got a hole, it sounded like the hottest car in town. Walter didn't believe in new cars, and Mom didn't care. I was the only one interested in something with shine and glitter, I guess, since I'd had to give up on the horse. I needed to satisfy myself somehow, and I still thought it was going to be something with four legs or four wheels. I had no idea it was going to be Donnie until he came to lean over the engine one day while I was checking the oil. He took the dipstick out of my hand and wiped it clean between two fingers he rubbed off on his jeans while he stuck the stick back in and pulled it out again. Squinting in the sunlight at the light new oil, he nodded as if we'd come to some essential agreement and put it back in the hole. I was watching his tan arm with the veins popping and the hair bleached blond, the thick wrist with that bone sticking up and it made my stomach hollow with want.

You keep your engine tight, he said lifting the air filter off and checking the white folds for dirt. Big mother, isn't it? He screwed the wingnut down and jiggled the hoses, running his hands down their lengths for tears. Think I could drive her sometime? He pressed the fan belt for give and nodded with satisfaction. Turn it on, he instructed.

We won money almost from the start, drag racing Mom's car on the blacktop three miles away in the middle of the night. Donnie put on a glass pack muffler, leg pipes, and dual exhausts, then went to work on the engine. Walter watched us out of the corner of his eye, kept Donnie working late as possible, and Mom fell in love with the UPS man.

The first time we did it wasn't in the backseat of the car though. It was in the middle of Heison's oatfield. We'd won a hundred and fifty dollars that night from some guys from Iowa City, and they'd gotten so pissed we'd had to take off and hide. Wasn't hard since we knew every farm and field road in the county, and we'd been necking on most of them. That night the wind was blowing hot with an edge of cool rain we could smell from someplace not too far away, so we flung open the car doors and ran into the middle of the field and lay down making angels in poor Heison's oats. In the morning, he'd think it was deer and threaten to go hunting out of season, but we didn't care. The grain was coming ripe and it smelled nutty and sweet as the wind pushed it around and about us like big heavy waves of hissing water. Donnie undid the only button fastening his shirt, and when I saw that smooth tan chest and stomach, I knew what I was going to do. I sat up and pulled my T-shirt over my head. He shrugged out of his shirt, and the wind moaned in the trees on either side of the field, tossing the sound back and forth over our heads as he lay down on top of me, and I licked the salt sweet sweat on his cheek as sandpapery as a cat's tongue. Then I let him put his thick oil-dark fingers everywhere he wanted.

Afterwards we lay there side by side while the storm came up and lightning struck the cornfield on the other side of the trees, and we could feel the razor jolt ripping along the ground in all directions. We made love again in the muddy oats, naked, our clothes drowned somewhere beside us. At dawn we drove home, and Walter and Mom met us at the door. Donnie moved in that day. It only took ten days to get us married. I was sixteen. Donnie was nineteen. But that isn't the car I'm talking about.

I don't know how we moved from drag racing to oval tracks. Probably the junked racer we got the year J.E was born. I'd just turned eighteen and was still running the salvage. Donnie and I had our own trailer now. Not a double-wide, but it was enough. We had the twenty acres, the garage, and the office to run around in, and Mom and I spent time together too, so I never felt confined or anything. Some days, I admit, while I was nursing J.P., I'd sit at the kitchen window and look out across my cars and think of them as horses, grazing in the snow there, pawing to get down to last summer's grass, their coats shaggy as sheepdogs. I had bays and blacks mostly, with one or two chestnuts or grays. But mostly I liked the good reliable colors, nothing too fancy, nothing that showed dirt or too much personality. I'd read that the browns were best, that all other horses wanted to be brown, that's why the palominos and whites kept rolling in the dirt. It could be true, I decided, leaning into the tugging weight of J.P. at my nipple. It would be nice to go out there and call and have your horses come galloping up to the fence for a carrot. To be able to pat their warm chests, to bury your face in their thick necks, to feel their hot breath blowing on the back of your head. The cars looked forlorn out there in the winter, the only tracks from the dogs trotting up and down the rows, inspecting the ranks like visiting generals. The deer don't bother coming in the salvage yard. People work less on their cars that time of year, too, so it could be peaceful and lonely out there, especially when I was nursing. That winter Mom got a job in town at the drugstore, so she wasn't around much either. That way she could see the UPS man more often, I guess, though I didn't know it at the time.

The racecar showed up on the back of a flatbed from Mason City. "Lady says to tell you she doesn't want to see this thing again," the driver announced and backed the rig through the gates. I had him put it right up front so I could go over it when I had time without having to wade through the deep snow. Donnie could use the tractor to drag it back down with the others later. But that's not what happened. I fell asleep after J.P. was done nursing, and by the time I woke up and got us both bundled for the outdoors, it was well past lunch and Donnie was back from his morning job driving school bus for the kindergartners. He'd found the number two red and black Pontiac and was already inside trying to fix the ignition box. Thank you, oh thank you, thank you, he crawled out the window and kissed me and J.P enough that I couldn't tell him the truth. And so Donnie came to believe that I'd given him the Christmas present he'd always wanted, and I came to be the biggest liar in the family. At least I was then.

So we went racing, taking Walter with us too when he could find some-one to work weekends at the station. Mom was working long hours in town, or so we thought, and we were too busy to notice all the changes that were taking place. Me, I thought it was Dwight Yoakam she was in love with, and what was the harm of that, I'd ask Donnie late at night at the track, snuggling in our truck bed camper, J.P in his own little bed on top of the flip-down table we ate at.

Once in a while we'd win, but it wasn't anything like the drag racing we'd done. We were broke all the time, borrowing from Mom and Walter, taking extra jobs, the both of us, finding J.P.'s clothes and toys in the second-hand stores, rummage and yard sales. Donnie had that true believer look in his eyes, though, and I don't think he noticed how it was going for the baby and me. I'd spend my time trying to rustle up deals on parts off flyers I'd make during the week at home, and trying to line up what Donnie needed for his car too. I took to keeping J.P. on a piece of clothesline tied around his waist and mine. Got dirty looks for that, and some laughs, but it was safety really. We were both about half deaf from the roaring engines. But I remembered what it was like all those years before when I'd wanted a horse more than anything else in the world and how it had seemed like both the easiest and the hardest, most distant thing that could happen, and I could not deny Donnie that one little corner of his dream.

Then we went through a time when everything seemed to click. Walter was helping with the engine and Donnie was driving like Richard Petty. Our life started moving faster, we bought a newer pickup and then a decent used car for me. We went to bigger tracks and got to know some of the other driv-ers and their families. The crowds started cheering for us once in a while. That lasted a year and a half, with our dreams tumbling out hot and fresh like clothes from the dryer. We would move up, get into newer cars, we'd get a team, we'd find sponsors, and so on. We'd just won at Mason City, and Donnie had decided to spend the Fourth at home because the next month he'd be gone part of every week.

He and Walter wanted to go to our town's annual Demolition Derby and take J.P. He was old enough, they said. I backed out. I was tired, I told them, wanted time to just sit and go over the books on the salvage yard and talk to Mom. And I remember we all looked around at Mom like we'd forgotten she existed, and in a way I guess she had. She'd been disappearing so gradually, we hadn't noticed, not even Walter, though as I say that, I don't believe that part is true. Walter would have noticed. He just might not have been able to say anything. There she was, Mom, with this forced little smile on her thin face and her pale blue eyes so long gone you could tell they weren't seeing any of us sitting around the table of her house. She was already out the door, down the walk, past the heavy tire scallops of her fence, stepping into the UPS man's brand new Camaro, a too-good-to-be-true gold yellow. But I wouldn't see that for several more hours yet. You go ahead, she smiled. I'm fine. We can watch the fireworks from the garage roof and when you come home, we'll have some ice cream and beer.

It's the small lies we come to hold against a person, I've decided. Not that she wouldn't be there when they came home, that she'd leave me to face Walter by myself, but that she promised them ice cream she already knew she didn't have in the freezer. Ice cream and beer, that should've been a tip-off, don't you think? Even her Ozarks hillbilly relatives knew better than to offer up a combination like that. What were we thinking, all of us?

So, like I said, when I came back from checking the books on the salvage yard, which Walter and Pugh did not bother keeping worth a darn, there was Mom packing. Wasn't much to say, really. At least I didn't try to say much. She was the determined one in our family, and she had that restlessness. I was a grown woman with a family of my own to worry about. I thought she'd be back, or that I'd go see her. I thought all kinds of things as I wrapped the glass swan in her underwear three, four times and bedded it safely with her socks on top of her jeans and put her T-shirts on top of that. I wasn't thinking about Walter. Her happiness swept all those thoughts up and away like a good strong wind blowing the house clean again as she opened the door and ran down to meet the yellow Camaro's honking horn. I carried the black nylon bag myself and put it in the trunk when he popped the lid, saw it safely resting on jumper cables next to a lava lamp even I knew was cheesy. His clothes were in a cardboard box. I remember a white athletic sock with a frayed heel hanging over the edge, and I reached to tuck it back in but stopped myself because suddenly I couldn't touch anything of his, as if his things were too nasty in a personal, naked way. I slammed the trunk lid and leaned down to kiss her good-bye, only getting the glance of her ear for she turned away too quickly to laugh at something he said. And by the time she turned back, he was stepping on the gas and spewing gravel from the tires that stung my bare legs as the car burst away, suddenly tearing a hole too big to be closed again.

Walter and Donnie and J.R drove right by the wreck on their way home, hurrying to tell me about it. How they could still be excited by a wrecked car, I'll never know, but I didn't blame them, not at first. Not until they said it was a new yellow Camaro with the front end so crumpled they had to cut it in half to get the people out, and the rescue squad turned off the blinking lights after they loaded up the bodies. Kids, Walter said, and I couldn't look at him again for a month.

That was the end of our racing luck. I never understood how one thing got in the way of the other, and maybe it didn't, but maybe it did. We dug a hole of debt so deep we about drowned, and now even Walter's working twenty-four-seven to keep the bills at bay. We were all good to go, though in some strange way we didn't realize it, and then she went and took it away. So you know now that the remains of that Camaro are right inside the gate here where I can keep an eye on them. I never unpacked the trunk either, the one part of the car intact. I've left it there, the black nylon bag with the glass swan safely nestled in its dark sleep among her clothes. The UPS man's cardboard box molding and collapsing in the wet years since that dream arrived and took ahold of our lives. Because it's like Walter says, you pay for every mistake.

Patricia Smith

Man On the TV Say

Go. He say it simple, gray eyes straight on and watered,
he say it in that machine throat they got.
On the wall behind him, there's a moving picture
of the sky dripping something worse than rain.
Go, he say. Pick up y'all black asses and run.
Leave your house with its splinters and pocked roof,
leave the pork chops drifting in grease and onion,
leave the whining dog, your one good watch,
that purple church hat, the mirrors.
Go. Uh-huh. Like our bodies got wheels and gas,
like at the end of that running there's an open door
with dry and song inside. He act like we supposed
to wrap ourselves in picture frames, shadow boxes
and bathroom rugs, then walk the freeway, racing
the water. *Get on out.* Can't he see that our bodies
are just our bodies, tied to what we know?
Go. So we'll go. Cause the man say it strong now,
mad like God pointing the way outta Paradise.
Even he got to know our favorite ritual is root,
and that none of us done ever known a horizon,
especially one that cools our dumb running,
whispering urge and constant: *This way. Over here.*

Only Everything I Own

This is my house.
This was my grandfather's house.
This is my thin wood, spidered pane.
These are my cobwebs, my four walls,
my silverfish, my bold roaches.
I bury my hands in that little garden,
cool them in the broken earth.
My food comes from my garden.
At my table, I slice the peppers,

seed the tomatoes, chop mint,
rip bitter green into wooden bowls.
The tiny pine table is my whole kitchen,
daddy's legacy, my certain warm nurture.
I dream loud in this house. I pull my bed
down from that wall, and I fall to my knees
next to it to question this shelter.
I sleep while a limp breeze dies at the window,
waking to dawn tangled with my dust.
This is my house.

Let's step out into the steam,
sip new breath from Mason jars,
find a sleeping rhythm for our chairs.
Let's wait patiently for the rain.
That blistered sky has learned my days
and hates me for everything I have. As it should.

Inconvenient

Go.
What, again? What nuisance, this back and forth.
But even the blessed must bow to damp tantrums.
Some network blathering, ominous graphics,
and we pack the steamer with overnight,
lash the boat to its mooring, wrap the new guest house
up like some stern little package. And for what?
So some dreary witch with a name bigger than she's worth
can drip scare into nightfall, turn one day, maybe two,
into missed manicures, grayish harping, dull dinners
of canned soup. *Go.* And this time, again, it's serious.
What it is is just more windy yelping by wild-eyed anchors,
round-the-clock warnings followed by wet drumming
in the flower beds, stretched nerves, maybe a hint of mold.
At least twice a year, we deal with the plumped drama
of an oversold storm, watching as the sky bulges,
leaks melodrama, postpones our garden parties.

Best to consider this whole mess a holiday,
a simple trade, one home for its vacation version.
Best to stuff our luggage into the idling Lincoln

and wait while my husband revels in busywork,
clawing through his toolbox, hammering a thumbnail
and strengthening every room's surface with tape.
After he slides his pampered girth behind the wheel,
we point the car toward rumored sun, scan the sky
for signs. Again, we run. Left to me, I wouldn't budge.
Up here the dollar sings. We pay for this boredom.

What To Tweak

Italicized excerpts are from an Aug. 31, 2005 email from Marty Bahamonde
to his boss Michael Brown, head of the Federal Emergency Management Agency.
Bahamonde was one of the only FEMA employees in New Orleans at the time.

Aug. 31, 12:20 p.m. Re: New Orleans

Sir, I know that you know the situation is past critical. Here are some
things you might not know.

> Rainbows warp when you curse them.
> I have held a shiver of black child against my body.
> The word *river* doesn't know edges.
> God wouldn't do this.
> There's a Chevy growing in that tree.
> Here, I am so starkly white.
> Sometimes bullets make perfect sense.
> Eventually the concrete will buckle.
> They won't stop screeching at me.
> I have passed out all my gum.
> So many people are thirsty.
> A kid breathes wet against my thigh.
> He calls me father.

Hotels are kicking people out....

> No one is prepared for their sulking shadows.
> They sully sleek halls, leave smudges on grand glass.
> They double negative, sport clothes limp with ache.
> These people don't know this place,
> this costly harbor where they have always pointed,
> eyes bucked and overwhelmed,
> giddy with the conjure of mirrored silver

and whole cups dedicated to tea.
In the sudden midst of glorious this,
they fill their cavernous pockets with faith.
Why didn't we bolt the doors
before they began to dream?

thousands gathering in the streets with no food or water...

The weakened mob veers into the open for breath.
Ashy babies bellow, B-boys hurl gold-toothed *fuck its,*
everyone asks for food. And the heat singes art
on bare backs, sucks tears from parched skin.
It's true there is no food, but water is everywhere.
The demon has chapped their rusty ankles,
reddened the throats of babies, smashed homes to mist.
It is water that beats down without taking a breath
and points its dank mossy finger at their faith.
I have killed you, it patters.
I have bled you dry.

Hundreds still being rescued from homes.

Or not.
Death has an insistent iron smell, oversweet rot
loud enough to wither certain woods.
Behind sagging doors specters swirl,
grow huge-limbed, stink brilliance.
And up on the roofs of tombs,
sinking mothers claw the sky,
pray the rising river away from their scream.
The moon refuses to illuminate their overtures,
winking dim then winking shut.
From the papery peaks of three-flats,
shots and weeping in the starless dark.
If you listen, you can hear the dying.
It creaks odd and high,
a song slowly larger than the singer.

*Evacuation in process. Plans developing for dome evacuation but hotel
situation adding to problem. We are out of food and running out of
water at the dome. Plans in works to address the critical need.*

Stifle the stinking, shut down the cameras,
wave Dubya down from the sky.
Subtract the babies, unarm the flailers,

Hose that wailing bitch down!
Draw up a blueprint, consider detention,
throw them some cash from a bag.
Tell them it's God, ply them with preachers,
padlock the rest of the map.
Hand them a voucher, fly in some Colonel,
twist the volume knob hard.
Turn down the TV, distract them with vision,
pull out your hammer and nail.
Sponge off their shoulders, suckle their children,
prop them upright for the lens.
Tolerate ranting, dazzle with card tricks,
pin flags on absent lapels.
Try not to breathe them, fan them with cardboard,
say that their houses will rise.
Play them some music, swear you hear engines,
drape their stooped bodies with beads.
Salute their resilience, tempt them with future,
surrender your shoes to the mud.
Promise them trailers, pass out complaint forms,
draft a law wearing their names.
Say help is coming, say help is coming,
then say that help's running late.
Shrink from their clutches, lie to their faces,
explain how the levies grew thin.
Mop up the vomit, cringe at their crudeness,
audition their daughters for rape.
Stomp on their sleeping, outrun the gangsters,
pass out American flags.

DMAT staff working in deplorable conditions. The sooner we can get the medical patients out, the sooner we can get them out.

Breathing bladed, blood tinged black,
their stark diseases mystify, ooze unbridled.
Heat stuns their grip on history,
so they keep attempting to walk back
into remembered days of weather
that never grew more difficult than rain.
They crave the reign of simple delta,
when skinned pig, peppered collards,
and a bottle of red heat signaled a day gone right.
So they keep trying to walk, to force their feet

into the now-obscenity of a straight line,
to begin with that first blessing—*forward, forward,*
not getting the joke of their paper shoes,
not knowing the sidewalks are gone.

Brown:

Thanks for update. Anything specific I need to do

or tweak?

Golden Rule Days

Following Katrina, thousands of schoolchildren were forced to work through trauma while they adjusted to new schools, cultures and communities. Their reception has ranged from pity, to acceptance, to blatant exclusion.

I.

They keep touching him. They keep touching
him, as if they expect his surface to suddenly
wilt, as if they could actually feel the water
sloshing in place of a heart. Their thousand
hands are curved and comforting, heat cupped
in them like money, arid swipes in each of their
fingers. *We're sorry, we're sorry.* They keep
touching him, brushing past his scarred arms,
tugging lightly on his clothing, some boldly
reaching out for his cheek, *sorry, so sorry.*
And he wonders how long he can stand this
still, be this sort of trophy, how long he can stay
bended, going from one to the other, slipping
their winged feet into God's loafers, slipping
deftly into his role as child who drowns, again
and again, who opens his mouth to scream,
but river rushes in. His saviors believe with all
their hearts in soft rescues. They keep touching him.

II.

Her name is A-R-L-I-N-E, an old woman's name
from a grandmama's way of spelling,
and her shoes are smeared with her home
and laced with string. Too nappy and ashed
for first day, she walks in halting,
but dippin' bayou like she's got one fluid hip
and knows some real old music real well.
She is prepared to be anyone, anything.
With just a little warning, she can juggle
language, gone days, she can recite lines
scripted to staunch questions and add light
to her skin. Replace the *i* in her name with an *e*,
yes, start there, with what she is called. Then
shield her against the murdering rain, which
just keeps drumming her dizzy, naming her over.

III.

Carla rose from the black river
and was resurrected as refugee
pickininny
unfortunate swimmer
gasper
She woke up in the wrong country
her donated denims too snug
too not hers
their pocked hips made her
instantly recognizable as
Katrina girl
as plaits undone
as double negative
as hard case
loud on these white streets
and so easily summoned now
by snicker, the tooth suck, that noun.

Carla rose from the black river
unraveled, rattled,
unrhymed,

What's the matter

alone, unwhole, choking on gas
and rot

nigger

but what a caress
beneath the water's shifting

couldn't you

surface

swim?

Mark Nowak
_____

Excerpts from
$00/Line/Steel/Train

1.

The basic form is the frame; the photograph of the factory predates how every one (of the materials) will get used. **and I can remember Mark & I talking about the possibility of Lackawanna becoming a ghost town** Past (participle) past (participant) past (articulating) an incessant scraping (away). **and what would we do. You know—it wasn't just losing a job in the steel industry, but your entire life, the place that you grew up in was going to be gone.** As I scraped (grease, meat, omelettes), the (former) railroad workers and steel workers (still) bullshitting in the restaurant where for eight years I short-order cooked.

*

Who knew

the crisis

from the conditions—

presumably

the Capital [Who]

13.

The interruption of the closure, in this instance, but the frame: "LTV [Steel] was able to use its bankruptcy to reduce payments to productive workers." **In the old days when the city bus used to pull up to the factory gate, the driver would call out "butcher shop" or "slaughterhouse."** "In negotiations with the steelworkers union, LTV extracted more takebacks than other, presumably healthier steel companies were able to." **I can remember sitting around the lunch table, and everybody at that table, there must have been seven or eight people, had a finger or something missing.** "This gave LTV an advantage over its competitors." **Believe it or not, people felt it was kind of like a badge of honor that they had a finger or something missing, and that would be a topic of conversation.** "Bankruptcy became, through a cultural process that understood bankruptcy as failure, a condition for success."

*

Where are

yards   our

yards where our

no you cannot
yards [where] away

38.

They put me in hot places all summer, where not many men will stay; when it gets cool they layed [*sic*] me off; White men get my job...I have went to see the employment manager of the mill [and] all he says is their [*sic*] is no call for colored men. He has sent me to places in the mill where I have worked as good as any other man, but I can't get the job steady, on account of I am not [a] White man...I don't think it fair...I have a right to a living as well as anyone else, no mater what color I am...The basic form (the photograph of a factory inside this frame) does not discontinue.

*

Separate in/to
two tracks   two doors
doesn't America "Land

of the Free..."
know this two from history

154.

Forty years of hard work and what have I got to show for it? Nothing. Aerosol cans empty in the middle of the tracks is not conducting the train. I can't even speak proper. Working-class kids writing their names on a wall that is bound to erase them. When you're a steelworker (laughs), you don't get to speak the same language that you would do if you meet people in a bank or business office. On Blackrock Bridge (above Buffalo Creek)—where my grandfather took me fishing after he retired from Bethlehem—someone wrote (before the train came, before the bridge tore down) "FUCK WHITE PUNKS ON DOPE!"

*

When was fond of

making   Memorials

of the materials—

they go, history

shows, sometimes, South

257.

Because the (brake) past is used because the tearing (past) of the (brick) form is used is used because the fence (in) of the (goddamn) frame is used is used is utterly used against us and by us and upon us and for us is used is used in the present (past) future (form) we are used yet users yet used.

Every day you put your life on the line when you went into that iron house. Every day you sucked up dirt and took a chance on breaking your legs or breaking your back. And anyone who's working in there knows what I'm talking about.

*

-roads]

Closing

words   :

[Rail

James Cihlar

Lessons

I.

My father would lie on his side in front of the TV.
My eyes followed the line of his back
up the steady incline from his hip
to the point of his shoulder.

II.

We walked to the top of the hill to cut a Christmas tree.
My father anchored himself on the worn yellow cusp.
Our words moved us from one place to the next
as we dotted the lines from tree to tree.

III.

When I woke at midnight
and reached over to touch my brother,
my hand was stopped in the darkness
by my father's arms wrapped around him.

IV.

My sisters and I found a sick cat.
By day's end, it was dying,
and we asked my father what could be done.
Nothing, he told us.

V.

In winter I walked home from classes
and lay with my roommate in bed,
fully clothed under the blankets
as we fit ourselves to each other.

Lincoln Avenue

Start with the granite stones
laid at the base of the white post fence
with grapevines wound through.
Someone had to place them there.
Go to the English Ivy
trained up the green slate wall,
sheltered even in winter.
How hard would it be
to stay in one place, year after year,
locked into family
and father? Every day
is a prop against leaving,
until you feel the weight upon you:
sour water in the plastic wading pool,
the play-worn spot
where grass will never grow.
Some day it will all come crashing down,
and you will think,
I must give up to save myself.
Look at the terraced yard
where the weeping willow
has shrugged off its leaves.
I've left, too.
The light has retreated into windows,
and the day has put its color away.
Someone will have to go back
and pick up what has fallen.

Resolution

In the first dream
my guidance counselor
makes a clerical error
and I do not have enough credits.
So in middle life
I go back to high school.
But I forget to show up for class,
and I don't know how to study any more,

so I never graduate.
This dream repeats.

When I was a kid I was mad
my mother treated me like an adult,
blaming me for her lost chances.
But now I'm mad
that as a kid
I did not act like an adult
and take the wheel
or just speak up.

When I was in college and my mother called, drunk again,
stereo throbbing behind her,
Jimmy Jay?
The most I did then was say,
Listen, old lady, if you don't knock this off,
we will lock you up. Hear me?
Lock you up.
For years
she stopped calling
but kept on drinking.
What if I had honked the horn,
pulled the car over,
told her to stop
what really needed stopping?

She is gone now.
I even threw away her last letter,
mentioning my sister,
Vickie and her girls
have been wonderful.
What comes after?
I'll always be circling back.

In the other dream
I am still living at home
with all my sisters and brother,
under her roof. Once I get a job,
or once I save money,
or once I make a decision,
I can move out.
But that will never happen.
And I'm middle-aged and fearful,

holding my knees to my chin
on my old bunk bed,
waiting for her to crash
through the door.

Undoing

Unfamiliar with the logic of the physical world,
As a kid I did not understand repair.

My mother warned,
If you break that lamp

We can't replace it, but I couldn't believe her.
The world can't be that stingy,

Not the same world of tulips erupting from bulbs,
Moths emerging from cocoons, smooth upholstery

Cradling my cheek in the backseat of my father's Chevy
Driving back roads to supper clubs, cornflake-crusted

Fried chicken, doughy dinner rolls, so much food
I had to push the plate away. There must be

A scientific process by which something broken
Can be restored entirely, the mistake undone, nothing lost.

Today a commercial tells me that a fire in one room
Can damage a whole house. A woman drapes a shawl

Over a space heater and it announces flames.
I have littered the past year with anxiety,

And it is spilling over into the rest of the house.
Taking it on, my cat breaks a figurine on the vanity.

Make it like it never happened, the commercial promises.
Even if I glued the shards together, I would comprehend

The fissures webbing the porcelain, the pressure points of weakness,
Which is my undoing.

Having broken many things
In my life, I have grown to accept

We could undo anything if only we could forget.

Manikin

Not until later did they notice the items missing through the house, a quick dip of stuff more suggestive of an anthropologist than a thief: a baseball glove, a plate, one of a set of four figurines, a photo, a pen holder, a piece of jewelry. Specimens. All collected in a pillow case that was also missing—this was how they pieced it together—and the perpetrator, one of their own, made off in the night for who really knew where.

Van came downstairs that morning and found his mother, Brenda, seated at the kitchen table. Brenda sat limp in her chair as though stunned from her night's rest, but really she was caught in recoil at the contents of a brief note that had been left behind, the proof of the crime.

Brenda, Gone to Tulsa. Brad.

The note was pinned to the table with a salt shaker. The message had an odd rhythm to it, Van thought, like the notes of a descending scale. At fifteen, Van knew musical order when he heard it. Brad was his father. Had been his father. Already the tense was confusing. But while Brenda soaked in the pain of it, Van found the news easier to reconcile, and he took comfort in the thought that he would now join the ranks of children-of-broken-homes at school; they got more attention and better grades, and the bond between them seemed strong and incalculably deep from a distance.

Van sat next to Brenda. He had never before thought of her by her given name. She seemed quite young to him then—she was thirty-six—and he saw at once in her new station what she herself could not: the potential for something better than what she had managed thus far. A single square of sunlight from the window over the sink cut them both in half, warming Brenda's left side and Van's right.

"Tulsa," Brenda said, "is 'a slut' spelled backwards."

Van didn't say anything, first to determine whether she was correct, then to interpret it. She was suggesting Brad had left her for another woman, which was probably true. It was dismissal in the form of humorous quip, but it was a joke meant to convey fury with hyperbole.

They were silent until Kara arrived.

Kara, seventeen, tossed her hair as she read the note. The glowing strands dripped away from her fingers as she comprehended it, and Van couldn't help noticing it was sexy, that motion, and that it was designed that way. His sister was a sexy girl, but it wouldn't last her long or get her far.

"I'm not surprised," Kara said, sitting down. "Are you surprised?"

She meant either of them, Kara needing someone to speak at such a moment, needing discourse to fetter her angst. But neither Van nor Brenda spoke, and Kara stared at the tabletop. She was a popular girl, and Van could see that her first reaction, similar to his, was to weigh what effect this development would have on her relationships at school. Brad had not been a mean father. But nor had he compared to the loving patrons of television, the polite dads of Van's friends. He had approached the role, Van thought, as though it were a commercial spot. A bad poet would have said he loved with half a heart.

Kara picked up the salt shaker, the note's paperweight, and turned it as though it was a relic. Then she said, "Where's the pepper?"

It was gone. They began to notice the other items missing as well: a knife, an alarm clock, a canister of tennis balls, a stuffed animal, a telephone. They called to one another through the house to catalog the damages, but it was unclear whether they were performing simple stock work or attempting to diagnose the thief. The items Brad had left behind made a list as potentially revealing: photo albums, his dog, Christmas ornaments, $300, a .22 bolt-action target rifle. They returned to the kitchen once the inventory was complete.

"I should call the cops right now," Brenda said.

Her reaction was more interesting as twisted linguistics, Van thought.

"What for?" Kara said. "It's *his* stuff. Useless junk."

"He's crazy," Brenda said. "Walking off with a bunch of random crap."

The house, Van thought, sported a new and conspicuous quality of lightness. "It's not random," he said. "There's order. There's pattern."

Brenda gave a masculine guffaw. "You'll have to explain that one to me, Dr. Metaphysics."

There weren't any words that wouldn't aggravate her further. "It's like this," Van said, and with his finger he traced a circle on the table.

*

Over the next several days Van noticed heightened awareness in himself, increased emotional efficiency. He *felt* better, and knew that he felt better. It hit him like a virus. Brenda and Kara were infected as well, but they were too steeped in bitterness to notice. All three of them had been caught off guard by the theft and departure, and as though to avoid another shock they had assumed a mode of lingering crisis. It made them more calculating if more cold, more intense if less pleasant, more intelligent if not happy. Van had insight into Brad's spree: the items he had lifted were all easily replaced, the holes filling in quickly like sand filling a hole at the beach. It was part of the message.

The oddest behavior came from Brad's dog, Charlie, a Rottweiler. Charlie seemed genuinely afraid to nudge any of the remaining masters for food. The dog drank from the toilets for three days until Brenda took to filling its bowl.

At school, Van's teachers, as he had predicted, paid closer attention to him once word came down that Brad had abandoned them. Kara parlayed the news to a center stage moment among her friends, and one day after school Van's English teacher, Mr. Finger, called out to him near the buses and pulled him aside. Mr. Finger was young, twenty-eight, and Van knew for a fact that he had briefly dated the divorced mothers of two other students. Mr. Finger said that he had heard about Van's family's difficulties, and asked if Van had ever kept a journal.

"No," Van said.

"Well, you should," Mr. Finger said. "And you should write about *this*."

Van had no idea at all why he should write something down when there would be no one to read it. By the time Mr. Finger was done talking, Van's bus had squealed away from the school. The walk home was two miles with short cuts through two fenced yards and a small park. These neighborhoods looked liked paintings, Van thought as he passed through them, but not good ones. Clouds shifting in the near distance, high hills that gave a sense of secure walls, perfect homes and clean curbs and upright mailboxes with flags raised for urgent dispatches. It was hollow art. He imagined himself posed in such a work, a kid trudging along with no books, no fishing pole, no lunchbox, basketball, radio, or sidekick. Where, in such a painting, he thought, would such a boy be going?

"Hey!"

Van was in the park now, and the voice was hollered but far off yet. A man stood over near the swing sets, alone, much like a figure in a painting himself.

"Hey!" the man called again, and now his arm beckoned Van along with a huge curling motion.

Van started the walk over. The man put his hands in his pockets and kicked at the sandbox sand as he waited. The man wore a thick brown beard over most of his face. The rest of his hair was long and wavy. He gave a hip flick of his head when Van was in speaking distance, and a smile appeared within the ragged beard, a tool of truce.

"Can you do me a favor, dude?" the man said. He squeezed awkwardly into one of the swings, his hands clenching the rusted iron chains. "Push me."

"Push you?" Van said.

"Come on, man. I'm not a pervert. Look around. Shoot."

A number of houses backed onto the park and dozens of windows stared down at them, it was true. Still, Van thought, it was an odd way to make the point.

"I'm Sasquatch," the man said, reaching forward to offer his hand. "It's a nickname."

"Hi." Sasquatch's hand was doughy and warm from his pocket.

"Come on, just for a little bit. I forget how to get it going."

"You just kick your legs. How could you forget?"

"Indulge me, man," Sasquatch said. "What's it gonna cost you?"

He smiled. Van walked around behind him. Sasquatch wore a heavy old army coat, and Van placed his hands on the man's shoulder blades. Sasquatch tensed his body to accept the energy just as Van leaned and shoved and had the thought that Sasquatch had done this before. The man was on his way.

Van pushed him perhaps a dozen more times, heaving him forward and backing out of the way to avoid the return swing. Sasquatch was silent in flight, the wind inflating his jacket and parting his beard and hair. The chains of the swingset screeched like birds in pain. When the lunges of the swing brought the chains to parallel with the earth, Sasquatch called, "Enough!" Van stepped back. On the next rush forward, just at the peak of the swing's altitude and acceleration, Sasquatch pushed himself from the seat, continuing up perhaps another four feet in the air, floating there a moment as the swing twisted and jingled and fell away, and then he was sucked back to the earth to splash in the sandbox with a thud Van felt in his feet.

Sasquatch crumbled onto his side, but did not cry out or even grunt. He quickly got up and brushed the sand from his knees.
"Thanks, dude," he said, and walked off.

Van headed home. The house was empty. Brenda was still at work, and Kara was supposed to be at soccer practice but was probably smoking with her friends at the creek. Charlie appeared in the kitchen wagging his stub tail as though expecting Brad; the dog whined at Van and turned away. Van ate an orange, drank milk from the carton, and noticed that one of the refrigerator magnets was missing, another piece of Brad's loot, a small Rottweiler's head.

Van wandered out to the garage. The dank two-car was filled with junk, a heaping pile of stuffed boxes and small appliances broken just beyond Brad's knowledge of repair. Van circled the mound.

I am thinking quite well, he thought.

The first piece came from a basketball backboard that Brad had shaped from plywood but never hung over the garage door. The slope of the backboard at its apex matched nicely the curve of a set of imagined shoulders, and Van had only to sheer off the edges to give it the rough shape of an armless torso. The old tree saw he used barely managed the knots, and the floor was quickly covered with sawdust. Van sanded the frayed edges of the backboard with his palms, then found a short bit of pipe. He picked through Brad's tackle box of bolts and nuts until he found a match, then screwed the pipe into the board, holding the nut in place with his finger and twisting until he stabbed his own fingerprint. The pipe held. Van had a choice of three Christmas tree stands for a base, and picked the one whose spike fit the pipe best. The torso stood upright at dwarf-height, firm and solid, like something built to outlast the generation of its creator.

The next piece was the obvious choice: a Styrofoam wig head. He plucked it from a shelf and the saw tore into it, small bits of Styrofoam flying away like sparks from a difficult weld. The cut was done in seconds, a slit bisecting the base of its neck. Van fastened the head onto the top of the backboard, and the construction came to life now, the head's blank expression fed emotion by the addition of a body at scale.

Van backed away from it just as Kara appeared in the door to the kitchen. She was back lit, hair bound in pony tails that cut her age by a third. She stood on one leg, posing.

"Oh, God," she said. "What are you doing?"

"I don't know," Van said.

She stepped down into the garage. "What is it?"

Van opened his mouth to speak, but then thought that words would ruin whatever it was.

"It's a person," Kara decided. "It's Dad."

She wasn't right, but denying it wouldn't help. "There was a man in the park today," Van offered. "I walked home. There was someone I met."

"No," Kara said. "It's Brad. It's Dad." She was quiet a moment, and passed a toe through the layer of sawdust and Styrofoam bits on the cement floor. "Rice and corn," she said.

They were quiet in miscommunication. The garage filled with the faint sound of the television running in the far-off living room.

"It's a manikin," Brenda said later, when Kara dragged her into the garage after she'd come home from work. "What the hell's it for?"

Van, hands at his sides, shrugged. He liked the word—*manikin*.

"He's going to make it a girl," Kara tried now. "He's going to give it tits."

Brenda reached out to jostle the manikin, test its buoyancy. The figure had two sections of flimsy plastic tubing for arms now, and they wagged in tandem at Brenda's touch. "That true?"

"It's not a woman," Van said.

Brenda's eyes stayed with the manikin a moment. "Whatever," she said, and went inside.

*

The next day, Kara was already home when Van returned from school. Again he had walked, but today the park was empty. He stood before the shrine of the refrigerator, and Kara passed behind him carrying a large shovel, her feet trailing dirt from the back yard.

"What are you doing?" he asked.

"A project," she said, headed for her room. "Like your doll."

Silence solved the proclamation. It was Charlie. The dog had not appeared to investigate him. Brad's .22 leaned against the wall next to the sliding glass door that led out to the backyard. Its barrel was warm. Van stared out into the yard, but everything was the same. Back in the family room, Kara splayed herself across the sofa to read biology.

In the garage, Van unwound several coat hangers and threaded them through the manikin's arms to give them a stiff elbowish bend. One he turned slightly in, and the other he brought all the way up to the belly as though the manikin was about to check the time on a pocket watch. He found a brass back scratcher whose business end was a small clawed hand. He snapped it in Brad's vise, then wound it into the manikin's arm until it protruded just right. A kitchen implement became the other hand, some kind of prodder or scooper, and when it was in place it took imagination to see it as a hand even mildly deformed. But it was right.

He was digging in the pile for features for the manikin's face when he heard the phone ring. Brenda's shoes clacked across the kitchen plastic, and Van heard the pitch of her voice but not her words. In a moment, she appeared in the door.

"There's someone on the phone named Derek Finger. Your English teacher, right?"

"Yes," Van said.

"He says he wants to discuss your grade." She looked the manikin up and down, eyeing its development. Van realized that he wanted it to please her. "But he's just hitting on me, right?"

"Probably."

Brenda's face collapsed into consideration, recalling parent nights at school. "He's the kind of scrawny one, right? But cute."

"I guess so. Yeah."

She squinted out past the garage. Then she turned decisively and clacked back into the house.

*

Buttons pinned to the head for irises, smaller buttons pinned to them for pupils. A plastic set of Mr. Potato Head lips fixed to the mouth. A mop, rank and stiff with old scum, for hair. An old fedora, a pair of sunglasses, belt buckles for epaulets. A plaid of expired coupons staple-gunned into the ply-wood for a shirt. Another shirt on top of that. The manikin was Van's height now, legs of the same plastic tubing as its arms, threaded through a pair of blue jeans Brad had used for working in the yard. Croquet mallets for feet. Slippers slipped over them. The manikin began to look comfortable.

Mr. Finger was home one day after school. Van had not said anything to him in class for several days, and Mr. Finger had avoided calling on him be-tween writing assignments. Brenda and Mr. Finger were at tea in the kitchen when Van arrived home.

"He said something about Tulsa," Van heard Brenda say, as he pushed his bag into the clutter of the closet. "We heard from a lawyer and started getting checks, but who really knows?"

Mr. Finger had his hands wrapped around his teacup as though it were a chalice. He pressed his lips wisely. It was as ridiculous to see him away from his classroom, Van thought, as it would have been to see a monkey loping madly down the street.

"Hi, sweetie," Brenda said.

"Hi, Van," Mr. Finger said.

Van nodded.

"Van, show Derek your thing out there," Brenda said, nodding toward the garage. Then, to Mr. Finger, "He's working on the most interesting thing. He's so smart! What is it, anyway, honey?"

"It's a manikin," Van said.

"I'd be happy to take a look," Mr. Finger said. "Maybe we can give you some extra credit there, huh?"

"Give me a minute."

Van went out to the garage. The manikin wasn't done. He had come to realize that he was ashamed that he cared what others thought about it. He had gone to the park every day since that first, but he had not seen Sas-quatch again.

Kara entered the garage through the door that led to the side yard. "Oh," she said. She was struck by the sight of the manikin—she hadn't seen it since height had given it power. She stared for a moment and recovered.

"That's your teacher in there, right?" she said.

"Yeah," Van said. He began to sift through the pile for something to make the manikin perfect before Mr. Finger came through the door.

"I just read in an article today," Kara said, "where women whose hus-bands take off sometimes get really promiscuous all of a sudden. It has to do with natural selection and spreading the genome."

Van scanned for metaphor in the entrails of a blender. "Did you really kill Charlie?"

Kara smiled. "I took a shot at him. But I missed. He ran away. The little fucker had an escape planned the whole time. I filled in his hole so he can't come back."

Mr. Finger knocked on the door from the kitchen. "Can I come—out?" he called.

Kara rolled her eyes.

"Yeah," Van said.

"It's art," Mr. Finger said, after descending to the floor of the garage and taking a moment to examine the manikin. "We should get you talking to Mr. Reginald."

"I heard Mr. Reginald's a fairy," Kara said.

"That's not nice," Mr. Finger said.

Van did not want to talk to Mr. Reginald and he now regretted showing the manikin to anyone. The next moment was awkward for all of them. Kara left again through the side door without a word.

"Well," Mr. Finger said, "thanks for showing me your piece, Van." He climbed back into the house to where Brenda was waiting.

*

Van colored the face of the manikin blue with airplane model paint. Then he decided blue was the wrong color. He tried yellow to cover it, but it all started to turn green, and he stopped. He put the manikin's eyes back in, its glasses and lips. He changed the position of its arms so that they were raised in a pose of surrender. It made the manikin look frightened, but there was nothing he could do about it.

He finally saw Sasquatch again at a convenience store. The man behind the counter said "Hey, dude," when Van approached with a soda and a candy bar. Van looked at him closely. The man was clean shaven and his hair was cut, but it could have been Sasquatch cleaned up for the job, and his badge said **TRAINEE**. Van looked into his eyes as the man counted out the change, but there was only routine in the brief hospitable glance Van was granted before the next customer pushed up behind him. Still, it was enough of a look for Van to know that the manikin was a failure.

Brenda had a date with Mr. Finger that night. Van and Kara watched television as she prepared. Once she came out from the bedroom wearing a slip to ask her daughter's preference between two dresses.

"The black one's sluttier," Kara said.

Brenda wore the black. She touched her hair in the mirror near the front door as the minutes ticked down to Mr. Finger's arrival. "Everything's changed now, guys," she called to them. "I'll be back late."

When the car pulled into the drive, she left before Mr. Finger could come into the house.

"I don't like this," Kara said.

They watched television together for the rest of the night, until its bright signals punctured them and made them weary and became the flickering light of the house. Black settled across the neighborhood, and soon they were as tired and stiff as if they had lived the petty dramas unfolded before them. Kara had made some French fries, and the ravaged plate sat on the coffee table between them. Van had left the last of them for his sister, but she had done the same for him, and now it sat as lonely monument to their new cooperation.

"You're not working on your doll," Kara said, as though the hours of television had not happened at all.

"It's not a doll," Van said. "It's a piece."

"A piece of what?"

"A piece of art. A piece of everything else." Van had the remote and flashed through several channels, flipping past body parts: a flexed thigh, a bare breast, a hand. "Anyway, it's done."

"Really?"

He nodded at the screen, and Kara got up and walked to the garage. She was only gone a minute.

"I don't like it," she said.

Van didn't say anything.

"I'm sorry," she said. "It's almost one o'clock. Mom's not home."

"She said she would be late. It makes sense."

"I guess it does," Kara said. She smiled. "What do you think she's doing *right now*?"

"I don't know."

"I'm going to bed," Kara said.

*

Van had sat through most of an episode of a generation-old detective drama when he heard the noises in the garage. The tense mood of the television show edging toward its climax climbed out from the box, and the dark world of the house filled with its goofy portent. Sounds like rats, sounds like opossums rooting through refuse. Van tensed, and his mind began to pleasantly churn, and he realized that the flush of quickened thought he had experienced when Brad left had faded, and only returned to him now with the danger.

I am thinking well, he thought again.

He imagined first that it was Charlie returned home, looking for scraps, then more fantastically, that it was the manikin somehow come to life despite his failure to make it whole. He retrieved the .22 from its spot against the wall, where it had stood since he last touched it. He did not know whether it was loaded, but hefted it in what he hoped was the proper way and walked toward the garage.

It was Brad. The door from the kitchen opened silently, and Van's father was caught near the back of the garage looking through its central heap, just then deciding on an item to set silently into a large canvas bag already half full of pilfered goods. In a moment Brad noticed the light and his son standing above him with a rifle. The manikin stood between them, facing away from Van like a conspirator in the confrontation.

Brad had grown a beard. "You caught me," he said.

Van climbed down the steps to the garage floor, training the rifle generally ahead of him but not exactly pointing it. "Mom's gone."

"I know," Brad said. "I'm glad she's moving on."

"What are you doing?"

Brad looked around the garage as though his chore should be apparent. "I'm cleaning up a bit. What did you think I was doing?" He watched Van's reaction, and gestured at the manikin between them. "You made this, didn't you? A scarecrow. Almost worked. I nearly pissed my pants when I walked in here."

Scarecrow. "Actually, it's art."

"Art? I don't know. As art, I think it needs something."

"Maybe what it needs," Van said, "is in your bag."

Brad looked down at his bag. He looked odd with his new beard, scruffy and younger and dangerous, and somehow it allowed him to remain silent.

"How's Tulsa?"

"Tulsa," Brad said, "is over. I'm headed to Miami."

"Miami," Van said, "is 'I maim' spelled backwards."

Brad squinted and walked around the mound. "You better give me that rifle."

Van turned it around like a knife and handed it to him. Brad held the rifle in one hand and his sack in the other like a hunter with a dead turkey. He looked into his son's eyes for a moment with a weird glimmer of transcendence and goodbye. It was important not to look away, and Van held the stare until Brad nodded again at the manikin.

"Take that thing apart," he said. "You're not scaring anyone."

Then he ducked through the side door and out into the world.

Hilda Raz

Avoidance

Today I'd like to write about epistemology or quarks, the habits of the leech—so useful in medical treatment, a horror in the pond—the growth and development of the precious embryo, attended, monitored until the radiance and blood of birth, the crash of hardwood cultivated for lumber, delight as the oak falls through undergrowth, the whine of the saw, the layers peeling off into fans, falling through their own fragrance to muslin pallets, dust in the chilly air raising a grit halo—or the burble coffee falls from into the cup as you pour a refill—all paid for, earned, the morning deserved, the back seat of the car piled with book bags, their bright canvas a rainbow of good work done, evening hours invested, the lucky deposit on cabins in the Maine woods, moose, ponds, gravel paths and in the near distance the salt, the crash of an ocean contained by its verge of rock.

So consider the weight of the child in his mother's arms, the reds and yellows of the photos, the leisurely flow of language, no compression, nothing packed or forced, no attempt to move in, no microcosm/macrocosm, no abstractions tied into the concrete, no natural paths sealed over to retain or meander, no wretched friends to accompany on their final walks.

Consider the tick, then, veinless, says the biologist in the deep voice of the woman he was, *useful as a figure for survival, researchers crush them in vises under tons of pressure, in sealed hermetic chambers devoid of air, pumped free of all essentials—and the tick scurries out, alive, cheerful, the size of a grape.*

We all shudder, down to the last woman at this table of learning, old friends all, colleagues.

What to make of our profiles: age, religious preference, marital history, hobbies, our experience with Hale-Bopp, did we see the comet at all, note its tail as...what?

Said to Sarah, Ten

And scribes wrote it all down.
—GILGAMESH

There is no one to say why
this face on the scrap of newsprint,
The Times, is not the face of my brother.
No one to say why her cat wastes
in a nest on the sofa, shawl and heating pad.
It yawns and gapes and whines
and arches its back.

How long will it last? she asks,
meaning grief, and I haven't the heart
to say a lifetime. Daughter.

Epistemology, I said in the dark
to her father, my head on his arm,
is my favorite subject, how we know what we know.

It will take so long, she says at intermission.
We hold each other in our common arms.
Mother and daughter, we are bound by mucus
and blood, the spilling of waters, flesh,
and the uses of smooth muscle.
I don't have the answer. It wasn't wisdom
brought her to life. I did nothing.
Now we sit in the dark watching
the orderly art of the body. Dancing.
People sweat in service.

I tell her in the dark,
when we're gone, when they're gone
under the earth, when all out names are forgotten
this will continue, this dancing.

Trans

What do you care, she asked
at last, letting me get the good
from my hundred-dollar therapy time.
She's still your daughter. Whoops
she said going red all over the parts
I could see—face under permed hair
her neck chicken-wattled, even the top part
of her chest, the V between her bowling shirt button
(marked JAKE on the pocket) showing blush.
I sobbed, quiet at first, swallowing salt
then louder, wailing like some beached baby.

Son you mean, you old biddy, I croaked at last
crying a good ten bucks worth of earth time.
Who would have thought that little one
whose cheek turned away from my breast
would grow up HE. He started SHE,
a brilliant daughter.
                                    It's the age, she said
not meaning puberty because he was long past,
thirty at his last birthday, but the times: everything
possible: hormones, surgery, way beyond unisex
jeans at the Mall, those cute flannel button-down shirts.

What will I do I whispered so deep into misery
I forgot she was listening and I was paying.
                                    Afterwards on the bluffs at the heart
of the weirdest sunset since July 4th
I try to conjure his voice: "Mom
since sunup the sky's been dark but now we're talking
I see the sun come out perfect
for a walk and when we're through talking
I'm going out. Come with me?"
That voice: the same words and phrases, intonation
from me with his dad mixed in "like cake with too much
frosting," as my student said tonight in class. Be honest
here. Love is the word he said in closing. "I love you,
Mom." Transsexual—like life, not easy—in this century.
My kid. And me in the same boat with him, mine.

Aaron at Work / Rain

By the light box propped in the window,
bare chested, scars rosy in artificial sun,
he crouches over his workbench.
Dental tools in their holder at hand, silver discs,
his torch, the tiny saw. Light flares, breaks on
his earring as he turns his head,
frowns, dark eyebrows almost meeting.
He takes a watch from his jeans pocket,
rubs it absently over his beard, electricity.
The braid clings its beads as his head
turns, reading something. Now he rises, goes
to the cupboard, mixes wallpaper paste with water.
The pile of miraculous papers, shot metal
threaded with linen, he sorts to start
a papier-mâché hypodermic needle he's building on the table,
matches to the real one he used this morning,
adds it as a detail to the mask to change the meaning:
a revolution: what he's about. Out the window the black car
beads up rain. He never drives it. An emblem, but of what?
A memory of pain, his slouching walk just home from hospital?
Where is the child whose shoes I bought? Where the bread
we kneaded? Where our kitchen? Our dead?

Greg Hewett

Hymns to Nanan

1. 1960, Between the Devil and the Gulf of Mexico

Florida was never heaven—
that was Pennsylvania.
Waking to pull bright fruit
from trees for ambrosia,

and fish from the wide silver gulf
was somehow too simple when
hauling stones from the field for fences
and avoiding the poison

of rhubarb is all she had known.
But she went south for him,
taking me, a grandson, as keepsake,
or else the deceivingly prim

secretary would have taken everything
and left her with nothing but remorse.
Now j'lai and casting for marlin,
playing the greyhounds and horses

she has bet her soul will keep him.
Only the devil knows
how far the sylvan hills
and her mother's Quaker god lie

from these infernal beaches,
these hideous swamps,
the mermaids in Miami,
and the life that he has mapped.

2. 1964, Loaves and Fish Fry (and Roast Beef)

She tore old loaves to bits,
her weekly duty
to remind us of suffering
through years of scarcity.

Pouring milk over bowls of crumbs
she'd talk about the War
and the Depression like we were there,
like we'd be eager

as our Puritan ancestors
for this meager supper,
for this ritual humility
that somehow did taste better

than Friday's exceptional fish
or the ceremony of Sunday's
rare roast displayed
before our innocent eyes.

3. 1967, Salvation

She never entered any church
and her feuds with ministers
were legendary.
She angered her sisters

with her simple prophecy
that she'd find salvation's door—
eventually—and the devil
would have to deal with her directly.

I alone was congregation,
choir and presbytery
in her saltbox of worship
that held all mystery.

She preached to me her deity
while my heathen parents slept
with rhythms of Coltrane in their heads
and my brother and sister crept

through to watch cartoons.
She promised that if I stayed
I'd find heaven without them.
It was then I prayed.

4. 1968, Our Golgotha

The streets in town were all still brick,
a paltry legacy

of our Roman ways. She tore up
and down imperially

as I, her dwarf emperor,
sat hypnotized
by a whir under the wheels,
the humming of slaves.

Then I saw him right before us,
heading down the wooded slope,
a college student looking
like Jesus as I had hoped

in my picture bible mind he would:
regulation beard,
long hair, gaunt face, sandals,
and those eyes of love I feared

would take me beyond her rule
to a new divinity.
Because I was her chosen one
or she just wanted me

saved for the service my crew cut
clearly marked me for
when my number was up,
she whispered right there in the Ford:

If you ever become like him
I promise you I'll steal
into your room in the dead of night
and moon or no I'll slit

your lovely white throat like a lamb,
and when you meet your God
you will not have to forgive me
for I know what I do.

5. 1969, The Flood

Don't monkey around with the moon
was her firm opinion
of all the Apollo missions.
And just as soon

as those godless astronauts stepped
onto the silver sand
the river began rising fast
and it was out of our hands.

First the glass factory went.
That furnace big as hell
where her brothers had all slaved
was doused like a coal in a pail.

Then the water swallowed each street
she'd walked for butter and eggs, for love and grief,
and when there was no higher ground
she felt righteous, relieved.

The valley where she'd spent her life
vanished at the thousand-year mark
and after praying she surmised
this time there would be no ark.

6. 1978, The Last Word

Knowing she used the word *gay*
in the old-fashioned way,
I told her I was *homosexual*,
something clinical.

I didn't understand the word
had entered the lexicon
after she was born,
too late to enter

her backwoods vernacular,
and I was too modern to relate
to her biblical Sodomite,
so beside her gray bed I sat

looking into blind eyes,
touching her damp forehead,
serving a silence
too strong for last words.

That Which Holds Us Together, That Which Pulls Us Apart

THERE IS NO single definition of what it means to be an "American." For some, it means living in the U.S.A., perhaps a legal citizen, perhaps not. For others, it means coming from one of the Americas: North, Central, South, anywhere within the two continents. The sense of what defines an American can be derived from a vast and shifting catalog of influences, including cultural and social messaging, the constant pressure of normative behavior, collective prejudices and preferences, and individual experiences. Everywhere we turn, we're bombarded by sometimes subtle and oftentimes bombastic messages about what it means to be an American, how to act like an American, how to defend America, and who is and isn't a "real" American. There are constantly competing voices arguing about what defines the great experiment that is the United States of America. This social and cultural noise can make it difficult for anyone who defines herself as "American" to critically reflect on her own experiences, her sense of self and what shapes her identity. Most self-identified Americans have, to some extent, multiple identities, and are often pulled in several directions at once when someone asks, "Who are you? What are you?" or "Where do you come from?" The stories, poems, and prose in this section explore the lives of individuals who find themselves at intersections, places where one sense of self clashes with another, where one individual or group tries to gain control over another. The work simultaneously defines what it means to be American, and defies any easy definition of that label. The United States is a living organism, never at rest, and never the same thing twice. It exists because of the dynamic play between unity and tension. This sense of *tensegrity* is what holds up the work in this section, with each piece defining, in moments of clarity, an individual's sense of an American self, filled with conflict, confidence and a myriad of unanswered questions.

Adrienne Rich

---

excerpts from

"An Atlas of the Difficult World"

I

A dark woman, head bent, listening for something
—a woman's voice, a man's voice or
voice of the freeway, night after night, metal streaming downcoast
past eucalyptus, cypress, agribusiness empires
THE SALAD BOWL OF THE WORLD, gurr of small planes
dusting the strawberries, each berry picked by a hand
in close communion, strawberry blood on the wrist,
Malathion in the throat, communion,
the hospital at the edge of the fields,
prematures slipping from unsafe wombs,
the labor and delivery nurse on her break watching
planes dusting rows of pickers.
Elsewhere declarations are made: at the sink
rinsing strawberries flocked and gleaming, fresh from the market
one says: "On the pond this evening is a light
finer than my mother's handkerchief
received from her mother, hemmed and initialed
by the nuns in Belgium."
One says: "I can lie for hours
reading and listening to music. But sleep comes hard.
I'd rather lie awake and read."   One writes:
"Mosquitoes pour through the cracks
in this cabin's walls, the road
in winter is often impassable,
I live here so I don't have to go out and act,
I'm trying to hold onto my life, it feels like nothing."
One says: "I never knew from one day to the next
where it was coming from: I had to make my life happen
from day to day.   Every day an emergency.
Now I have a house, a job from year to year.
What does that make me?"
In the writing workshop a young man's tears
wet the frugal beard he's grown to go with his poems

hoping they have redemption stored
in their lines, maybe will get him home free.   In the classroom
eight-year-old faces are gray.   The teacher knows which children
have not broken fast that day,
remembers the Black Panthers spooning cereal.

———————————

I don't want to hear how he beat her after the earthquake,
tore up her writing, threw the kerosene
lantern into her face waiting
like an unbearable mirror of his own.   I don't
want to hear how she finally ran from the trailer
how he tore the keys from her hands, jumped into the truck
and backed it into her.   I don't want to think
how her guesses betrayed her—that he meant well, that she
was really the stronger and ought not to leave him
to his own apparent devastation.   I don't want to know
wreckage, dreck and waste, but these are the materials
and so are the slow lift of the moon's belly
over wreckage, dreck, and waste, wild treefrogs calling in
another season, light and music still pouring over
our fissured, cracked terrain.

———————————

Within two miles of the Pacific rounding
this long bay, sheening the light for miles
inland, floating its fog through redwood rifts and over
strawberry and artichoke fields, its bottomless mind
returning always to the same rocks, the same cliffs, with
ever-changing words, always the same language
—this is where I live now.   If you had known me
once, you'd still know me now though in a different
light and life.   This is no place you ever knew me.
But it would not surprise you
to find me here, walking in fog, the sweep of the great ocean
eluding me, even the curve of the bay, because as always
I fix on the land.   I am stuck to earth.   What I love here
is old ranches, leaning seaward, lowroofed spreads between rocks
small canyons running through pitched hillsides
liveoaks twisted on steepness, the eucalyptus avenue leading
to the wrecked homestead, the fogwreathed heavy-chested cattle
on the blond hills.   I drive inland over roads

closed in wet weather, past shacks hunched in the canyons
roads that crawl down into darkness and wind into light
where trucks have crashed and riders of horses tangled
to death with lowstruck boughs.   These are not the roads
you knew me by.   But the woman driving, walking, watching
for life and death, is the same.

II

Here is a map of our country:
here is the Sea of Indifference, glazed with salt
This is the haunted river flowing from brow to groin
we dare not taste its water
This is the desert where missiles are planted like corms
This is the breadbasket of foreclosed farms
This is the birthplace of the rockabilly boy
This is the cemetery of the poor
who died for democracy   This is a battlefield
from a nineteenth-century war   the shrine is famous
This is the sea-town of myth and story   when the fishing fleets
went bankrupt   here is where the jobs were   on the pier
processing frozen fishsticks   hourly wages and no shares
These are other battlefields   Centralia   Detroit
here are the forests primeval   the copper   the silver lodes
These are the suburbs of acquiescence   silence rising fumelike
            from the streets
This is the capital of money and dolor whose spires
flare up through air inversions whose bridges are crumbling
whose children are drifting blind alleys pent
between coiled rolls of razor wire
I promised to show you a map you say but this is a mural
then yes let it be   these are small distinctions
where do we see it from is the question

IV

Late summers, early autumns, you can see something that binds
the map of this country together: the girasol, orange gold-
            petalled
with her black eye, laces the roadsides from Vermont to
            California
runs the edges of orchards, chain-link fences
milo fields and malls, schoolyards and reservations

truckstops and quarries, grazing ranges, graveyards
of veterans, graveyards of cars hulked and sunk, her tubers the
                    jerusalem artichoke
that has fed the Indians, fed the hobos, could feed us all.
Is there anything in the soil, cross-country, that makes for
a plant so generous?   *Spendthrift* we say, as if
accounting nature's waste.   Ours darkens
the states to their strict borders, flushes
down borderless streams, leaches from the lakes to the curdled foam
down by the riverside.

Waste.   Waste.   The watcher's eye put out, hands of the
                    builder severed, brain of the maker starved
those who could bind, join, reweave, cohere, replenish
now at risk in this segregate republic
locked away out of sight and hearing, our of mind, shunted aside
those needed to teach, advise, persuade, weigh arguments
those urgently needed for the work of perception
work of the poet, the astronomer, the historian, the architect of
                    new streets
work of the speaker who also listens
meticulous delicate work of reaching the heart of the desperate
                    woman, the desperate man
—never-to-be-finished, still unbegun work of repair—it cannot
                    be done without them
and where are they now?

XIII *(DEDICATIONS)*

I know you are reading this poem
late, before leaving your office
of the one intense yellow lamp-spot and the darkening window
in the lassitude of a building faded to quiet
long after rush-hour.   I know you are reading this poem
standing up in a bookstore far from the ocean
on a grey day of early spring, faint flakes driven
across the plains' enormous spaces around you.
I know you are reading this poem
in a room where too much has happened for you to bear
where the bedclothes lie in stagnant coils on the bed
and the open valise speaks of flight
but you cannot leave yet.   I know you are reading this poem

as the underground trains loses momentum and before running
                    up the stairs
toward a new kind of love
your life has never allowed.
I know you are reading this poem by the light
of the television screen where soundless images jerk and slide
while you wait for the newscast from the *intifada*.
I know you are reading this poem in a waiting-room
of eyes met and unmeeting, of identity with strangers.
I know you are reading this poem by fluorescent light
in the boredom and fatigue of the young who are counted out,
count themselves out, at too early an age.   I know
you are reading this poem through your failing sight, the thick
lens enlarging these letters beyond all meaning yet you read on
because even the alphabet is precious.
I know you are reading this poem as you pace beside the stove
warming milk, a crying child on your shoulder, a book in your
                    hand
because life is short and you too are thirsty.
I know you are reading this poem which is not in your language
guessing at some words while others keep you reading
and I want to know which words they are.
I know you are reading this poem listening for something, torn
                    between bitterness and hope
turning back once again to the task you cannot refuse.
I know you are reading this poem because there is nothing else
                    left to read
where you have landed, stripped as you are.

1990–1991

Kristin Naca

Speaking English Is Like

Brown and beige and blonde tiles set in panels of tile across the
    bathroom floor.

Wakes curled into the pavement by traffic, the asphalt a slow, gray tide.

A loose floorboard hiding the gouges chunked out of the floor.

Tawny red curtains hamstrung in the quick, morning light.

Her body oils like sage in a shirt, in the bed sheets.

Pigeons on a line and in the gutters.

The staple that misfires and jams the hammer.

The tender, black wick at the top of a candle's waxy lip.

The lonely woman secretly dying her curtains red at the Laundry Factory.

The purple and purple-blue berry sacks tethered to a blackberry rind.

Branches lolled by the weight of voluminous, tender sacks.

The path along the lake lit up with the pitch of purple stars.

Mouthfuls of lavender at the height of August.

Her lips, red gathering in the creases when she puckers.

Endings that are dirty tricks and also feathers.

Red water out the pipes, teeming from the rusty gutters.

The curtain flicker in the leafy, August breeze.

The ghostly cu-cu echoing through the purple night, under stars.

Uses for Spanish in Pittsburgh

What use is there for describing
Bloomfield's hard-sloping rooftops this way?
Or that the church steeples beam upward, inexpertly
toward God. What difference does it make
to say, the chimney pipes peel their red skins,
or *las pieles rojas*, exposing tough steel underneath.

What good, then, for Spanish,
its parity of consonants and vowels—
vowels like a window to the throat,
breath chiming through the vocal chords.
And what good is singing to describe
this barrio's version of the shortened sky,
el cielo cortado—power lines crisscrossing
so high, that blue only teases through them.

And what for fog *la niebla arrastra*,
creeping down *los calles inmoviles*
before the bank and grocery store open.
Y por la zapatería on Liberty Avenue,   *And by the shoemaker's*
a lady's boot for a street sign.

What use to remember in any language
my father was a Puerto Rican shoe salesman.
From his mouth, he'd dangle a ropy, ashy cigarette.
He spoke good English and knew when to smile.
With his strong fingers he'd knot shoes like *redes*,   *fishing nets*
knew three kinds of knots so lady customers
could buy the shoes they loved to look at
but really shouldn't have worn.

At home, Dad kept his *lengua íntima*
to himself. His Spanish not for children,
only older relatives who forced him to speak,
reminded, *Spanish means there's another person
inside you.* All beauty, he'd argue, no power in it.
Still, I remember, he spoke a hushed Spanish
to customers who struggled in English, the ones
he pitied for having no language to live on.

So many years gone, what use to invent
or question him in Pittsburgh? The educated one,
why would I want my clumsy Spanish to stray
from the pages of books on outward? My tongue,
he'd think so untrue and inarticulate. Each word
having no past in it. What then? Speaking Spanish
to make them better times or Pittsburgh
a better place. *En vez de regresar la dura realidad*   *Instead of returning*
del pasado. And then, if I choose to speak like this   *to the hard reality*
who will listen?   *of the past*

Grocery Shopping
with My Girlfriend
Who Is Not Asian

Through the doors gleam pyramids
of apples, peaches, broccoli hybrids.
I pronounce a name in Minh, *kài lán*,
pull back its leaves, and reveal small,
white flowers. All to watch her mouth
the words and make white flowers
translations. She asks what *uppo* is
and I tell her how my auntie grew
the woody fruit by foot-long beans,
tomatoes my father claimed to grow
on his own. If she needs more, I'll list
ingredients like a poem, like garlic
onion, ground pork, and potatoes.
Vegetables I don't have words for
stew for an hour in that poem.

We don't last long before the blitz
of shiny packaging overwhelms her.
One sea green cellophane submits
to a lime, pea, then a teal wrapper,
the lucky elephant or lotus stamp,
the photographs of curious

food items that luxuriate in broth,
a cartoon sketch of a boy's face
above some steam lines and a bowl—
delight the angle that his eyes slant
as he devours the noodles. Brands
we differentiate by script, each lilt
depicts the path a language takes
to conquer, infiltrate, or drift.
Some brushstrokes end in a tip
sharp as my tongue when I dish out
old-fashioned, Asian lady barking.

The aisles feed into a basin where
aquariums line the walls, and fish
glint beneath fluorescent light bulbs.
When I say, *So gorgeous, I feel guilty
eating them*, that's not the half of it.
Next week, we trade-in excess beauty
to shop at the markets my Mother
took me—and I still shop as though
my girlfriend and I had never met,
where we fish beans from boxes;
dodge old ladies throwing elbows
at the fruit bins; scales unraveling
off a fish when a butcher knocks
the daylights out of it. And in time
come the meals we dine on chicken
that stinks of piss-soaked feathers.

Speaking Spanish Is Like

A bird in a tree sings to a parrot in a cage, next door.

As the needle skids it plays the grooves carved in the record vinyl.

In front of the butcher shop a man, the name of a woman tattooed on his chest.

The letters on his skin gone green from too many years.

C H R I S T I N A. Who is this woman on the skin?

On the edge of town, green gusts escape the aging smoke stacks.

The smell of her in a pillowcase delays her leaving.

A green mouth, the taste of rastro[1] on her tongue and lips.

A pulp of stars through the sieve of Nebraska's thick, black sky.

People inside this town call it, "Lincoln-comma-Nebraska."

The bird in the tree takes flight when the parrot joins in.

On a night without stars, we drive, no traction to the sky's smooth terrain.

O spinning wheels! No one dies from a broken heart too quickly.

Only echoes of sweat and the rest of her gone.

---

1. *los rastros*: meat packing plants

Sherman Alexie

Indian Education

FIRST GRADE

My hair was too short and my U.S. Government glasses were horn-rimmed, ugly, and all that first winter in school, the other Indian boys chased me from one corner of the playground to the other. They pushed me down, buried me in the snow until I couldn't breathe, thought I'd never breathe again.

They stole my glasses and threw them over my head, around my outstretched hands, just beyond my reach, until someone tripped me and sent me falling again, facedown in the snow.

I was always falling down; my Indian name was Junior Falls Down. Sometimes it was Bloody Nose or Steal-His-Lunch. Once, it was Cries-Like-a-White-Boy, even though none of us had seen a white boy cry.

Then it was a Friday morning recess and Frenchy St. John threw snowballs at me while the rest of the Indian boys tortured some other *top-yogh-yaught* kid, another weakling. But Frenchy was confident enough to torment me all by himself, and most days I would have let him.

But the little warrior in me roared to life that day and knocked Frenchy to the ground, held his head against the snow, and punched him so hard that my knuckles and the snow made symmetrical bruises on his face. He almost looked like he was wearing war paint.

But he wasn't the warrior. I was. And I chanted *It's a good day to die, it's a good day to die*, all the way down to the principal's office.

SECOND GRADE

Betty Towle, missionary teacher, redheaded and so ugly that no one ever had a puppy crush on her, made me stay in for recess fourteen days straight.

"Tell me you're sorry," she said.

"Sorry for what?" I asked.

"Everything," she said and made me stand straight for fifteen minutes, eagle-armed with books in each hand. One was a math book; the other was English. But all I learned was that gravity can be painful.

For Halloween I drew a picture of her riding a broom with a scrawny cat on the back. She said that her God would never forgive me for that.

Once, she gave the class a spelling test but set me aside and gave me a test designed for junior high students. When I spelled all the words right, she crumpled up the paper and made me eat it.

"You'll learn respect," she said.

She sent a letter home with me that told my parents to either cut my braids or keep me home from class. My parents came in the next day and dragged their braids across Betty Towle's desk.

"Indians, indians, indians." She said it without capitalization. She called me "indian, indian, indian."

And I said, *Yes, I am. I am Indian. Indian, I am.*

THIRD GRADE

My traditional Native American art career began and ended with my very first portrait: *Stick Indian Taking a Piss in My Backyard.*

As I circulated the original print around the classroom, Mrs. Schluter intercepted and confiscated my art.

Censorship, I might cry now. *Freedom of expression*, I would write in editorials to the tribal newspaper.

In third grade, though, I stood alone in the corner, faced the wall, and waited for the punishment to end.

I'm still waiting.

FOURTH GRADE

"You should be a doctor when you grow up," Mr. Schluter told me, even though his wife, the third grade teacher, thought I was crazy beyond my years. My eyes always looked like I had just hit-and-run someone.

"Guilty," she said. "You always look guilty."

"Why should I be a doctor?" I asked Mr. Schluter.

"So you can come back and help the tribe. So you can heal people."

That was the year my father drank a gallon of vodka a day and the same year that my mother started two hundred different quilts but never finished any. They sat in separate, dark places in our HUD house and wept savagely.

I ran home after school, heard their Indian tears, and looked in the mirror. *Doctor Victor*, I called myself, invented an educations, talked to my reflection. *Doctor Victor to the emergency room.*

FIFTH GRADE

I picked up a basketball for the first time and made my first shot. No. I missed my first shot, missed the basket completely, and the ball landed in the dirt and sawdust, sat there just like I had sat there only minutes before.

But it felt good, that ball in my hands, all those possibilities and angles. It was mathematics, geometry. It was beautiful.

At that same moment, my cousin Steven Ford sniffed rubber cement from a paper bag and leaned back on the merry-go-round. His ears rang, his mouth was dry, and everyone seemed so far away.

But it felt good, that buzz in his head, all those colors and noises. It was chemistry, biology. It was beautiful.

Oh, do you remember those sweet, almost innocent choices that the Indian boys were forced to make?

SIXTH GRADE

Randy, the new Indian kid from the white town of Springdale, got into a fight an hour after he first walked into the reservation school.

Stevie Flett called him out, called him a squawman, called him a pussy, and called him a punk.

Randy and Stevie, and the rest of the Indian boys, walked out into the playground.

"Throw the first punch," Stevie said as they squared off.

"No," Randy said.

"Throw the first punch," Stevie said again.

"No," Randy sad again.

"Throw the first punch!" Stevie said for the third time, and Randy reared back and pitched a knuckle fastball that broke Stevie's nose.

We all stood there in silence, in awe.

That was Randy, my soon-to-be first and best friend, who taught me the most valuable lesson about living in the white world: *Always throw the first punch.*

SEVENTH GRADE

I leaned through the basement window of the HUD house and kissed the white girl who would later be raped by her foster-parent father, who was also white. We both lived on the reservation, though, and when the headlines and stories filled the papers later, not one word was made of their color.

Just Indians being Indians, someone must have said somewhere and they were wrong.

But on the day I leaned through the basement window of the HUD house and kissed the white girl, I felt the good-byes I was saying to my entire tribe. I held my lips tight against her lips, a dry, clumsy, and ultimately stupid kiss.

But I was saying good-bye to my tribe, to all the Indian girls and women I might have loved, to all the Indian men who might have called me cousin, even brother.

I kissed that white girl and when I opened my eyes, she was gone from the reservation, and when I opened my eyes, I was gone from the reservation, living in a farm town where a beautiful white girl asked my name.

"Junior Polatkin," I said, and she laughed.

After that, no one spoke to me for another five hundred years.

EIGHTH GRADE

At the farm town junior high, in the boys' bathroom, I could hear voices from the girls' bathroom, nervous whispers of anorexia and bulimia. I could hear the white girls' forced vomiting, a sound so familiar and natural to me after years of listening to my father's hangovers.

"Give me your lunch if you're just going to throw it up," I said to one of those girls once.

I sat back and watched them grow skinny from self-pity.

Back on the reservation, my mother stood in line to get us commodities. We carried them home, happy to have food, and opened the canned beef that even the dogs wouldn't eat.

But we ate it day after day and grew skinny from self-pity.

There is more than one way to starve.

NINTH GRADE

At the farm town high school dance, after a basketball game in an overheated gym where I had scored twenty-seven points and pulled down thirteen rebounds, I passed out during a slow song.

As my white friends revived me and prepared to take me to the emergency room where doctors would later diagnose my diabetes, the Chicano teacher ran up to us.

"Hey," he said. "What's that boy been drinking? I know all about these Indian kids. They start drinking real young."

Sharing dark skin doesn't necessarily make two men brothers.

TENTH GRADE

I passed the written test easily and nearly flunked the driving, but I still received my Washington State driver's license on the same day that Wally Jim killed himself by driving his car into a pine tree.

No traces of alcohol in his blood, good job, wife and two kids.

"Why'd he do it?" asked a white Washington State trooper.

All the Indians shrugged their shoulders, looked down at the ground.

"Don't know," we all said, but when we look in the mirror, see the history of our tribe in our eyes, taste failure in the tap water, and shake with old tears, we understand completely.

Believe me, everything looks like a noose if you stare at it long enough.

ELEVENTH GRADE

Last night I missed two free throws which would have won the game against the best team in the state. The farm town high school I play for is nicknamed the "Indians," and I'm probably the only actual Indian ever to play for a team with such a mascot.

This morning I pick up the sports page and read the headline: INDIANS LOSE AGAIN.

Go ahead and tell me none of this is supposed to hurt me very much.

TWELFTH GRADE

I walk down the aisle, valedictorian of this farm town high school, and my cap doesn't fit because I've grown my hair longer than it's ever been. Later, I stand as the school board chairman recites my awards, accomplishments, and scholarships.

I try to remain stoic for the photographers as I look toward the future.

Back home on the reservation, my former classmates graduate: a few can't read, one or two are just given attendance diplomas, most look forward to the parties. The bright students are shaken, frightened, because they don't know what comes next.

They smile for the photographer as they look back toward tradition.

The tribal newspaper runs my photograph and the photograph of my former classmates side by side.

POSTSCRIPT: CLASS REUNION

Victor said, "Why should we organize a reservation high school reunion? My graduating class has a reunion every weekend at the Powwow Tavern."

Kenny Fries

_____

excerpts from

The History of My Shoes
and the Evolution of Darwin's Theory

Still Disabled

" Take off your shoes," Dr. Mendotti says.

For the first time in close to eight years, Social Security has decided it needs a medical review to discern if, according to their rules, I am still disabled.

Still disabled?

Specifically, I was born without fibula, with sharp anterior curves of the tibia, and flexion contractures of the knees. Also absent were two toes and posterior calf bands on each foot. There was no scientific explanation for this situation; no medical name for the condition. Medical records simply state that I was born with "congenital deformities of the lower extremities." Despite numerous childhood surgeries, those bones are still missing—and since around the time I turned twenty-eight, because of the almost three-inch leg length discrepancy, my increasingly weakening lower back sends a constant flow of low-grade pain throughout my body.

Dr. Mendotti's office is in Enfield, Connecticut, a half-hour drive from Northampton, Massachusetts, where I live. It is a building shared by many different doctors, more like a building housing a small town's bureaucratic departments than medical offices. The structure feels makeshift, as if these were temporary quarters until funds were raised to build a new building, but somehow as the years went on the funds never materialized. The examination room, where a secretary has placed me, looks as worn as my shoes. As worn as the disheveled, portly Dr. Mendotti who, after doing a double take at the examination room door—as though he, a specialist in the field, has never seen someone with legs and feet like mine before—has ordered me to take off my shoes, then disappeared somewhere down the hall.

Alone, I watch the clock across the room. The black second hand moves through black numbers around the unornamented white face of the institutional clock, a clock like the one in every classroom and every hall in P.S. 200, my elementary school on Benson Avenue in the Bath Beach section, between Bay Ridge and Coney Island in Brooklyn, and once again I am eight years old, staring at the P.S. 200 clock, its thin black second hand making its sixty-second round over and over and over again. In front of my third grade classroom, Mrs. Krimsky, my silver-haired teacher, is telling my class about Charles Darwin, his theory of evolution, the survival of the fittest.

At her mention of this phrase, sharp to my skin as a surgeon's knife, I instinctively reach beneath my desk and clutch my legs, protectively lifting them so my shoe-clad feet rest against the edge of my chair.

What am I afraid of? Other children's stares? Amputation? Panic-stricken, I wonder as I grow older how will I be able to walk, let alone realize my childhood dreams of becoming a basketball player, a foreign diplomat, a United States senator. Forget about dreams, with these deformed legs and feet. How will I survive?

Now, sitting in the doctor's office, I realize this clock does not tell the correct time. I know it is later than one P.M. because I left my house in Northampton at one P.M. I look at the brown, padded examination table with its familiar, unwelcoming rolled white paper to show it is clean, as well as a small black stepping stool nearby. Above, on a shelf, are five models—two white, three beige—of legs, the kind that show not only the bones, but the ligaments and tendons as well. I have always been fascinated by these models because, although I know which bones I am missing, neither my doctors nor numerous physical therapists have ever been able to tell me which ligaments and tendons my legs do contain. When I've fallen and torn something in my right knee, my doctor and I have never been sure whether it is the meniscus or the anterior cruciate ligament that I have torn, or whether it was some soft tissue adapted solely for the odd orthopedic configuration of my legs.

"Why did they send you to me?" Dr. Mendotti asks, as I take off my shoes and socks. Does he actually want me to answer?

"Wow," he breathes a mixture of pity and surprise. I wish I could recoil my legs, like the legs of the Wicked Witch of the East that curled underneath Dorothy's house which fell from the sky, when Glinda the Good Witch of the North removed the Wicked Witch's ruby slippers.

But in this situation, wanting to keep my Medicare and other benefits, I cannot curl up my legs. I must not only go through being examined by a doctor who has never seen a body like mine before, but in this situation I must act as if my disability is the worst thing that could have ever happened, when the truth is, this examination, Dr. Mendotti's stare, are much more difficult to endure.

"You can walk on those? How can I describe this to them? They won't believe me," Dr. Mendotti says, after I've given him a cursory history of the congenital deformities of my legs. "I'll have to take some photos." Decisively, he gets up, goes to the door and out into the hallway, where he talks to his secretary. "That old Polaroid must be around somewhere. You've got to come in and see this."

Dr. Mendotti returns and asks me to roll up my pants to reveal more of my legs. "You really should be using Canadian crutches to walk," he tells me. "With the right shoes I walk just fine," I want to tell him.

"There must be doctors in Hartford who can do something for you. They work with children like you," he says.

"I'm okay as I am," I do not say.

But am I okay? This has become a recurrent question ever since, after enduring a year of back pain and knee problems, I went to see Dr. Victor Frankel, the former assistant of my childhood orthopedic surgeon.

"We can use the Ilizarov procedure," Dr. Frankel had suggested. "We cut the shell, the cortex of the bone, but leave the bone's marrow cavity, which contains important blood vessels necessary to the formation of new bone, intact. The Ilizarov apparatus consists of wires put through the bone, and external rings that are kept under a great deal of tension to apply slow traction so the nerves, muscles, tendon, and bone can grow."

As I listened to Dr. Frankel's description, my fingers reached for the four-inch scar on the right side of my knee, a remnant from the unsuccessful surgery he performed in 1966. "Theoretically, your lower back pain is caused by the length discrepancy between your legs. I can surgically line up your right foot, which now juts out from your leg at almost ninety degrees, into normal weight-bearing position, and, using the Ilizarov method, I can achieve bone growth in your right leg, making it almost as long as the left."

I have had five major reconstructive surgeries since I was born, and I did not need my searching fingers to remind me I did not want to endure another. My mind searched for an alternative. "And if I decide not to have surgery?"

"A cane would help, " Dr. Frankel offered. "I'd also suggest adding three inches to your right shoe—but only an eighth, maybe a quarter of an inch at a time, so your spine won't overcompensate. That could cause more pain and disorientation than you're experiencing now."

Seven years have passed since I rejected Dr. Frankel's surgical solution. But now, with my back pain increasing and new problems developing with my right knee and my left foot, had the time come when my asymmetrical body, with or without properly fitted shoes, had reached the apex of what it could do, of where it could take me?

Sitting in Dr. Mendotti's office, in yet another of the seemingly endless number of medical examinations, I begin to question whether or not the costs of avoiding surgery have become too great.

Dr. Mendotti takes a photo and the camera noisily releases it. From my vantage point the photo seems very yellow, as antiquated as the camera. "That should show them," he says. "Even with photographic documentation, you wouldn't believe the mistakes they make. I wish there was more I could do for you."

I smile.

Job done, Dr. Mendotti has clipped the photo to a manila folder and is now standing at the door. "If they deny you," he says with too much concern, "give me a call." The doctor pauses at the door, then he turns back to me and says: "I shouldn't say this to you, but if you ever need medication, you let me know."

I take my cane, get up, and, not paying attention to his final offer, pass the secretary's desk. I open the door and go out into what serves as the doctor's waiting room. As I make my way to my car, my limp seems more pronounced than usual.

Although the sky is full of white billowy clouds, the day seems much brighter than I remembered it an hour ago.

You can walk on those? I keep hearing Dr. Mendotti say, his words with their underlying disbelief, repeating over and over. It is as if I, too, believe that my being able to get the short way from the doctor's office to my car must be some sort of miracle. Through some act of God—not to mention doctors, shoemakers, persevering parents, and some innate drive of my own—I am able to stand here with the assistance of a cane and twenty-year-old orthopedic shoes. In this suburban world of office parks and strip malls, I am sure that if I look up I will see cherubic angels, hear them trumpeting the proof of the miracle of my being alive at all. But I don't see angels. I don't hear trumpets. Driving on I-91, I hear the words of poet Gerard Manley Hopkins: *Glory be to God for dappled things—*. I check the sky to see if it looks *couple-colored as a brindled cow,* and am thankful for Hopkins's poem celebrating *all things counter, original, spare, strange.*

But when I arrive home, I keep seeing the clock that did not tell the right time in Dr. Mendotti's office. I hear his offer of medication. Even then, I knew what he was offering, the "help" he couldn't ever voice out loud. The medication was not for pain but in case I decide that the pain is too much and I do not want to survive.

Survival of the fittest.

Somehow, I know Dr. Mendotti's reaction was not based on my pain or on my body. His reaction was based on his misunderstanding of what it means to survive in an often inhospitable world. He assumed I could not walk without crutches, although I have walked without crutches my entire life. Was Dr. Frankel's surgical solution based on the same assumptions? I have not had surgery since I was ten years old. Isn't the pain of the surgery far worse than the pain I live with now? Was I wrong to believe there had to be another way for me to adapt to my body's changes?

My childhood questions of survival are answered by Hopkins's question: how do each of us become *swift, slow; sweet, sour; adazzle, dim*? Disabled, nondisabled, I add to Hopkins's list. And I realize I am just beginning to understand what survival of the fittest actually means.

Bodies of Water

Sitting at the edge of my local YMCA pool, I think again of Hopkins's question: *swift, slow; sweet, sour; adazzle, dim...fickle, freckled, who knows how?* I rock back and forth, feel the rough, stuccoed cement chafe the back of my thighs.

Unlike the pool at Lansman's Bungalow Colony in the Catskills in up-state New York, where my family spent thirteen of my childhood summers, there are no comforting steps leading down into this water, just two silver-gray metal holds one above the other—not even a ladder—on each side of the pool's shallow end. There is no way to ease in, body part by body part, ever so slowly, as I have been doing ever since I learned to swim.

I close my eyes and imagine I am swimming like the lone other swimmer in the pool this morning. I imagine the water against his body as he glides, hand over head, hand over head, one stroke after the next, until he reaches the other end of the pool. Swimming, back stretched, no pressure on my legs, the water neutralizing weight, is easier for me than walking.

With my palms, I spread water on my thighs. The fingers on my left hand gently knead my left thigh. When has this thigh developed so much muscle? Bending my knee, I stretch out my left leg its entire twenty-two-inch length and notice, as if for the first time, how the ligament running up my leg on the outside between my knee and thigh will not fully extend. Three inches longer than my right leg, my left leg never has the opportunity to reach its potential elongation.

My left leg outstretched over the shallow end of the pool, I begin to run my hand from sole to hip, the entire length of my leg. The lone swimmer, having finished his laps, grabs for a metal rung and lifts himself out of the pool. I watch the water drip from his well-toned chest, from his washboard stomach, his sculpted thighs, forming a substantial puddle on the floor.

Above the hips my body could be described just like everybody else's. *Your body—okay, at least your upper parts—can look like his.*

The comparison to the now-departed swimmer does the trick, and in one motion I am skimming the water's surface, making my way up the length of the pool. But as I move my body through the water I am reminded that I do not swim correctly. Afraid the chlorine will sting my allergy-ridden eyes, never sure how to breathe smoothly, holding my breath when under water, releasing my breath when above, when swimming I keep my head out of the water. My feet, for years strong enough to perform daily tasks, and to travel, do not have a propulsive kick when swimming, leaving the bulk of my body's water work to my arms and upper torso.

Lap 20. I think about the idea of normal in relation to the well-toned swimmer who by now, having showered, I imagine is in the locker room drying his naked body. When imagining this naked man I also imagine myself among the men in the locker room who are surreptitiously, some more overtly, gazing at this man's beauty. And by such a measuring gaze, disabled and nondisabled, designate ourselves as *other*, the beautiful man as the *norm*, if not some unreachable Greek ideal. Some of us spend our entire lives as the beholder, the one who gazes, trying to achieve for ourselves this abstract, ultimately fictitious notion of what we should be, an ideal which being a projection—*if, if , only if*—evaporates as if it were the water of which our bodies, and the world in which our bodies inhabit, are mostly comprised.

Lap 30. One more lap and my swim will be over. I do not use the metal rungs at the side of the pool. With my palms flat against the surface where only an hour ago I sat on the edge of the pool, I lift myself from the water.

As I make my way from the pool into the shower I think about my travels, my personal history in relation to the fantasy of the ideal, the reality that can never be the norm. With all these thoughts moving fast through my mind it is as if I am still weightless.

When I was in my early twenties, when I was a graduate student in New York, as well as during my first years after graduate school living in San Francisco, I had success finding sexual partners in bars. When I first started going to bars I planted myself at a table or on a stool at the bar and stayed in one place as long as possible. When I saw someone I wanted to get to know, I stayed put, as frozen to the barstool as I was this morning to the concrete edge of the YMCA pool. Even when I had to go to the bathroom I put it off for as long as I could to avoid making my disability noticeable by standing up and walking around the bar. By deciding to remain stationary, to my mind I made myself nondisabled. As soon as I walked I felt I would become disabled.

Only once during my years of going to the bars did a man decide not to go home with me after he noticed my legs. That one time, after I had been talking with this guy most of the evening, long after it had become obvious we would leave the bar together and go back to where one of us lived, when I got up and he saw that I stood just over five feet tall, he immediately decided not to leave the bar with me. When I stood up, this man who a moment before had been running his finger up and down the length of my arm, became flustered and without saying a word walked to the other side of the bar. As far as I know, only this once in my years of going to bars were my legs actually a disability. And what made me disabled was not my bodily impairment but this man who decided to disable my body by choosing, for whatever reasons that were his own, not to have sex with me that night. Isn't it true that a dark-haired man who is rejected by a potential partner who is attracted only to blonds is, in that situation, disabled by another's predilections and not by the color of his hair?

Crucial to this understanding is: What is a disability? Who is disabled? Who decides? Sometimes, as was my experience with that man in that bar, the decision is made by someone who seizes the power of naming. And, at other times, I have to admit, the disabling agent has been none other than myself.

No longer drinking alcohol, allergic to smoky places, and no longer interested in meeting men this way, I stopped going to bars. When I moved to Northampton, I found out my cholesterol was way too high and my doctor recommended I swim for cardiovascular exercise. So I joined the YMCA, which had a good pool and was close to where I lived.

During the late morning and early afternoon, the YMCA is nearly empty. Most who use the facilities during these hours are elderly Eastern European men. Long dormant hybrid languages of the recent past are whispered in the locker room and showers.

When I began my cholesterol-lowering regimen, I noticed a few men my age who swam every other day the same time as I did. After my almost-an-hour swim, in the showers or in the locker room, I was surprised that many of these men took an obviously sexual interest in me. Why in bars where I was fully clothed did I usually go unnoticed, but when my lower body was revealed naked in the showers at the YMCA did men consistently pursue me? Were my expectations of how men react to my disability that out of line? Had I internalized all the negative body imagery, the stereotypes, the fear of disability to the point where I could no longer think clearly about the effect my body's difference had in the world?

When I reach the showers, the swimmer with whom I compared myself is gone. Through the spraying water, I hear Gerard Manley Hopkins's question—*fickle, freckled, who knows how?*—and staring down at my feet, my childhood question—why was I born missing bones in my both of my legs?—returns. Why was it so difficult for me to realize that I could compete successfully—indeed, survive—in this overtly physical world? Why do each of us spend so much of our resources on changing what we look like, changing who we are? And, as if in answer, I speak Hopkins's words: *All of our beauty should be past change.*

Elizabeth Alexander

_____

Fugue

1. Walking (1963)

after the painting by Charles Alston

You tell me, knees are important, you kiss
your elders' knees in utmost reverence.

The knees in this painting are what send the people forward.

Once progress felt real and inevitable,
as sure as the taste of licorice or lemons.
The painting was made after marching
in Birmingham, walking

into a light both brilliant and unseen.

2. 1964

In a beige silk sari
my mother danced the frug
to the Peter Duchin Band.

Earlier that day
at Maison Le Pelch
the French ladies twisted

her magnificent hair
into a fat chignon
while mademoiselle watched,

drank sugared, milky tea,
and counted bobby pins
disappearing in the thick-

ness as the ladies worked
in silence, adornment
so grave, the solemn toilette,

and later, the bath,
and later, red lipstick,
and later, L'Air du Temps.

My mother without glasses.
My mother in beige silk.
My mother with a chignon.
My mother in her youth.

3. 1968

The city burns. We have to stay at home,
TV always interrupted with fire or helicopters.
Men who have tweedled my cheeks once or twice
join the serial dead.

Yesterday I went downtown with Mom.
What a pretty little girl, said the tourists, who were white.
My shoes were patent leather, all shiny, and black.
My father is away saving the world for Negroes,
I wanted to say.

Mostly I go to school or watch television
with my mother and brother, my father often gone.
He makes the world a better place for Negroes.
The year is nineteen-sixty-eight.

4. 1971

"Hey Blood," my father said then
to other brothers in the street.
"Hey, Youngblood, how you doin'?"

"Peace and power," he says,
and, "Keep on keepin' on,"
just like Gladys Knight and the Pips.

My stomach jumps: a thrill.
Sometimes poems remember small things, like
"Hey, Blood." My father
still says that sometimes.

5. The Sun King (1974)

James Hampton, the Sun King
of Washington DC
erects a tinfoil throne.
"Where there is no vision, the people perish."
Altar, pulpit, lightbulbs.

My 14th and "U," my 34 bus, my weekday winos,
my white-robed black Israelites
on their redstone stoops,
my graffiti: "Anna the Leo as 'Ice,'"
my neon James Brown poster
coming to the DC Coliseum
where all I will see is the circus,
my one visit to RKO Keith's Theater
to see *Car Wash*
and a bird flew in, and mania,
frantic black shadow on the screen,
I was out of the house in a theater full of black folks,
black people, black movie, black bird,
I was out, I was free, I was at RKO Keith's Theater
at 14th and "U"
and it was not *Car Wash* it was the first
Richard Pryor concert movie
and a bird flew in the screen
and memory is romance
and race is romance,
and the Sun King loves
in Washington, DC.

Overture: Watermelon City

Philadelphia is burning and watermelon is all that can cool it,
so there they are, spiked
atop a row of metal poles,
rolling on and off pickup trucks,
the fruit that grows longest,
the fruit with a curly tail, the cool fruit,
larger than a large baby, wide
as the widest green behind, wide
vermilion smile at the sizzling metropole.
Did I see this yesterday? Did I dream
this last night? The city is burning,
is burning for real.

When I first moved here I lived two streets over
from Osage, where it happened, twelve streets down.

I asked my neighbors, who described
the smell of smoke and flesh,
the city on fire for real.
How far could you see the flames?
How long could you smell the smoke?
Osage is narrow, narrow
like a movie set: urban eastern seaboard,
the tidy of people who work hard for very little.

Life lived on the porch,
the amphitheater street.
I live here, 4937 Hazel Avenue, West Philly.
Hello, Adam and Ukee,
the boys on that block
who guarded my car, and me.
They called him Ukee because
as a baby he looked
like a eucalyptus leaf.
Hello, holy rollers
who plug in their amps,
blow out the power in the building,
preach to the street from the stoop.
Hello, crack-head next-door neighbor
who raps on my door after midnight
needing money for baby formula,
she says, and the woman
who runs in the street
with her titties out, wailing.
Hello, street. Hello, ladies
who sweep their front porches each morning.
In downtown Philadelphia
there are many lovely restaurants,
reasonably priced.
Chocolate, lemon ice,
and hand-filled cannolis
in South Philly.
Around the corner
at the New Africa Lounge
in West Philadelphia
we sweat buckets
to hi-life and zouk,
we burn.

Brian Turner

Observation Post #71

Balad, Iraq

Owls rest in the vines of wild grapes.
Eucalyptus trees shimmer.
And from the minaret, a voice.

Each life has its moment. The sunflowers
lift their faces toward dawn
as milk cows bellow in a field of trash.

I have seen him in the shadows.
I have watched him in the circle of light
my rifle brings to me. His song
hums in the wings of sand flies.
My mind has become very clear.

Here, Bullet

If a body is what you want,
then here is bone and gristle and flesh.
Here is the clavicle-snapped wish,
the aorta's opened valves, the leap
thought makes at the synaptic gap.
Here is the adrenaline rush you crave,
that inexorable flight, that insane puncture
into heat and blood. And I dare you to finish
what you've started. Because here, Bullet,
here is where I complete the word you bring
hissing through the air, here is where I moan
the barrel's cold esophagus, triggering
my tongue's explosives for the rifling I have
inside of me, each twist of the round
spun deeper, because here, Bullet,
here is where the world ends, every time.

AB Negative (The Surgeon's Poem)

Thalia fields lies under a gray ceiling of clouds,
just under the turbulence, with anesthetics
dripping from an IV into her arm,
and the flight surgeon says *The shrapnel*
cauterized as it traveled through her
here, breaking this rib as it entered,
burning a hole through the left lung
to finish in her back, and all of this
she doesn't hear, except perhaps as music—
that faraway music of people's voices
when they speak gently and with care,
a comfort to her on a stretcher
in a flying hospital en route to Landstuhl,
just under the rain at midnight, and Thalia
drifts in and out of consciousness
as a nurse dabs her lips with a moist towel,
her palm on Thalia's forehead, her vitals
slipping some, as burned flesh gives way
to the heat of blood, the tunnels within
opening to fill her, just enough blood
to cough up and drown in; Thalia
sees shadows of people working
to save her, but cannot feel their hands,
cannot hear them any longer,
and when she closes her eyes
the most beautiful colors rise in darkness,
tangerine washing into Russian blue,
with the droning engine humming on
in a dragonfly's wings, island palms
painting the sky an impossible hue
with their thick brushes dripping green...
a way of dealing with the fact
that Thalia Fields is gone, long gone,
about as far from Mississippi
as she can get, ten thousand feet above Iraq
with a blanket draped over her body

and an exhausted surgeon in tears,
his bloodied hands on her chest, his head
sunk down, the nurse guiding him
to a nearby seat and holding him as he cries,
though no one hears it, because nothing can be heard
where pilots fly in blackout, the plane
like a shadow guiding the rain, here
in the droning engines of midnight.

Night in Blue

At seven thousand feet and looking back, running lights
blacked out under the wings and America waiting,
a year of my life disappears at midnight,
the sky a deep viridian, the houselights below
small as match heads burned down to embers.

Has this year made me a better lover?
Will I understand something of hardship,
of loss, will a lover sense this
in my kiss or touch? What do I know
of redemption or sacrifice, what will I have
to say of the dead—that it was worth it,
that any of it made sense?
I have no words to speak of war.
I never dug the graves in Talafar.
I never held the mother crying in Ramadi.
I never lifted my friend's body
when they carried him home.

I have only the shadows under the leaves
to take with me, the quiet of the desert,
the low fog of Balad, orange groves
with ice forming on the rinds of fruit.
I have a woman crying in my ear
late at night when the stars go dim,
moonlight and sand as a resonance
of the dust of bones, and nothing more.

Ray Gonzalez

Praise the Tortilla, Praise Menudo, Praise Chorizo

for Juan Felipe Herrera

I praise the tortilla in honor of El Panson
who hit me in school every day,
made me see how the bruises on my arms looked
like the brown clouds on my mother's tortillas.
I praise the tortilla because I know they
fly into our hands like eager flesh of the one we love,
soft yearnings we delight in biting as we tear
the tortilla and wipe the plate clean.

> I praise the menudo as the visionary food,
> the *tripa y posole* tight flashes of color we see
> as the red *caldo* smears across our notebooks,
> our lives going down like the empty bowls
> of menudo with the *chili pequin* of our poetic dream

I praise the chorizo and smear it across
my face and hands, the dayglow brown of it
painting me with desire to find out why
the chorizo sizzled in the pan and covered the house
with a smell of growing up I will never have again,
the chorizo burrito hot in my hands
when I ran out to play and show the vatos
it was time to cut the chorizo,
tell it like it is before *la manteca* runs
down our chins and drips away.

The Magnets

On turning forty

They draw me closer like the hands
of one grandmother I kissed upon
visiting her in the barrio.
The magnets make me look at my waist,
wonder why the ache is in the street,
houses giving off stinking air,
a magnetic field collecting old newspapers,
broken-down cars, alleys where
the drummer cowers before he beats
on his bag of beer cans.

I visit the irrigation canal that
churns green and flows beyond the streets,
wait for the alligator to swim by,
the one released from the plaza long ago.
I feel the pull toward mongrel dog,
the clicking of the magnets in the church,
an attraction for open doorways.

*

I remove the magnet from my neck,
a medal of a denied saint.
It eases the pull toward the barbed-wire fence.
I will never witness the migration of bats again,
stand at the entrance of the caverns
as bats shoot out of the opening,
the evening bristling with their intelligence,
the black cloud a mass of sound.

The sky bruises against the horizon
of yucca plants surrounding
the cavern, erect as magnets,
miles of yucca encircling the poles
as if their silhouettes protect
the tunnel, clear it of wind
that pulls me into the hole.

*

He tells me to believe what I have seen.
He insists magnetic force comes from the blade,
the woman wanting us to keep something for her.
He says magnets are missing metals
from an underground wound,
a husband's wrist broken by a slammed car hood,
loyal dance of an old couple watching the street.

He says tortillas and menudo sometimes attract flies.
He learned red chili kills all life.
He insists magnets let him sleep fulfilled,
delicious food he fixes
long after his wife has died.
He says magnets get stronger when he peels
the pods to find no difference
in the seeds of hunger and the seeds of love.

*

I climb the rocks because the minerals are there.
I climb to where I buried the sea shell,
rusted can, and pencil twenty-eight years ago.
I climb the rocks because I am allowed one mountain.
I climb to readjust the magnets,
stand and look down.
I clear my chest of a fist never encountered up here.
I climb to set my foot on the humming slab.
I climb to survive when I touch my heart.
I climb before deciding I must bend and dig.

These Days

These years the border closes,
mojados sent back to be found as bodies in the river,
or the cut-off head hanging in the tree.
The gang in the barrio where I work sprays
graffiti on my office door, symbols I don't understand.
The English and Spanish don't belong to me.
They vibrate in drive-by shootings,
boys gasping with laughter and the gun,
betting on who will get shot or dance in prison.

Inside a mountain,
a man gets up and wonders what happened to
the *cuento* passed to him about madness
of a family who fled here, building a stone bridge
to hold water that saved them, made their corn grow.
Water seeps into the man's ears when he lies down.
It trickles into the room where he grows old,
water weeping out of the saguaro so he can cup his hands.

The hills contain graves of Mejicanos,
the rumor my father's ancestors were throat-cutting thieves
buried without markers on their graves.
I read about the psychic in the Alamo who encountered
spirits of Mejicanos forced into Santa Ana's army to die.
He contacts Bernardo y Juan Vargas, brothers trapped
156 years as tourists step on them,
soldiers revealing they want to rest in peace.
The psychic asks if the ghost of John Wayne dwells here.
The brothers tell him Wayne wanders among the dead,
never speaks because he can't find
the spirits of the Texas heroes.

I wave to the gang member we hired
to paint a mural on our center wall,
his arms finishing the blue and yellow feathers
on the Aztec face he created,
showing me how the man trapped in the mountain
can find his way out when I enter the old house to find
he is a muralist mixing color from
the burned mirrors under our familiar floors.

Marvin Bell

I Didn't Sleep

I didn't sleep in the light. I couldn't sleep
in the dark. I didn't sleep at night. I was awake
all day. I didn't sleep in the leaves or between
the pages. I tried but couldn't sleep
with my eyes open. I couldn't sleep indoors
or out under the stars. I couldn't sleep where
there were flowers. Insects kept me up. Shadows
shook me out of my doziness. I was trying hard.
It was horrible. I knew why I couldn't sleep.
Knowing I couldn't sleep made it harder to try.
I thought maybe I could sleep after the war
or catch a nap after the next election. It was
a terrible time in America. Many of us found
ourselves unable to sleep. The war went on.
The silence at home was deafening. So I
tried to talk myself to sleep by memorizing
the past, which had been full of sleepiness.
It didn't work. All over the world people
were being put to sleep. In every time zone.
I am busy not sleeping, obsessively one might say.
I resolve to sleep again when I have the time.

Bagram, Afghanistan, 2002

The interrogation celebrated spikes and cuffs,
the inky blue that invades a blackened eye,
the eyeball that bulges like a radish,
that incarnadine only blood can create.
They asked the young taxi driver questions
he could not answer, and they beat his legs
until he could no longer kneel on their command.
They chained him by the wrists to the ceiling.
They may have admired the human form then,
stretched out, for the soldiers were also athletes
trained to shout in unison and be buddies.
By the time his legs had stiffened, a blood clot
was already tracing a vein into his heart.
They said he was dead when they cut him down,
but he was dead the day they arrested him.
Are they feeding the prisoners gravel now?
To make them skillful orators as they confess?
Here stands Demosthenes in the military court,
unable to form the words "my country." What
shall we do, we who are at war but are asked
to pretend we are not? Do we need another
naïve apologist to crown us with clichés
that would turn the grass brown above a grave?
They called the carcass Mr. Dilawar. They
believed he was innocent. Their orders were
to step on the necks of the prisoners, to
break their will, to make them say something
in a sleep-deprived delirium of fractures,
rising to the occasion, or, like Mr. Dilawar,
leaving his few possessions and his body.

Messy

Morning's old news from another time zone.
Another video, last night's big-eyed child
cradled by a weary soldier or firefighter
across battle lines and a shifting border.
Off the walkway to step around the water
where the shopkeeper is hosing the concrete,
the aspirate knocking of the stream, shaped
by contained pressure, ups the ante because
I have bet on consciousness to be awake
even as the sales of armament overtake
the shopkeeper and the street vendor, reduced
to cleaning the neighborhood underneath
the saw-sound of engines above the cloud cover.
Yes, it all goes together, it is messy. The story
of a child rescued from the destroyed city
for a better life omits the residue. I have inside me
the click of a single round squeezed off
in a sniper-scope war, and the tidal thudding
of wave after wave of bombers melting steel
and the puncturing whoosh of bunker missiles
and the painting of napalm and the spray of
cluster-bombing, which returns me between wars
to the ideal, the sublime, the transcendent,
the transformative and the aesthetic escapes
of the mind from a cracked and patched heart.
I am only seventy, think what it means to be
twenty and the sidewalk taking you past dry goods
and home apothecaries, past a pocket of cold
at the ice cream window, past the hissing espresso,
and at the far end the dark of the movie house
telling a story that never happened. I am my insides,
as you are, try to tell me the paycheck is bigger
than the hole in your gut where peace used to be.

Poem Post-9/11/01

Eastern Long Island

The air has been torn by helicopter blades.
The sky tries to heal itself but the rotors keep churning.
The late-night disc jockey sits in a hot spot spinning songs.
Exhausted gas falls from idling autos parked by the bay.
The stocks were up, as they say, "modestly."
This is the national news, supported by people like you.
I wake up with whoever is talking on the air.
I cannot see the rooftops or the basements that pepper their reports.
The attics of my neighbors lean with the weight of fading memories.
My totems, a polished piece of hematite.
A triangle of carved Chinese jade.
A medical necklace.
The basic moral questions.
For example, is a total commitment to the life force demonic?
For example, is ethics a luxury of circumstance?
For example, how thin is ice?
Dark chocolate, they say, is the better for being bittersweet.
Try to see where you are, oppressed by the thumping of the copters.
A promise has been made to air an entire season of the mortuary show.
A man in a three-piece suit steps on the edge of a shovel to break ground
        for a community garden.
The tall Whalers Church standing stark white surrounds a resonant cavity.
You can picture the boats jostling the waves and the whale tail slapping.
When the harpoon hits, the exhalation shakes the tide, then the
        exaltation.
When disturbed, the otherwise free-flowing air terrifies, come nor'easters.
The disc jockey can't smooth it over when the helicopters come.
The parked lovers lose the moment.
The words from the front lines return to us chopped up.
We could have told one another before this din began.

David Mura

First Generation Angels

They lived behind the firehouse and Little Saigon Auto.
In the spring he sat on the porch while his mother,
the manicurist at Khan's salon, clipped his hair.
Smells of lilac, exhaust. A siren sucking up the distance.
A black corona drops to his shoulders. An impatient sigh.

How soon he vanished from her. Like his father staring
from the couch at the color TV, his black veteran's cap
from the surplus store sliding a mask over his eyes.
Five sisters, three brothers. Smells of *pho* and coriander.
While he's gone to fry stacks of tortillas at Little Tijuana's

With lean bad ass cheeks. Hair pomaded back. A thin mustache.
You know then he's written poems decrying *Miss Saigon*.
His life as Nuprin, a little yellow pill for your pains.
His uncle dead years ago in a paddy. VC bullet in his brow.
He and his poems will read next week at Patrick's Cabaret.

But if you look from your salsa and he's not in the kitchen?
You fear he's sitting in a room with the social worker,
the clock above ticking, the lawyer not yet arrived, and he
recording his story, muttering I've outlived all your stories,
man. Eyes like a panther. A caged bird. A jaded small boy.

Back in the apartment his mother conjures with the shaman,
rocks to and fro for the spirits, so far from Laos hills,
herbal hallucinations that once brought them forth.
Hot blood wrung from a rooster's neck. Ancestral prayers.
Her head wrapped in a black cloth, her eyes dry weeping.

Then you know he's not Vietnamese. That Mai was with him.
That she was the one shouting, *Shoot him, shoot the motherfucker.*
And the other girl screaming. He staring at the dark pool.
Man, I didn't know you could bleed that much...How'd they find us:
The words won't translate. Like years ago, winter at the window—

He's looking down University, his head echoing with
his father's nightmares, his mother's weeping. He marks
the tire tracks, a cop car sluicing past. Then its nothing

but snow and snow and snow, and each flake a small angel
sprouting wings in the dark, spiraling down upon us all.

The Young Asian Women

The young Asian women are shaving their heads,
piercing eyelids and ears. They stare holes
in curators, shop clerks and geisha chasers,
bubble gum snapping like caps in their jaws.
Their names? Juliana, Vong, Lee, and Lily.
Could be Mina from the outskirts of Tokyo
but more likely she's Nkauj'lis of the famous
or infamous Lyfongs (depending on your clan
and your anti-Communist persuasions).
Check out that siren named Sonia, too in love
with her looks, a nasty curl of Seoul
in her smile. Or if her name is Hoa,
she's tough as her mother, bad girl, bitch,
it doesn't matter, she'll survive like nettles
flower in what ditch she finds herself, with
or without a man, or her lesbian lover who left
for Alaska, the smell of bear shit on the trail.
With her Taiwanese aunt, digs tales of Toisan
ladies, dragons and the water marsh where bandit
ghosts steal years with a kiss, talking tongues
down your throat to your belly, slipping
a demon seed inside you to grow. Oh, they're
like that, these young women, their art alive
like Thai hot sauce on your tongue, hurtling hurt
with a half pint gleaming on the night stand.
They know how mysteriously the body is written,
how thundering colors of Benetton befit
statistics on garment workers in the Third
and First Worlds. They know *Woman Warrior*,
bell hooks, how the moon waxes red like
the sheets where they write out scripts, stories,
and poems, unwrapping their dreams before
you, a palm of paint, pearls, I-Ching stones.
With boots black and buckled, their jeans frayed,
lips bruised purple or incandescent red,
their bodies at the dance club cut into hip-hop.

Their voices are hoarse after nights on the floor,
their faces smeared with sweat. Their cheeks aglow.
They scare the pants off the young men they know.

Father Blues for Jon Jang

Way back in the fifties
    when Chinaman was a chink
        and chance a Chinaman's dance,

and Charlie Chan still yellowed
    his wizened fat face in a cinema
        of blue-eyed blondes;

with white boys blowing blues
    as angel-headed hipsters
        coked and toked their dreams

on the road, in Beat Bay cafés;
    back when Chinatown
        danced *Flower Drum Song*—

Well, once in that glorious decade,
    my father's rising, Ph.D.
        in chemistry, crashing

glass ceilings of Fluor Corporation
    with brains and acumen
        and easygoing laugh,

and like any white blue-blooded American
    screening *Leave it to Beaver*,
        Reed, and *Father Knows Best*,

father had to score a house,
    and no one could call him
        Hey By, Hop Sing,

or Peter the cranky *Bachelor Father* houseboy,
    forget those Stepin Fetchit
        chinky figures of fun, Baba

got a house jones, come hell or highwater
    so he banked bids on house after
        house all across this city,

and after every bid they told him
> politely—or impolitely, it didn't really matter—Solly!
>> Charlie Chinaman,

you don't stand a chance!
> Even if your offer bounces higher than the price,
>> even if you send the price soaring

like the homers of the Say Hey
> Kid blasting over the fence,
>> no way, wing-wong, NO WAY!

—But never a man to trip "No," Baba
> steered a white friend to bid on this house, higher
>> than the asking,

and his proxy copped the house,
> taking commission on the side,
>> and now we're living high on the hog

on a hill over Chinatown and the Bay
> and father queued for Vice President, better salaries,
>> bigger cars, the whole shebang...

And then. And then: SLAM—HEADLINE:
> June 29, 1956, *New York Times*:
>> *126 Die in Plane Crash*

down the Grand Canyon, the
> decades largest disaster, larger
>> than any other for me

with my father aboard, Baba's
> remains mangled beyond
>> recognition in the crumpling

crush of metal, pyres of high octane
> flames. And Woo's Funeral Parlor
>> serviced what was left,

and, inside Woo's roaring oven,
> a small stellar blast
>> seared my father

down to a vase of ash, slipped
> inside a lacquered wooden box,
>> and my mother, three months

pregnant, hauled it in
        to be interred in the Glendale Cemetery,
                her other arm tugging along, barely

two, a toddler teetering from the Chevy,
        half conscious
                something was now amiss, amid

rolling lawns and slabs of stone
        and the office where my mother stood, waiting
                to tomb what was left

of father in a vault,
        and I don't know why, don't
                savvy, my mother

crying, screaming, yanking
        me out of that office, cursing in Chinese
                the white man behind the desk,

and only years later do I catch my father
        couldn't be buried there once
                they made my mother, once

they scried her eyes, her skin, her
        lithe dark figure, her eyes, her skin
                in the boy beside her,

and the moral charts, I suppose,
        what I've carted to this day—
                "It don't matter if you're flamed

down to ash, just primal dust,
        you still a Chinaman, you might as well
                blow your life, your music that way

—Oh Chinaman Chinaman Chinaman blues..."

Minneapolis Public

There are 150 first languages in our schools
and so many aliens even E.T. would go unnoticed,
though if your tongue moved one way in the land of your birth
it must move another now, awkward at first.

There are blacks here who've never been to Africa;
Africans who've never heard a Baptist prayer,
much less the solemn dirges of Lutherans
or how the artist formerly known is some sort of Prince.

In the anthology of American Buddhist poetry
you will find not one face of a Tibetan
but they are here with girls and boys named Tenzin
and one, my son's good friend, throws a hard mean spiral.

Esmir is not the name of a girl but a Bosnian
boy who crouches at a table and glues a lamp together
and later with my other son conspires on a book—"A Touch
of Rabies"—a heartbreaking tale of good dogs gone bad.

(Why tell a soul of the sieges that brought him here
or stories of the Dali Lama and the temples destroyed
or troops of the warlords in the streets of Somalia,
the borders dividing death from safety if not evil and good?)

Say you're Egyptian or Haitian: Here you're singular,
not part of a Big Apple ghetto. If you're Chinese,
most likely you're adopted, or else your parents study
engineering at the U. And have I mentioned the Mexicans?

In *West Side Story* the rumble starts with Puerto Ricans
and working-class whites in a high-school gym;
this year Maria's still Natalie Wood white to Jamaica's
half-black Anita, and the Jets sport blacks, one Tibetan,

and my *happa* daughter who still doesn't question
such casting, or why *Bye Bye Birdie* last year
just might not be the choice of half the school
for a song and dance they could take on as their own.

Still at the spring school dance J. Lo and Ja Rule
set the awkward bump and grind of junior high girls
and the boys watch on the sidelines as boys that age do,
whether Bosnian, black, white, Somali, Tibetan.

I'm told we live in the Land of Great Lake Woebegon
where all the women are strong, all the men good-looking,
and the children above average—and, I always add,
everyone's white. Hey, Tenzin, Nabil, go tell Garrison:

Not now. Not quite.

Scott Russell Sanders

Under the Influence

My father drank. He drank as a gut-punched boxer gasps for breath, as a starving dog gobbles food—compulsively, secretly, in pain and trembling. I use the past tense not because he ever quit drinking but because he quit living. That is how the story ends for my father, age sixty-four, heart bursting, body cooling and forsaken on the linoleum of my brother's trailer. The story continues for my brother, my sister, my mother, and me, and will continue so long as memory holds.

In the perennial present of memory, I slip into the garage or barn to see my father tipping back the flat green bottles of wine, the brown cylinders of whiskey, the cans of beer disguised in paper bags. His Adam's apple bobs, the liquid gurgles, he wipes the sandy-haired back of a hand over his lips, and then, his bloodshot gaze bumping into me, he stashes the bottle or can inside his jacket, under the workbench, between two bales of hay, and we both pretend the moment has not occurred.

"What's up, buddy?" he says, thick-tongued and edgy.

"Sky's up," I answer, playing along.

"And don't forget prices," he grumbles. "Prices are always up. And taxes."

In memory, his white 1951 Pontiac with the stripes down the hood and the Indian head on the snout jounces to a stop in the driveway; or it is the 1956 Ford station wagon, or the 1963 Rambler shaped like a toad, or the sleek 1969 Bonneville that will do 120 miles per hour on straightaways; or it is the robin's-egg blue pickup, new in 1980, battered in 1981, the year of his death. He climbs out, grinning dangerously, unsteady on his legs, and we children interrupt our game of catch, our building of snow forts, our picking of plums, to watch in silence as he weaves past into the house, where he slumps into his overstuffed chair and falls asleep. Shaking her head, our mother stubs out the cigarette he has left smoldering in the ashtray. All evening, until our bedtimes, we tiptoe past him, as past a snoring dragon. Then we curl in our fearful sheets, listening. Eventually he wakes with a grunt, Mother slings accusations at him, he snarls back, she yells, he growls, their voices clashing. Before long, she retreats to their bedroom, sobbing—not from the blows of fists, for he never strikes her, but from the force of words.

Left alone, our father prowls the house, thumping into furniture, rummaging in the kitchen, slamming doors, turning the pages of the newspaper with a savage crackle, muttering back at the late-night drivel from television. The roof might fly off, the walls might buckle from the pressure of his rage.

Whatever my brother and sister and mother may be thinking on their own rumpled pillows, I lie there hating him, loving him, fearing him, knowing I have failed him. I tell myself he drinks to ease an ache that gnaws at his belly, an ache I must have caused by disappointing him somehow, a murderous ache I should be able to relieve by doing all my chores, earning A's in school, winning baseball games, fixing the broken washer and the burst pipes, bringing in money to fill his empty wallet. He would not hide the green bottles in his tool box, would not sneak off to the barn with a lump under his coat, would not fall asleep in the daylight, would not roar and fume, would not drink himself to death, if only I were perfect.

I am forty-two as I write these words, and I know full well now that my father was an alcoholic, a man consumed by disease rather than by disappointment. What had seemed to me a private grief is in fact a public scourge. In the United States alone some ten or fifteen million people share his ailment, and behind the doors they slam in fury or disgrace, countless other children tremble. I comfort myself with such knowledge, holding it against the throb of memory like an ice pack against a bruise. There are keener sources of grief: poverty, racism, rape, war. I do not wish to compete for a trophy in suffering. I am only trying to understand the corrosive mixture of helplessness, responsibility, and shame that I learned to feel as the son of an alcoholic. I realize now that I did not cause my father's illness, nor could I have cured it. Yet for all this grown-up knowledge, I am still ten years old, my own son's age, and as that boy I struggle in guilt and confusion to save my father from pain.

*

Consider a few of our synonyms for *drunk*: tipsy, tight, pickled, soused, and plowed; stoned and stewed, lubricated and inebriated, juiced and sluiced; three sheets to the wind, in your cups, out of your mind, under the table; lit up, tanked up, wiped out; besotted, blotto, bombed, and buzzed; plastered, polluted, putrefied; loaded or looped, boozy, woozy, fuddled, or smashed; crocked and shit-faced, corked and pissed, snockered and sloshed.

It is a mostly humorous lexicon, as the lore that deals with drunks—in jokes and cartoons, in plays, films, and television skits—is largely comic. Aunt Matilda nips elderberry wine from the sideboard and burps politely during supper. Uncle Fred slouches to the table glassy-eyed, wearing a lamp shade for a hat and murmuring, "Candy is dandy but liquor is quicker." Inspired by cocktails, Mrs. Somebody recounts the events of her day in a fuzzy dialect, while Mr. Somebody nibbles her ear and croons a bawdy song. On the sofa with Boyfriend, Daughter giggles, licking gin from her lips, and loosens the bows in her hair. Junior knocks back some brews with his chums at the Leopard Lounge and stumbles home to the wrong house, wonders foggily why he cannot locate his pajamas, and crawls naked into bed with the ugliest girl in school. The family dog slurps from a neglected martini and wobbles to the nursery, where he vomits in Baby's shoe.

It is all great fun. But if in the audience you notice a few laughing faces turn grim when the drunk lurches on stage, don't be surprised, for these are the children of alcoholics. Over the grinning mask of Dionysus, the leering mask of Bacchus, these children cannot help seeing the bloated features of their own parents. Instead of laughing, they wince, they mourn. Instead of celebrating the drunk as one freed from constraints, they pity him as one enslaved. They refuse to believe in vino veritas, having seen their befuddled parents skid away from truth toward folly and oblivion. And so these children bite their lips until the lush staggers into the wings.

My father, when drunk, was neither funny nor honest; he was pathetic, frightening, deceitful. There seemed to be a leak in him somewhere, and he poured in booze to keep from draining dry. Like a torture victim who refuses to squeal, he would never admit that he had touched a drop, not even in his last year, when he seemed to be dissolving in alcohol before our very eyes. I never knew him to lie about anything, ever, except about this one ruinous fact. Drowsy, clumsy, unable to fix a bicycle tire, throw a baseball, balance a grocery sack, or walk across the room, he was stripped of his true self by drink. In a matter of minutes, the contents of a bottle could transform a brave man into a coward, a buddy into a bully, a gifted athlete and skilled carpenter and shrewd businessman into a bumbler. No dictionary of synonyms for drunk would soften the anguish of watching our prince turn into a frog.

*

Father's drinking became the family secret. While growing up, we children never breathed a word of it beyond the four walls of our house. To this day, my brother and sister rarely mention it, and then only when I press them. I did not confess the ugly, bewildering fact to my wife until his wavering walk and slurred speech forced me to. Recently, on the seventh anniversary of my father's death, I asked my mother if she ever spoke of his drinking to friends. "No, no, never," she replied hastily. "I couldn't bear for anyone to know."

The secret bores under the skin, gets in the blood, into the bone, and stays there. Long after you have supposedly been cured of malaria, the fever can flare up, the tremors can shake you. So it is with the fevers of shame. You swallow the bitter quinine of knowledge, and you learn to feel pity and compassion toward the drinker. Yet the shame lingers in your marrow, and, because of the shame, anger.

*

For a long stretch of my childhood we lived on a military reservation in Ohio, an arsenal where bombs were stored underground in bunkers, vintage airplanes burst into flames, and unstable artillery shells boomed nightly at the dump. We had the feeling, as children, that we played in a mine field, where a heedless footfall could trigger an explosion. When Father was drinking, the house, too, became a mine field. The least bump could set off either parent.

The more he drank, the more obsessed Mother became with stopping him. She hunted for bottles, counted the cash in his wallet, sniffed at his breath. Without meaning to snoop, we children blundered left and right into damning evidence. On afternoons when he came home from work sober, we flung ourselves at him for hugs, and felt against our ribs the telltale lump in his coat. In the barn we tumbled on the hay and heard beneath our sneakers the crunch of buried glass. We tugged open a drawer in his workbench, looking for screwdrivers or crescent wrenches, and spied a gleaming six-pack among the tools. Playing tag, we darted around the house just in time to see him sway on the rear stoop and heave a finished bottle into the woods. In his good night kiss we smelled the cloying sweetness of Clorets, the mints he chewed to camouflage his dragon's breath.

I can summon up that kiss right now by recalling Theodore Roethke's lines about his own father in "My Papa's Waltz":

> *The whiskey on your breath*
> *Could make a small boy dizzy;*
> *But I hung on like death:*
> *Such waltzing was not easy.*

Such waltzing was hard, terribly hard, for with a boy's scrawny arms I was trying to hold my tipsy father upright.

For years, the chief source of those incriminating bottles and cans was a grimy store a mile from us, a cinder block place called Sly's, with two gas pumps outside and a moth-eaten dog asleep in the window. A strip of flypaper, speckled the year round with black bodies, coiled in the doorway. Inside, on rusty metal shelves or in wheezing coolers, you could find pop and Popsicles, cigarettes, potato chips, canned soup, raunchy postcards, fishing gear, Twinkies, wine, and beer. When Father drove anywhere on errands, Mother would send us kids along as guards, warning us not to let him out of our sight. And so with one or more of us on board, Father would cruise up to Sly's, pump a dollar's worth of gas or plump the tires with air, and then, telling us to wait in the car, he would head for that fly-spangled doorway.

Dutiful and panicky, we cried, "Let us go in with you!"

"No," he answered. "I'll be back in two shakes."

"Please!"

"No!" he roared. "Don't you budge, or I'll jerk a knot in your tails!"

So we stayed put, kicking the seats, while he ducked inside. Often, when he had parked the car at a careless angle, we gazed in through the window and saw Mr. Sly fetching down from a shelf behind the cash register two green pints of Gallo wine. Father swigged one of them right there at the counter, stuffed the other in his pocket, and then out he came, a bulge in his coat, a flustered look on his red face.

Because the Mom and Pop who ran the dump were neighbors of ours, living just down the tar-blistered road, I hated them all the more for poisoning my father. I wanted to sneak in their store and smash the bottles and set fire to the place. I also hated the Gallo brothers, Ernest and Julio, whose jovial faces shone from the labels of their wine, labels I would find, torn and curled, when I burned the trash. I noted the Gallo brothers' address, in California, and I studied the road atlas to see how far that was from Ohio, because I meant to go out there and tell Ernest and Julio what they were doing to my father, and then, if they showed no mercy, I would kill them.

*

While growing up on the back roads and in the country schools and cramped Methodist churches of Ohio and Tennessee, I never heard the word *alcoholism*, never happened across it in books or magazines. In the nearby towns, there were no addiction treatment programs, no community mental health centers, no Alcoholics Anonymous chapters, no therapists. Left alone with our grievous secret, we had no way of understanding Father's drinking except as an act of will, a deliberate folly or cruelty, a moral weakness, a sin. He drank because he chose to, pure and simple. Why our father, so playful and competent and kind when sober, would choose to ruin himself and punish his family, we could not fathom.

Our neighborhood was high on the Bible, and the Bible was hard on drunkards. "Woe to those who are heroes at drinking wine, and valiant men in mixing strong drink," wrote Isaiah. "The priest and the prophet reel with strong drink, they are confused with wine, they err in vision, they stumble in giving judgment. For all tables are full of vomit, no place is without filthiness." We children had seen those fouled tables at the local truck stop where the notorious boozers hung out, our father occasionally among them. "Wine and new wine take away the understanding," declared the prophet Hosea. We had also seen evidence of that in our father, who could multiply seven-digit numbers in his head when sober, but when drunk could not help us with fourth-grade math. Proverbs warned: "Do not look at wine when it is red, when it sparkles in the cup and goes down smoothly. At the last it bites like a serpent, and stings like an adder. Your eyes will see strange things, and your mind utter perverse things." Woe, woe.

Dismayingly often, these biblical drunkards stirred up trouble for their own kids. Noah made fresh wine after the flood, drank too much of it, fell asleep without any clothes on, and was glimpsed in the buff by his son Ham, whom Noah promptly cursed. In one passage—it was so shocking we had to read it under our blankets with flashlights—the patriarch Lot fell down drunk and slept with his daughters. The sins of the fathers set their children's teeth on edge.

Our ministers were fond of quoting St. Paul's pronouncement that drunkards would not inherit the kingdom of God. These grave preachers assured us that the wine referred to during the Last Supper was in fact grape juice. Bible and sermons and hymns combined to give us the impression that Moses should have brought down from the mountain another stone tablet, bearing the Eleventh Commandment: Thou shalt not drink.

The scariest and most illuminating Bible story apropos of drunkards was the one about the lunatic and the swine. Matthew, Mark, and Luke each told a version of the tale. We knew it by heart: When Jesus climbed out of his boat one day, this lunatic came charging up from the graveyard, stark naked and filthy, frothing at the mouth, so violent that he broke the strongest chains. Nobody would go near him. Night and day for years this madman had been wailing among the tombs and bruising himself with stones. Jesus took one look at him and said, "Come out of the man, you unclean spirits!" for he could see that the lunatic was possessed by demons. Meanwhile, some hogs were conveniently rooting nearby. "If we have to come out," begged the demons, "at least let us go into those swine." Jesus agreed, the unclean spirits entered the hogs, and the hogs rushed straight off a cliff and plunged into a lake. Hearing the story in Sunday school, my friends thought mainly of the pigs. (How big a splash did they make? Who paid for the lost pork?) But I thought of the redeemed lunatic, who bathed himself and put on clothes and calmly sat at the feet of Jesus, restored—so the Bible said—to "his right mind."

When drunk, our father was clearly in his wrong mind. He became a stranger, as fearful to us as any graveyard lunatic, not quite frothing at the mouth but fierce enough, quick-tempered, explosive; or else he grew maudlin and weepy, which frightened us nearly as much. In my boyhood despair, I reasoned that maybe he wasn't to blame for turning into an ogre: Maybe, like the lunatic, he was possessed by demons. I found support for my theory when I heard liquor referred to as "spirits," when the newspapers reported that somebody had been arrested for "driving under the influence," and when church ladies railed against that "demon drink."

If my father was indeed possessed, who would exorcise him? If he was a sinner, who would save him? If he was ill, who would cure him? If he suffered, who would ease his pain? Not ministers or doctors, for we could not bring ourselves to confide in them; not the neighbors, for we pretended they had never seen him drunk; not Mother, who fussed and pleaded but could not budge him; not my brother and sister, who were only kids. That left me. It did not matter that I, too, was only a child, and a bewildered one at that. I could not excuse myself.

*

On first reading a description of delirium tremens—in a book on alcoholism I smuggled from the library—I thought immediately of the frothing lunatic and the frenzied swine. When I read stories or watched films about grisly metamorphoses—Dr. Jekyll becoming Mr. Hyde, the mild husband changing into a werewolf, the kindly neighbor taken over by a brutal alien—I could not help seeing my own father's mutation from sober to drunk. Even today, knowing better, I am attracted by the demonic theory of drink, for when I recall my father's transformation, the emergence of his ugly second self, I find it easy to believe in possession by unclean spirits. We never knew which version of Father would come home from work, the true or the tainted, nor could we guess how far down the slope toward cruelty he would slide.

How far a man *could* slide we gauged by observing our back-road neighbors—the out-of-work miners who had dragged their families to our corner of Ohio from the desolate hollows of Appalachia, the tightfisted farmers, the surly mechanics, the balked and broken men. There was, for example, whiskey-soaked Mr. Jenkins, who beat his wife and kids so hard we could hear their screams from the road. There was Mr. Lavo the wino, who fell asleep smoking time and again, until one night his disgusted wife bundled up the children and went outside and left him in his easy chair to burn; he awoke on his own, staggered out coughing into the yard, and pounded her flat while the children looked on and the shack turned to ash. There was the truck driver, Mr. Sampson, who tripped over his son's tricycle one night while drunk and got so mad that he jumped into his semi and drove away, shifting through the dozen gears, and never came back. We saw the bruised children of these fathers clump onto our school bus, we saw the abandoned children huddle in the pews at church, we saw the stunned and battered mothers begging for help at our doors.

Our own father never beat us, and I don't think he ever beat Mother, but he threatened often. The Old Testament Yahweh was not more terrible in his wrath. Eyes blazing, voice booming, Father would pull out his belt and swear to give us a whipping, but he never followed through, never needed to, because we could imagine it so vividly. He shoved us, pawed us with the back of his hand, as an irked bear might smack a cub, not to injure, just to clear a space. I can see him grabbing Mother by the hair as she cowers on a chair during a nightly quarrel. He twists her neck back until she gapes up at him, and then he lifts over her skull a glass quart bottle of milk, the milk running down his forearm, and he yells at her, "Say just one more word, one goddamn word, and I'll shut you up!" I fear she will prick him with her sharp tongue, but she is terrified into silence, and so am I, and the leaking bottle quivers in the air, and milk slithers through the red hair of my father's uplifted arm, and the entire scene is there to this moment, the head jerked back, the club raised.

When the drink made him weepy, Father would pack a bag and kiss each of us children on the head, and announce from the front door that he was moving out. "Where to?" we demanded, fearful each time that he would leave for good, as Mr. Sampson had roared away for good in his diesel truck. "Someplace where I won't get hounded every minute," Father would answer, his jaw quivering. He stabbed a look at Mother, who might say, "Don't run into the ditch before you get there," or, "Good riddance," and then he would slink away. Mother watched him go with arms crossed over her chest, her face closed like the lid on a box of snakes. We children bawled. Where could he go? To the truck stop, that den of iniquity? To one of those dark, ratty flophouses in town? Would he wind up sleeping under a railroad bridge or on a park bench or in a cardboard box, mummied in rags, like the bums we had seen on our trips to Cleveland and Chicago? We bawled and bawled, wondering if he would ever come back.

He always did come back, a day or a week later, but each time there was a sliver less of him.

*

In Kafka's *The Metamorphosis*, which opens famously with Gregor Samsa waking up from uneasy dreams to find himself transformed into an insect, Gregor's family keep reassuring themselves that things will be just fine again, "When he comes back to us." Each time alcohol transformed our father, we held out the same hope, that he would really and truly come back to us, our authentic father, the tender and playful and competent man, and then all things would be fine. We had grounds for such hope. After his weepy departures and chapfallen returns, he would sometimes go weeks, even months without drinking. Those were glad times. Joy banged inside my ribs. Every day without the furtive glint of bottles, every meal without a fight, every bedtime without sobs encouraged us to believe that such bliss might go on forever.

Mother was fooled by just such a hope all during the forty-odd years she knew this Greeley Ray Sanders. Soon after she met him in a Chicago delicatessen on the eve of World War II, and fell for his butter-melting Mississippi drawl and his wavy red hair, she learned that he drank heavily. But then so did a lot of men. She would soon coax or scold him into breaking the nasty habit. She would point out to him how ugly and foolish it was, this bleary drinking, and then he would quit. He refused to quit during their engagement, however, still refused during the first years of marriage, refused until my sister came along. The shock of fatherhood sobered him, and he remained sober through my birth at the end of the war and right on through until we moved in 1951 to the Ohio arsenal, that paradise of bombs. Like all places that make a business of death, the arsenal had more than its share of alcoholics and drug addicts and other varieties of escape artists. There I turned six and started school and woke into a child's flickering awareness, just in time to see my father begin sneaking swigs in the garage.

He sobered up again for most of a year at the height of the Korean War, to celebrate the birth of my brother. But aside from that dry spell, his only breaks from drinking before I graduated from high school were just long enough to raise and then dash our hopes. Then during the fall of my senior year—the time of the Cuban missile crisis, when it seemed that the nightly explosions at the munitions dump and the nightly rages in our household might spread to engulf the globe—Father collapsed. His liver, kidneys, and heart all conked out. The doctors saved him, but only by a hair. He stayed in the hospital for weeks, going through a withdrawal so terrible that Mother would not let us visit him. If he wanted to kill himself, the doctors solemnly warned him, all he had to do was hit the bottle again. One binge would finish him.

Father must have believed them, for he stayed dry the next fifteen years. It was an answer to prayer, Mother said, it was a miracle. I believe it was a reflex of fear, which he sustained over the years through courage and pride. He knew a man could die from drink, for his brother Roscoe had. We children never laid eyes on doomed Uncle Roscoe, but in the stories Mother told us he became a fairy tale figure, like a boy who took the wrong turning in the woods and was gobbled up by the wolf.

The fifteen-year dry spell came to an end with Father's retirement in the spring of 1978. Like many men, he gave up his identity along with his job. One day he was a boss at the factory, with a brass plate on his door and a reputation to uphold; the next day he was a nobody at home. He and Mother were leaving Ontario, the last of the many places to which his job had carried them, and they were moving to a new house in Mississippi, his childhood stomping grounds. As a boy in Mississippi, Father sold Coca-Cola during dances while the moonshiners peddled their brew in the parking lot; as a young blade, he fought in bars and in the ring, seeking a state Golden Gloves championship; he gambled at poker, hunted pheasants, raced motorcycles and cars, played semi-professional baseball, and, along with all his buddies—in the Black Cat Saloon, behind the cotton gin, in the woods—he drank. It was a perilous youth to dream of recovering.

After his final day of work, Mother drove on ahead with a car full of begonias and violets, while Father stayed behind to oversee the packing. When the van was loaded, the sweaty movers broke open a six-pack and offered him a beer.

"Let's drink to retirement!" they crowed. "Let's drink to freedom! to fishing! hunting! loafing! Let's drink to a guy who's going home!"

At least I imagine some such words, for that is all I can do, imagine, and I see Father's hand trembling in midair as he thinks about the fifteen sober years and about the doctors' warning, and he tells himself *Goddamnit, I am a free man,* and *Why can't a free man drink one beer after a lifetime of hard work?* and I see his arm reaching, his fingers closing, the can tilting to his lips. I even supply a label for the beer, a swaggering brand that promises on television to deliver the essence of life. I watch the amber liquid pour down his throat, the alcohol steal into his blood, the key turn in his brain.

*

Soon after my parents moved back to Father's treacherous stomping ground, my wife and I visited them in Mississippi with our five-year-old daughter. Mother had been too distraught to warn me about the return of the demons. So when I climbed out of the car that bright July morning and saw my father napping in the hammock, I felt uneasy, for in all his sober years I had never known him to sleep in daylight. Then he lurched upright, blinked his blood-shot eyes, and greeted us in a syrupy voice. I was hurled back helpless into childhood.

"What's the matter with Papaw?" our daughter asked.

"Nothing," I said. "Nothing!"

Like a child again, I pretended not to see him in his stupor, and behind my phony smile I grieved. On that visit and on the few that remained before his death, once again I found bottles in the workbench, bottles in the woods. Again his hands shook too much for him to run a saw, to make his precious miniature furniture, to drive straight down back roads. Again he wound up in the ditch, in the hospital, in jail, in treatment centers. Again he shouted and wept. Again he lied. "I never touched a drop," he swore. "Your mother's making it up."

I no longer fancied I could reason with the men whose names I found on the bottles—Jim Beam, Jack Daniels—nor did I hope to save my father by burning down a store. I was able now to press the cold statistics about alcoholism against the ache of memory: ten million victims, fifteen million, twenty. And yet, in spite of my age, I reacted in the same blind way as I had in childhood, ignoring biology, forgetting numbers, vainly seeking to erase through my efforts whatever drove him to drink. I worked on their place twelve and sixteen hours a day, in the swelter of Mississippi summers, digging ditches, running electrical wires, planting trees, mowing grass, building sheds, as though what nagged at him was some list of chores, as though by taking his worries on my shoulders I could redeem him. I was flung back into boyhood, acting as though my father would not drink himself to death if only I were perfect.

I failed of perfection; he succeeded in dying. To the end, he considered himself not sick but sinful. "Do you want to kill yourself?" I asked him. "Why not?" he answered. "Why the hell not? What's there to save?" To the end, he would not speak about his feelings, would not or could not give a name to the beast that was devouring him.

In silence, he went rushing off the cliff. Unlike the biblical swine, however, he left behind a few of the demons to haunt his children. Life with him and the loss of him twisted us into shapes that will be familiar to other sons and daughters of alcoholics. My brother became a rebel, my sister retreated into shyness, I played the stalwart and dutiful son who would hold the family together. If my father was unstable, I would be a rock. If he squandered money on drink, I would pinch every penny. If he wept when drunk—and only when drunk—I would not let myself weep at all. If he roared at the Little League umpire for calling my pitches balls, I would throw nothing but strikes. Watching him flounder and rage, I came to dread the loss of control. I would go through life without making anyone mad. I vowed never to put in my mouth or veins any chemical that would banish my everyday self. I would never make a scene, never lash out at the ones I loved, never hurt a soul. Through hard work, relentless work, I would achieve something dazzling—in the classroom, on the basketball floor, in the science lab, in the pages of books—and my achievement would distract the world's eyes from his humiliation. I would become a worthy sacrifice, and the smoke of my burning would please God.

It is far easier to recognize these twists in my character than to undo them. Work has become an addiction for me, as drink was an addiction for my father. Knowing this, my daughter gave me a placard for the wall: WORKAHOLIC. The labor is endless and futile, for I can no more redeem myself through work than I could redeem my father. I still panic in the face of other people's anger, because his drunken temper was so terrible. I shrink from causing sadness or disappointment even to strangers, as though I were still concealing the family shame. I still notice every twitch of emotion in the faces around me, having learned as a child to read the weather in faces, and I blame myself for their least pang of unhappiness or anger. In certain moods I blame myself for everything. Guilt burns like acid in my veins.

*

I am moved to write these pages now because my own son, at the age of ten, is taking on himself the griefs of the world, and in particular the griefs of his father. He tells me that when I am gripped by sadness he feels responsible; he feels there must be something he can do to spring me from depression, to fix my life. And that crushing sense of responsibility is exactly what I felt at the age of ten in the face of my father's drinking. My son wonders if I, too, am possessed. I write, therefore, to drag into the light what eats at me—the fear, the guilt, the shame—so that my own children may be spared.

I still shy away from nightclubs, from bars, from parties where the solvent is alcohol. My friends puzzle over this, but it is no more peculiar than for a man to shy away from the lions' den after seeing his father torn apart. I took my own first drink at the age of twenty-one, half a glass of burgundy. I knew the odds of my becoming an alcoholic were four times higher than for the sons of non-alcoholic fathers. So I sipped warily.

I still do—once a week, perhaps, a glass of wine, a can of beer, nothing stronger, nothing more. I listen for the turning of a key in my brain.

Heid E. Erdrich

Guidelines for the
Treatment of Sacred Objects

If the objects emit music,
and are made of clay or turtle shell,
bathe them in mud at rainy season.
Allow to dry, then brush clean
using only red cloth or newspaper.
Play musical objects from time to time.
Avoid stereotypical tom-tom beat
and under no circumstances dance or sway.

If objects were worn as funerary ornament,
admire them verbally from time to time.
Brass bells should be called *shiny*
rather than *pretty.* Shell ear spools
should be remarked upon as *handsome,*
but beads of all kinds can be told,
simply, that they are *lookin' good.*

Guidelines for the treatment of sacred objects
composed of wood, hair (human or otherwise)
and/or horn, include offering smoke,
water, pollen, cornmeal or, in some instances,
honey, chewing gum, tarpaper
and tax incentives.

If an object's use is obscure,
or of pleasing avian verisimilitude,
place rocks from its place of origin
within its display case. Blue-ish rocks
often bring about discovery, black rocks
soothe or mute, while white rocks irritate mildly.
All rocks must return to their place of origin
whenever they wish. Use only volunteer rocks,
or stones left by matri-descendant patri-tribalists.

Guidelines for the treatment of sacred objects
that appear or disappear at will
or that appear larger in rear view mirrors,
include calling in spiritual leaders such as librarians,
wellness-circuit speakers and financial aide officers.

If an object calls for its mother,
boil water and immediately swaddle it.
If an object calls for other family members,
or calls collect after midnight, refer to tribally
specific guidelines. Reverse charges.

If objects appear to be human bone,
make certain to have all visitors stroke
or touch fingertips to all tibia, fibula
and pelvis fragments. In the case of skulls,
call low into the ear or eyeholes, with words
lulling and kind.

If the bones seem to mock you
or if they vibrate or hiss,
make certain no mirrors hang nearby.
Never, at anytime, sing *Dem Bones*.

Avoid using bones as drumsticks
or paperweights, no matter
the actions of previous Directors or Vice
Directors of your institution.

If bones complain for weeks at a time,
roll about moaning, or leave chalky outlines,
return them instantly to their place of origin,
no questions asked. C.O.D.

The Theft Outright

after Frost

We were the land's before we were.
Or the land was ours before you were a land.
Or this land was our land, it was not your land.

We were the land before we were people,
loamy roamers rising, so the stories go,
or formed of clay, spit into with breath reeking soul—

What's America, but the legend of Rock 'n' Roll?

Red rocks, blood clots bearing boys, blood sands
swimming being from women's hands, we originate,
originally, spontaneous as hemorrhage.

Un-possessing of what we still are possessed by,
possessed by what we now no more possess.

We were the land before we were people,
dreamy sunbeams where sun don't shine, so the stories go,
or pulled up a hole, clawing past ants and roots—

Dineh in documentaries scoff dna evidence off.
They landed late, but canyons spoke them home.
Nomadic Turkish horse tribes they don't know.

What's America, but the legend of Stop 'n' Go?

Could be cousins, left on the land bridge,
contrary to popular belief, that was a two-way toll.
In any case we'd claim them, give them some place to stay.

Such as we were we gave most things outright
(the deed of the theft was many deeds and leases and claim stakes
and tenure disputes and moved plat markers stolen still today . . .)

We were the land before we were a people,
earthdivers, her darling mudpuppies, so the stories go,
or emerging, fully forming from flesh of earth—

The land, not the least vaguely, realizing in all four directions,
still storied, art-filled, fully enhanced.
Such as she is, such as she wills us to become.

Butter Maiden and Maize Girl Survive Death Leap

Even now, Native American Barbie gets only so many roles:
Indian Princess, Pocahontas, or, in these parts, Winona—
maiden who leapt for brave love from the rock where eagles mate.

In my day, she might have played Minnehaha, laughing waters,
or the lovely one in the corn oil ads: "We call it maize . . ."
Or even Captain Hook's strangely erotic Tiger Lily.

Oh, what I would have done for a Chippewa Barbie.
My mother refused to buy tourist souvenir princesses
in brown felt dresses belted with beads, stamped Made in China.

"They're stunted," Mom would say. Her lips in that line
that meant she'd said the last word. She was right, those dolls
were stubby as toddlers, though they wore women's clothes.

Most confusing was the feather that sprouted at the crown
of each doll's braided hair. "Do they grow there?"
a playmate once asked, showing me her doll from Mount Rushmore.

I recall she gazed at my own brown locks then stated,
"Your mother was an Indian Princess." My denial came in an instant.
My mother had warned me: "Tell them that our tribe didn't have any royalty."

But there was a problem of believability, you see, a crumb of fact
in the fantasy. Turns out, Mom had floated in the town parade
in feathers, raven wig and braids, when crowned the college "Maiden."

Her escort was the college "Brave" they chose each autumn.
Oh, Mom . . . you made it hard on us, what you did at 18—
and worse, the local rumor that it was *you* on the butter box!

You on their toast each morning, you the object of the joke,
the trick boys learned of folding the fawn-like Butter Maiden's
naked knees up to her chest to make a pair of breasts!

I cannot count the times I argued for Mom's humble status.
How many times I insisted she was no princess, though a beauty
who just happened to have played along in woodland drag one day.

I wonder, did my sisters have to answer for the princess? Did you?

Couldn't we all have used a real doll, a round, brown, or freckled,
jeans and shawl-wearing pow-wow teen queen? A life-like Native Barbie—
better yet, two who take the plunge off lover's leap in tandem and survive.

The Lone Reader and Tonchee Fistfight in Pages

Have I not been your faithful sidekick?
Have I not been your faithful Indian guide?
Have I been, at least, your Sacajawea,
hankering for her mother tongue, slogging,
baby on the back and all? Your insider
reading the trail, trailing the readings
so as to point a way? Forgive me,
Kein No Sabe. You know not what
you know not, I know.
I do not mean to keep from you
tribal secrets, tribal sec-texts,
secret tribes or textual innuendo.
Only, my tongue refuses to fork, fork you
off into the path not-to-be-taken—
for that has made all our differences.

Mark Doty

Charlie Howard's Descent

Between the bridge and the river
he falls through
a huge portion of night;
it is not as if falling

is something new. Over and over
he slipped into the gulf
between what he knew and how
he was known. What others wanted

opened like an abyss: the laughing
stock-clerks at the grocery, women
at the luncheonette amused by his gestures.
What could he do, live

with one hand tied
behind his back? So he began to fall
into the star-faced section
of night between the trestle

and the water because he could not meet
a little town's demands,
and his earrings shone and his wrists
were as limp as they were.

I imagine he took the insults in
and made of them a place to live;
we learn to use the names
because they are there,

familiar furniture: *faggot*
was the bed he slept in, hard
and white, but simple somehow,
queer something sharp

but finally useful, a tool,
all the jokes a chair,
stiff-backed to keep the spine straight,
a table, a lamp. And because

he's fallen for twenty-three years,
despite whatever awkwardness
his flailing arms and legs assume
he is beautiful

and like any good diver
has only an edge of fear
he transforms into grace.
Or else he is not afraid,

and in this way climbs back
up the ladder of his fall,
out of the river into the arms
of the three teenage boys

who hurled him from the edge—
really boys now, afraid,
their fathers' cars shivering behind them.
Headlights on—and tells them

it's all right, that he knows
they didn't believe him
when he said he couldn't swim,
and blesses his killers

in the way that only the dead
can afford to forgive.

Tiara

Peter died in a paper tiara
cut from a book of princess paper dolls;
he loved royalty, sashes

and jewels. *I don't know,*
he said, when he woke in the hospice,
I was watching the Bette Davis Film Festival

on Channel 57 and then—
At the wake, the tension broke
when someone guessed

the casket closed because
he was in there in a big wig
and heels, and someone said,

You know he's always late,
he probably isn't here yet—
he's still fixing his makeup.

And someone said he asked for it.
Asked for it—
when all he did was go down

into the salt tide
of wanting as much as he wanted,
giving himself over so drunk

or stoned it almost didn't matter who,
though they were beautiful,
stampeding into him in the simple,

ravishing music of their hurry.
I think heaven is perfect stasis
poised over the realms of desire,

where dreaming and waking men lie
on the grass while wet horses
roam among them, huge fragments

of the music we die into
in the body's paradise.
Sometimes we wake not knowing

how we came to lie here,
or who has crowned us with these temporary,
precious stones. And given

the world's perfectly turned shoulders,
the deep hollows blued by longing,
given the irreplaceable silk

of horses rippling in orchards,
fruit thundering and chiming down,
given the ordinary marvels of form

and gravity, what could he do,
what could any of us ever do
but ask for it?

Homo Will Not Inherit

Downtown anywhere and between the roil
of bathhouse steam—up there the linens of joy
and shame must be laundered again and again,

all night—downtown anywhere
and between the column of feathering steam
unknotting itself thirty feet above the avenue's

shimmered azaleas of gasoline,
between the steam and the ruin
of the Cinema Paree (marquee advertising

its own milky vacancy, broken showcases sealed,
ticket booth a hostage wrapped in tape
and black plastic, captive in this zone

of blackfronted bars and bookstores
where there's nothing to read
but longing's repetitive texts,

where desire's unpoliced, or nearly so)
someone's posted a xeroxed headshot
of Jesus, permed, blond, blurred at the edges

as though photographed through a greasy lens,
and inked beside him, in marker strokes:
HOMO WILL NOT INHERIT. *Repent & be saved.*

I'll tell you what I'll inherit: the margins
which have always been mine, downtown after hours
when there's nothing left to buy,

the dreaming shops turned in on themselves,
seamless, intent on the perfection of display,
the bodegas and offices lined up, impenetrable:

edges no one wants, no one's watching. Though
the borders of this shadow-zone (mirror and dream
of the shattered streets around it) are chartered

by the police, and they are required,
some nights, to redefine them. But not now, at twilight,
permission's descending hour, early winter darkness

pillared by smoldering plumes. The public city's
ledgered and locked, but the secret city's boundless;
from which do these tumbling towers arise?

I'll tell you what I'll inherit: steam,
and the blinding symmetry of some towering man,
fifteen minutes of forgetfulness incarnate.

I've seen flame flicker around the edges of the body,
Pentecostal, evidence of inhabitation.
And I have been possessed of the god myself,

I have been the temporary apparition
salving another, I have been his visitation, I say it
without arrogance, I have been an angel

for minutes at a time, and I have for hours
believed—without judgment, without condemnation—
that in each body, however obscured or recast,

is the divine body—common, habitable—
the way in a field of sunflowers
you can see every bloom's

the multiple expression
of a single shining idea,
which is the face hammered into joy.

I'll tell you what I'll inherit:
stupidity, erasure, exile
inside the chalked lines of the police,

who must resemble what they punish,
the exile you require of me,
you who's posted this invitation

to a heaven nobody wants.
You who must be patrolled,
who adore constraint, I'll tell you

what I'll inherit, not your pallid temple
but a real palace, the anticipated
and actual memory, the moment flooded

by skin and the knowledge of it,
the gesture and its description
—do I need to say it?—

the flesh *and* the word. And I'll tell you,
you who can't wait to abandon your body,
what you want me to, maybe something

like you've imagined, a dirty story:
Years ago, in the baths,
a man walking into the steam,

the gorgeous deep indigo of him gleaming,
solid tight flanks, the intricately ridged abdomen—
and after he invited me to his room,

nudging his key toward me
as if perhaps I spoke another tongue
and required the plainest of gestures,

after we'd been, you understand,
worshipping a while in his church,
he said to me, *I'm going to punish your mouth.*

I can't tell you what that did to me.
My shame was redeemed then;
I won't need to burn in the afterlife.

It wasn't that he hurt me,
more than that; the spirit's transactions
are enacted now, here—no one needs

your eternity. This failing city's
radiant as any we'll ever know,
paved with oily rainbow, charred gates

jeweled with tags, swoops of letters
over letters, indecipherable as anything
written by desire. I'm not ashamed

to love Babylon's scrawl. How could I be?
It's written on my face as much as on
these walls. This city's inescapable,

gorgeous, and on fire. I have my kingdom.

Beginners

The year Miss Tynes enrolled our class
in the Object of the Month Club,
a heavy box arrived each month
from the Metropolitan Museum.
What emerged once—when volunteers
opened each latch, and one lucky girl

lifted the wooden lid away—
was an Egyptian cat, upright on its haunches,
unapproachable, one golden earring flashing,
a carved cartouche between its legs.
Miss Tynes read a translation of the hieroglyphics
and a paragraph depicting the glory

of thousands of mummies ranged on shelves
in the dark—cased and muslined cats,
ibis, baboons—their jewelry ready to offer
any sliver of sunlight back, if it ever touched them.
Later, the cat ruled the back of the room,
fixed on a countertop beside a model

of the planets and a display of moths.
When we'd finished out work it was all right
to go and stand beside it,
even, if we were careful, to touch it.
I'd read a story in which two children
drank an emerald medicine from a pharmacy urn,

forgot their parents, and understood
the speech of cats. Their adventures were nocturnal
and heroic, and their cat became, I think,
the King of Cats, and was lost to them,
so they drank red medicine from the drugstore urn,
and returned to the human world

of speech. I cried, not for their lost pet
but for the loss of language, and my father
forbade me sad books. Some days, after school,
I'd go to my friend Walter's, and we'd play

a simple game: because he was smaller than me,
though no younger, Walter would be the son.

He'd take off his shirt and sit in my lap;
I'd put my arms around him
and rub his stomach, and he would pretend
to cry or be content, liking my hands.
We were ten, or eight. It's too easy
to think of our game as sex before we knew

what bodies could do, before bodies could do
much. There was something else,
at least for me: the pleasure
of touching what became pure form,
not Walter anymore but the sensation
of skin over supple muscle. I was the heroic

father, I loved—not him, exactly,
with his narrow crewcut head which reminded me,
even then, of a mouse—but the formal thing
he'd become, in his room, with the door closed.
We never changed roles; I was the good lover,
I fathered him. We knew enough to keep

the game private, less out of guilt
than a sense of something exposure
might dilute. It was like the way the children
in my class touched the cat, even talked to it,
hesitantly, beginners in a new language,
maybe imagined it might speak back to us.

Though it was the perfect confidant,
since it could take in anything
and remain calm and black and golden
until it packed away in the varnished box
to another school, where other children
might lean toward it and whisper,
until it was more ancient, with all it knew.

Art Lessons

Bored with the still life her painting teacher
has composed—Oaxacan vase and copper
bowl, ragged sunflowers—my mother takes a long scrap
of watercolor paper and sketches whatever

emerges first: five Chinese horses.
Each a few quick strokes of black ink.
Sun on their fluid and restless shoulders,
they seem to be running out her sudden rebellion.

She'll never paint like this again.
Though the future doesn't matter now, not while these five
unstoppable animals—angry, perfect—derive
their strength from refusal and hurry off the page.

This isn't the lesson, the art teacher says,
and likes the painting anyway.

*

What if she'd continued that sheer
pleasure of refusal? No bruised years?
No little paintings of dark and smoldering
lilacs again and again, no vodka blurring

every afternoon to a troubled sheen?
No ice and then no glass: a disease.
Do I still believe that will alone
could have cured her? No one was home,

the world was slick, slurred. Everything's erased,
purposefully forgotten, impossible now to read.
Twenty years and still it's hard to breathe.
Could I let it in, all I still can't say?

That's the lesson: art is remembering, and turning away.
And the poem, refused, hurries off the page.

*

The sets of slides my parents ordered
came wrapped in beautifully marbled
paper. Projected on our largest wall,
heat from the bulb rippling the image a little,

they offered worlds: a Renaissance prince taut and alien
as his hawk; breath, in a Botticelli, blooming
into the millefiori of spring; Tintoretto's
palpable silk. When my father questioned Caravaggio's

—boy, was he, lavish hair and ambiguous smile framed
with grape leaves?—I felt a sense of shame,
though I couldn't have said why.
I was to learn to name the art,

though the lesson ran deeper: this resonant intelligence,
this order, couldn't have come from people like us.

Didn't my parents see that?
We lived in a tract house, in Tucson,
Arizona, and I never heard anyone say *marbled*
or *Veronese*. I liked to stand

in the blasted grass of the backyard and study,
through my father's binoculars, the lavender bulk
of the mountains, the two sharp spires in the cleft
of one peak I thought of as a cathedral,

the shadowy place beneath them a door.
We'd take Sunday drives into the desert
and I saw remnants of some age grander than ours
in every wind-turned pinnacle,

as if the desert were classical,
demanding, framed. I wanted a world

constructed to be read, with an arch,
a tiny human figure in one corner to lend meaning
or scale. I didn't know art
was a world lost from the very beginning.

Now my mother's buried in a desert cemetery
irrigated into lawn, dominated
by the unforgettable outline of those mountains. My family
was a ruined gesture, a building that collapsed,

a few years after the art lessons,
into brutality and incoherence.
I wished myself no one's
son, compromised, airy as the monuments

magnified over the Naugahyde sofa, with no context
to embrace or erase. When I visited my father last
we drove to the Grand Canyon, with his new wife,
who has made him happy, and who narrated
every bit of landscape along the way.
And watching the foreign, arid cliffs, it was just the same,

as if I knew something my parents did not: what lay
around us had only been mistaken
for random stones. On a narrow spar over the canyon's
terrifying layers of color, I imagined

I was surrounded by ruins, doors
carved with the reliefs of their vanished inhabitants, doors
that yet would open, if only we could find them,
onto hidden chambers, the heartbreakingly

perfect colonnades. Mother, Father,
listen: I was not born but made.

Javier O. Huerta

Toward a Portrait of the Undocumented

The economy is a puppeteer
manipulating my feet.

(Who's in control when you dance?)
Pregnant with illegals, the Camaro
labors up the road; soon, I will be born.

I am the heat
captured by infrared eyes.

(Had you no life before this?)
(Are you not the source of that warmth?)

I am a night shadow; when la migra
shines spotlights, I disperse.

A body snatcher, I steal faces
and walk among the people, unnoticed.

I wear anonymity like an oversized
trench coat; now and then, I flash.

(Is your name perverse?)
(Is your skin not your own?)
(Are you not flesh?)

Read me: I am a document
without an official seal.

(Who authored you?)

Blasphemous Elegy for May 14, 2003

exhale: breathe out, give off, let out, send forth, throw out, cast out, blow,
blast, fan, gasp, heave, huff, pant, puff, whiff, whisper, whistle, sigh,
wheeze, disembogue, expectorate, expel, ooze
the abandoned trailer exhaled a ninety-nine headed beast

ella me espera en Houston
ella me espera en Houston
ella me espera en Houston
ella me espera en Houston

ella me espera en Houston
ella me espera en Houston
ella me espera en Houston
ella me espera en Houston

ella me espera en Houston
ella me espera en Houston
ella me espera en Houston

ella me espera en Houston
ella me espera en Houston
ella me espera en Houston

I modestly propose that every year on the 14th day of May as a way
to memorialize the 19 journeys we hold our breath—better yet, that
we abstain from breathing—for a period of 24 hours so that one year
we might come to asphyxiate the 14th of May. I offer this proposal not
for the sake of vengeance but for the sake of proving to ourselves that
we are indeed, more than human.

José Felicito Figueroa Guitiérrez edad desconocida de Honduras
Catarino González Merino edad desconocida de México
Mateo Salgado Pérez edad desconocida de México
Héctor Ramírez Robles 34 años de México
Chelve Benítez Jaramillo edad desconocida de México
Rogelio Domínguez Benítez edad desconocida de México
Jorge Mauricio Torres Herrera 15 años de El Salvador
Roberto Rivera Gámez 24 años de Juventino Rosas, Guanajuato
Serafín Rivera Gámez 34 años de Juventino Rosas, Guanajuato
Elisendo Cabanas González 27 años de Tulcingo del Valle, Puebla
Marco Antonio Villaseñor Acuña 5 años de la Ciudad de México
José Anotonio Villaseñor León 31 años de la Ciudad de México

Edgar Gabriel Hernández Zúñiga 17 años de Cárdenas, San Luis Potosí
Juan Carlos Castillo Loredo 20 años de Cárdenas, San Luis Potosí
Ricardo González Mata 24 años de Plan de Iguala, San Luis Potosí
Oscar González Guerrero 18 años de Plan de Iguala, San Luis Potosí
José Luís Ramírez Bravo 21 años de Ajuchitlán del Progreso, Guerrero
Juan José Morales 24 años de Nuevo Leon
Augusto Stanley Vargas 31 años de Republica Dominicana

gentlemen,
that the beast
ran
off terrified I
do not
believe nor
do I
believe that
it gnawed off
its limp
and lifeless heads
besides
such a beast
would
have ninety-nine
stomachs
each
full of urine
and sweat
yet its
hunger
and thirst
would continue
what nonsense
understand
this clearly
there is
no beast
only
an indeterminate
number of survivors
19 bodies
and
an infinity of noses

inhale: drag, draw in, gasp, inspire, insufflate, respire, sniff, suck in, absorb, consume, annihilate, appreciate, rejoice in, relish, revel in, devour

the abandoned trailer inhaled our teddy bears

affair aware bare bear beware billionaire blare care chair compare concessionaire dare debonair declare despair disrepair doctrinaire ensnare extraordinaire fair forswear foursquare glare hair hare heir impair lair mare millionaire pair pear prayer prepare questionnaire rare repair scare share snare solitaire spare square stair stare tear their there they're unaware underwear unfair ware wear where

Parece que va a llover. No hay para atrás. De amor. Síganme. Es un fenómeno. El cielo se está rublando. La necesidad de nuestros países. Los buenos. A esta triste canción. Vi fotos del niño. No contraban. Hay una linda región. No sé si sería eso. Con mi astucia. Para darle vida. Asinas. Una mancha y un ramo. Tengo todos mis movimientos. Ni modo. Las mismas pesadillas. Unieron sus almas. Mi cuñado y sus dos tíos. Yo no los maté. Ay, Mamá, me estoy mojando. Pi pipi pipi. En la eternidad. Perfectamente calculados. Luego cambian la página. Nunca te podré olvidar. Ya ya ya ya ya.

Eric Gansworth

The Rain, the Rez, and Other Things

1. Step by Step

Rain (and)
    still more
        rain.

"If you're an Indian,
why don't you do us a rain . . ."
I bet you could finish
that sentence, even without
prompting from our studio
audience, even without
calling on your life
line. I bet, even though
you are perhaps not Indian
and have not stood
in the dry August sun
with white men
so sweaty they've soaked
their white T-shirts
straight through to the point
the patch of thick
hair covering their
belly and chest
and heart is visible
and showing
their teeth
in that smile
        (not smile)
you know the end of that
sentence is "dance,"
but I only infrequently
dance with white people

and never in hopes
of rain because once
a thing like that
starts, you never know
when it is going to stop.

2. *Who's Who*

Rain

    (and)

         still

            more
            rain.

It started sometime
that peppery afternoon, maybe
even as I spoke
to a roomful of high-school Indians
considering college
as a real alternative
having dinner with one
of their chaperones from home
who asked after my siblings
as thunder pressed onto the drums
in our ears
so she could find me on the reservation
chart of Who's Who, and she said
"Okay, okay, I went to school
with your oldest brother, how
is he doing, these days, anyways?"
and not knowing Ma was likely shaking
you, trying desperately
to wake
you from your last sleep,
at that moment
I said, "Oh, you know
fine, just fine,"
(and still)
excused myself to stand
before the crowd trying

to inspire them by informing
them how hard it is
going to be to engage
higher education in an institution
not suited to their histories
and I initially plan to make
some joke about the Indian Higher
Education Conference being held
on April First, but discretion
uncharacteristically overtakes me
as their lives will be full
of pranks in the coming four years
at least, and this is one way
they do not need a head start.

3. That Long Pause

Rain

    (and)

        still

           more
           rain.

It is
like the one
where you count
between lightning
flash and thunder grumbling
out its disdain that it always comes
second, and that its place
is the nature of things.

You know the pause, that odd
silence even daredevils
fear, the one
bridging sentence
fragments you do not want
connected, wishing you
had a flaming
sword, to sear the first
half clear away from
the second in that gap

where, if you act fast
enough, you might
almost silence what you know
is coming or fall to your own
sad departure before you
are forced to hear
the end.

It is the one
where the person offers
a chair before telling you
the things they know, and you
have absolute certainty
that is never
a good sign.

Okay, so in this
case, it's me, not
you, me, not you,
and the first words
out of her mouth, that person
offering me that chair,
and then those words, the ones
before the pause,
are "Your brother . . ."
and I can almost see
the ellipsis trailing
from her lips as she
decides how to
continue as if
she needed to.

Of course she needed
to, the details, certainly, were
of the sort I couldn't guess
in fact, hadn't
guessed, knowing in abstraction
one of my four brothers was
dead I guessed twice
wrong before she delivered
his name, codifying the moment
but really, did those details
matter all that much?

What mattered was
that one of my four brothers
was dead and I was wrapping
up a speaking engagement
seven hours away, and the rain
had begun, and no matter
what time I got
back home, or how fast
I drove or how much I wanted
to believe my family was playing
the ultimate April Fool's Day gag, he was still
going to be dead
when I arrived home at two
in the morning on April 2nd
and they would all be still
up, waiting to help me
confirm over and over that
he was not there, to confirm
his empty place, for myself
and for others when
my brother's phone began
ringing as the sky lightened
and I started that repetitious
phrase, myself, speaking
into the receiver, sending
this phrase out across the lines
and into the world, daring
the person on the other end to hang
up before it was too late: "My brother . . ."

4. These Fields Are Not Forever

Rain

   (and)
      still
         more)

       rain.

That afternoon found me
killing time before

my obligation
at a record store called
Strawberry Fields in the small college
town of Potsdam, where I had
found, over the counter,
like in pharmacies where they keep
those drugs that are
only almost dangerous enough
to be by prescription only
a bootleg set of CDs called
From Kinfauns to Chaos
that documented the beginning
of the Beatles' departure
from one another starting
with acoustic demos for the White
Album and ending with a relentless
chronicling of John working
Revolution into the mixing
board while Yoko chatters
into the feedback mic
and I threw it in the car
so I could listen to it
later, after I had sung
for my supper
a soundtrack for my impromptu
drive home over slick
roads shining taillights
streaming from other cars
guiding me back to you
thinking of the way
you moved out one day
telling me I could have any
Beatles albums you left behind
as some sort of a consolation prize
not knowing I was selecting
some of the last
recorded moments
of cohesion a different group
of brothers held
with one another.

5. Are These the Moments Eastman Was Thinking of?

Rain

    (and)
        still
           more)

                rain.

like that November night
five months before
when it should have been
cold enough for snow
but we were glad for it
anyway, counting each
small blessing
as we find them standing
at a family
party, our aunt and uncle's
fiftieth anniversary, conducted
in a fire hall just off
the reservation, and while
Squid leaps to a table and commences
with an impromptu late Elvis
imitation we have
the longest conversation we've
engaged in more years than either
can remember, in which we reveal
that silence does not equal ignorance

that the way we think of each
other when we do
and it does not occur
as rarely as either
of us had assumed it
is the way we first grew
to know each other in

absence

(and still)

more absence.

The first memories
I have of you
are not really of you
technically you are
a dark, skinny man
in a series of photographs.

Ma kept you tucked
into the mirror
she used every morning
getting ready to clean
the houses of white
people in Lewiston
whose nineteen-year-
old sons were probably still
in college and not half
a world away posing
for photo ops proving
to everyone back home
that they were
indeed still alive
delivering evidence
like in some kind of
hostage/ransom situation
and though we couldn't afford meat
for sandwiches let alone
any influence that might
have kept your number
from coming up
in the draft lottery
we bought film, loaded
our own ammunition
and pressed those triggers
reminding you of the way
things were at home
so you might find us again
when you zeroed out,
so you would remember us
that we might harbor
in some corner
when your head was filled

with the unspeakable
truths, you in infantry
me in infancy
each making our way
in those strange places
our eyes tried to focus on.

And here you are
sixteen years later
we sit at the same dinner
table, and I am beginning
college, reading *Deliverance*
for a class, and you say "you know
what that book's about?" but you
don't wait for me
to guess "rape of the land"
not that I would have, but I could
see it that way as soon as you
said it, but could also see you
had been told that interpretation
in a literature class, and have
repeated it to yourself hoping
you would understand
what that meant at some point,
which was strange since you had
experienced that particular metaphor
first hand, without the aid
of James Dickey, or even Burt
Reynolds for that matter.

And here you are
fifteen years before
on the nights shortly after you
arrived home, shouting for your rifle
every morning at 3:00 A.M. and on the days
distributing the hats you brought
with you across the world, letting
us play with them but keeping their histories
mute as you pose all of us
our eyes hidden beneath
the brims' shadows on the front
porch and I wonder, after you
have developed them, if you have

the urge to mail them back
across the world address
them to that piece
of you left behind in the jungles
(where it rained every day for a year)
that none of us knows is even missing.

And here you are
on that day your divorce was more
true than it had been, before
abstract, something that might be
occurring but perhaps not
and you and I sit
on the picnic table you had
built at some point, though
I'd not known you for
carpenterly ambitions and out
of nowhere, we have our first
and only conversation about Vietnam
when you say "I was in the back
of the chopper, a door gunner, you know
and we were leaving the bush, relieved, you know
and the guy in the passenger's seat, you know
he just slumped over, you know
a bullet had come up through
the floor, traced the spine of his flak
jacket, snuck up under his helmet
and made the back of his head
just disappear, there one
minute, gone the next, but that's just
the way life is, you know, no,
I don't guess you do, yet," you said
informing me how we all accrue loss
and the ways in which we are
frequently unprepared.

And here you are
laid out in a borrowed ribbon
shirt, a borrowed eagle
feather beaded with the colors
of Vietnam between your folded hands
because we could not find the one
you'd been given, knowing you could

really hide things well when you wanted
and in the bouquet above your head
the heart shaped container holding
a dozen roses slips suddenly
and all the water rains out
into the casket as Walter the minister
begins, and yes, I know this
is a clichéd image, but we can't always
make these moments our own
and as we work our way
up, to see you one last time
before they close the lid, .
when I touch your hand with its borrowed
feather, it is as cold
as it was that November night
five months before, when you pressed
it to my shoulder, whispered drunken
confessions we would never speak of
and someone yelled for us to look
up and a flash filled the room. Did you
ever see that picture? I haven't.

6. Walter the Minister Tells Us How It Is

He says something in Tuscarora and since
his mother was the language teacher
we are inclined to believe him though
we did not understand one word, and are
thankful, sort of, when he translates.
It is four days later, and we still have
not seen the sun, and Walter alleges the Creator
is washing away the tracks you made in your time
with us, and we all know one fact for certain.
There will be rain
                    and still
                              more rain.

Yusef Komunyakaa

---

excerpts from

"Autobiography of My Alter Ego"

You see these eyes?
                    You see this tongue?
You see these ears?
                    They may detect a quiver
in the grass, an octave
                    higher or lower—
a little different, an iota,
                              but they're still no different
than your eyes & ears.
                    I can't say I don't know
how Lady Liberty's
                    tilted in my favor or yours,
that I don't hear what I hear
                              & don't see what I see
in the cocksure night
                    from Jefferson & Washington
to terrorists in hoods & sheets
                              in a black man's head.
As he feels what's happening
                    you can also see & hear
what's happening to him.
                    You see these hands?
They know enough to save us.
                              I'm trying to say this: True,
I'm a cover artist's son,
                    born to read between the lines,
but I also know that you know
                              a whispered shadow in the trees
is the collective mind
                    of insects, birds, & animals
witnessing what we do to each other.

* * * * * * * * *

Iraq? Well, as I said before:
                     If you start me talking,
I'll tell everything I know,
               & now I'll say this:
Please, America,
            let's forget the old warfare
of skin color and hair.
                 I can see a gutted palace in Hue,
dust devils rising from the ashes
                     of Operation Phoenix. Gods
fighting other gods.
             The looting & pillage
of museums in Baghdad—
               the shattering of a porcelain pig
with a ball-peen hammer.
                 Looters running with engraved images
& figures, statues, icons, & cuneiforms
                     stained with the blood
& shit of war. Some are messengers
                 of the dead, trying to hide
treasures from the infidels,
               as if we're the last horde
of barbarians storming the gates.
                 Other's, of course,
are filling orders for this blue jug
               of Sumerian clay shaped & fired
on the bank of the Euphrates,
               or that statue lying like a dead child
in a heap of rubble,
             the shadow of a desert
ram burned into it.

                    ****

The blond poster girl
            of this war, I can't
remember her name. Amy,
               Melissa, Jennifer, Jessica?
Like a captivity story
             that circles back, corralled
inside the brain—Indian braves
                 riding ponies into the sunset

with a white woman.
            But when this poster girl
Refused any false honors
                & medals, she disappeared
from the headlines & magazine covers.
                She could still hear
the old Iraqi woman
            whispering in her ear
as the doctors worked
                in their bloodstained room,
& maybe a question
            hummed inside her head:
Why is our enemy
            always dark-skinned,
always surrendering an arm
                & a leg for a tooth,
a child for an eye?

                ****

Ah, Abu Ghraib.
            Guantanamo. Lord,
if the dead could show us
            where the secret graves are
we'd walk with bowed heads
                along the Mason-Dixon Line
till we're in a dusty prison yard
                in Angola or Waycross,
or we're near the Perfume River
                or outside Ramadi. You see,
the maps & grids flow together
                till light equals darkness:
an eye, a nose, an ear, a mouth
                telling a forbidden story,
saying, Sir, here's the skin
            growing over a wound,
& this is flesh interrogating a stone.

Philip Bryant

1959, Loomis Avenue

The intimate smell that belongs
to the poor and nobody else
drifts out into the streets
at dusk.
My cousin and I
play in the yard
where I soon notice there
is no grass, just a
clean dirt patch leading
to the alley. Our voices
reverberate among the other
sounds of the street as we kick
beer cans and throw shreds
of broken pop bottles through
the humid August air.
It is 1959. There are no
cries of bloody murder yet,
no guns or sirens or
ghostlike figures
dragging the street for a corpse to fix,
only the sound of children's
voices playing in
the growing rubble,
the smell of cooking collards
and friend chicken and the
Naugahyde-laminated family
Bible propped on the reading
table in the living room.
My cousin—with beautifully braided
pigtails and clean cotton blouse
so stiffly starched white on Sundays
she almost cracks as she moves—
jumps double dutch on the
sidewalk, her small brown legs turn
perfect loops over the old laundry ropes
in the almost darkness.

She looks to me as if she
were suspended in air,
and I imagine her ascending to
heaven to receive Jesus,
like the preacher on the radio said
late that Sunday night: "He will
receive us as little children."
As the streetlights come on
and the sky fades into turquoise blue,
a few ominous stars appear on the horizon,
and I hear my aunt's slow, solid-hipped
southern drawl
through the darkness
calling us home.

Akhenaten

I

I went there
to see her at the Robert Taylor Homes
on 35th Street and Federal.
It was like I'd
gone into a great earthen tomb—
all hollowed out, cool, dark, and foul smelling,
with glistening wet walls.
Sounds were sorrowful baritone,
baleful bass,
all brought low to the ground
scraping the bottom of the barrel:
desperate shouts and screams,
cries, followed by harsh
muffled laughter.
I timidly knocked on your door
and it opened
to your sad, dark, bug-torn eyes.
Enclosed within these tiny, concrete,
roach-infested rooms,
everything clogged for the afterworld:
old china,
a picture of Christ

over the old phonograph,
cheaply made French Provincial chairs
bought on time,
old magazines,
glass bowls,
goblets, dishes.
You smiled and simply
closed the door,
and we talked for hours
on your couch until dark;
and all that time,
I could only think about this
being one of my old recurring
nightmares
of Devil's Disciples,
Imperial Gangsters,
and Egyptian Lords,
and how would I get out
of here alive?
Then you calmly led me out
through the dark entryway
and in my behalf
appealed to those gangsters
who ran the building—
Tojo, Mikey, Casino.
You saying I was all right
because I was with you.
They were all waiting for something strange
to enter their own lives
and change them forever,
but they gave a nod—
I was small fish.

II

Years later, my wife
and I sat on a grassy knoll for hours
in the sweltering July sun
with tourists from Iowa, New York,
and California,
all waiting for a chance to glimpse
antiquity thousands of

years old—
Anubis, lead us to Akhenaten,
Nefertiti. We enter the
cool hollow hallway of
The Museum of Natural
Science and History. Among
the gold and bronze statuettes,
I see beautifully carved *your* face again
as you led me out by the
hand, kissing me good-bye
lightly on my cheeks,
letting me come back from the underworld
into the world of the living again—
safe and unscathed
for that moment.
I promised to return,
all the time knowing
I wouldn't come back to see you
as I watched you that evening enter antiquity
through that small dark entryway,
your perfectly carved face set in
white alabaster against the light,
as you disappeared from this life forever.

The Glue That Held
Everything Together

We were all
stuck to the same
glue in 1967,
sticky as a roll of flypaper
and we didn't know it yet. To us,
our world was coming
up roses—Chicago Vocational
had just won the public league football
championship with big Polacks from Hegewisch,
Bohunks from Blue Island,
and swift-footed
colored boys from the Southside,
and we were all shit and grit in our shops

pinging and panging
the industrial rag
that would send us
either to the blast furnaces
of Gary or Vietnam.
For some, it was
their salad days:
hair greased back
Dago style, tight black
Levi jeans, and a cigarette
dangling like a crucifix
from their mouths.
No one would tell us
we were stuck
on this desert island
for the rest of our lives
and there wasn't no use
in trying to get out either.
So, we buzzed over our
souped-up cars
and looked forward to
annual three-percent raises.
The tiny, ramshackle bungalows
were built below
the smoking mills that called
us even then—as we
stretched our wings
on Saturday nights
to impress our girls,
as fledglings often do, as if to fly
off with them somewhere,
but the glue that held
everything together back then
hardened fast as cement—
we flapped and flapped
but our wings got us nowhere.

Diane Wilson

---

excerpt from

Spirit Car: Journey to a Dakota Past

Step Back in Time

November 6, 2002
Lower Sioux Reservation, Minnesota

The motel clock on my bedside table read 4:10 am, too early to get up and too late to hope for more sleep. I lay still with my eyes closed, trying to recall the dream that woke me and left a feeling of anxious violence lingering in its wake. I threw back the covers, then pushed open the drapes so that I could at least see the prairie night sky and a few stars beyond the casino's bright lights.

My overnight bag sat on the luggage stand, neatly packed and ready for an early departure. I had left my notebooks on the table, along with a few reference books, to be packed quickly in the morning. My books detailed the history of the Lower Sioux Reservation where I was staying at the Jackpot Junction Casino in Morton, Minnesota, about three hours southwest of Minneapolis. Before falling asleep I reread the chapter on the 1862 Dakota War, a bloody conflict between Dakota Indians and white settlers that had been fought in this area. Those were the images that haunted my dreams.

In the morning, just before sunrise, I would meet my younger brother Dave in the motel lobby. He told me later that he could not sleep, that he too woke just after 4:00 AM. Sitting on the edge of his bed, he spent the rest of the night quietly plucking at his guitar.

I wondered how many other rooms were filled with people like us, who had come to be part of the first-ever Dakota Commemorative March. This event was planned to honor the Dakota who had been forced to walk 150 miles from the Lower Sioux reservation to a prison camp at Fort Snelling after the 1862 war. We were supposed to meet before daybreak at St. Cornelia's Church, not far from the casino motel, beginning the walk shortly after dawn. The group planned to walk more than twenty miles each day, regardless of weather, arriving at Fort Snelling the following week. The march would follow roughly the same route as the original, commemorating the 140th anniversary of a painful history that had never before been publicly acknowledged.

I had invited my brother to join me, but I had not known whether Dave would actually come until I spotted his car in the parking lot. I felt immense

relief. Neither of us knew anyone who was involved in planning or partici-
pating in this event. We checked in, then went in search of the group, which
was gathering somewhere in Morton for an evening meal and a sweat lodge
ceremony. Although the town of Morton is only a few blocks long, we could
not find anyone who knew anything about the March. Confused and uncertain, we agreed to stay the night. If the next morning did not go well, we
would find a way to leave early in the day.

Eleven years of retracing our family history had led me to the 1862 war,
but this long journey began with my mother, Lucille Dion Wilson. She was
enrolled on the Rosebud reservation in South Dakota, where she grew up.
Between the ages of ten and sixteen, she attended the Holy Rosary Mission
School, a boarding school on the Pine Ridge reservation. After moving to
Minneapolis, she eloped with Chuck Wilson, a tall Swede from central Minnesota, and raised five children in a white suburb. When I was growing up,
she told me that she was done with "all that," referring to her Indian heritage. "We were poor," she said. "I'm glad to be out of it." With a stubborn
lift of her chin, she then refused to say more. Her reluctance to speak about
her past, the silence that surrounded her years at boarding school, seemed
impenetrable.

At that time, I had no idea why boarding schools existed, nor any sense
of the history that surrounded the reservation system. Reading the word "as-
similation" in my history book at school inspired the same yawn-inducing,
this-is-dry-as-dirt reaction that I felt reading about history in general. Mani-
fest Destiny, Lewis and Clark, the 1862 Dakota War meant nothing to me.
Those events had all happened a long time ago to other people and had no
relevance to my life.

My mother, on the other hand, was a mystery. All of us kids kept asking
questions, trying to squeeze out whatever information we could get any time
we were alone with her. Her life, her unimaginable life, dangled before us like
a long thread reaching to the past, the single unraveled edge of something
that was much larger than we could even begin to guess.

One afternoon, my mother told me about being left for two years at
the boarding school until her family could afford to send for her. She would
repeat the story to my sister and my brothers, one at a time, without blame
or bitterness, as if to make a point, to teach a lesson. But she did not say,
in the usual way she and her sisters liked to end a story about a difficult
time in their lives, "We made the best of it." There was an undercurrent of
emotion that she had never acknowledged except in telling this one story.
For years afterwards, her words flashed their weak signal to me like a firefly
in the bushes. I knew that one day I would need to learn what they hid.

I pursued this story for years, retracing my family's trail across South
Dakota and Nebraska, where I gathered facts, anecdotes, and sepia-tinted

photographs of relatives faded to a ghost-like image, and I second-guessed history when the information dried up. The struggle to understand the gap between my mother's past and my life, and the leap she made from Pine Ridge to Golden Valley, led me to the 1862 war and the Lower Sioux reservation. What began as a simple question about my mother evolved into a search for understanding about culture and identity and family legacy.

At 5:00 AM I turned on the lamp and began to pack. The sun would not rise for at least another hour, and there was plenty of time before I would meet Dave in the lobby. On the desk lay the flyer that had come in the mail a month earlier, offering its scant details about the March. A line drawing from the June 1863 issue of *Harper's New Monthly Magazine* showed men and women from New Ulm attacking Dakota captives riding through town in a wagon. A shower of sticks and rocks fell on the Indians, while white women in long dresses stood poised to hurl more, their faces focused in rage upon their victims.

I had been surprised that so much attention would be given to an event that was little more than a footnote in history books. Most of the accounts focused on the six-week war that exploded in August 1862 on the Lower Sioux reservation from the frustrations of failed treaties. Hundreds of white settlers were killed and their farms were destroyed. When the war was over, much of the white population of Minnesota demanded that the Dakota people be forcibly removed from the state, regardless of which side they had supported during the war. The march was usually mentioned briefly as a four-mile train of about 1,700 Dakota, mostly women, children, and elders, who were forced to walk under military guard through towns filled with outraged settlers to a prison camp near the Mississippi River at Fort Snelling.

I had stumbled into this history two years earlier while searching for information about my great-great-grandmother, Rosalie Marpiya Mase, or Iron Cloud, a full-blood Dakota woman. After years of chasing my family's story, the trail finally led me to Rosalie, who lived directly across the Minnesota River from the Agency on the Lower Sioux reservation, where the war began. No one in my family knew much about Rosalie or her involvement in the war. I had only recently learned that when the fighting started, she and her French-Canadian husband, Louis LaCroix, had taken refuge at Fort Ridgely with the white settlers. Rosalie and her seven mixed-blood children were among the few Dakota who were not forced to march to Fort Snelling, who remained behind in Minnesota after the war.

Rosalie was the reason I had come to be part of the March. Although she was spared the traumatic experience of the March, she was involved in the violent war that had preceded it. My theory—which is how I understood history, by analyzing it—was that Rosalie's separation from her community was as harsh, in some ways, as that experienced by the people who were imprisoned at Fort Snelling. I was there because her survival had also come at a terrible cost.

What I did not know in those early morning hours was whether that tenuous connection to the March would be accepted by Dakota people whose families had lost everything, sometimes even their lives. I lay awake partly from the anxiety that comes from walking into a gathering of Indian people who are focused on remembering a violent and tragic part of the past. The Dakota War had inspired a deep hatred between whites and Indians, feelings that sometimes still lie just beneath the surface. My brother is dark like our mother, but I look like a middle-aged, middle-class, green-eyed *wasichu*.

My comfort, then, came from those notebooks and history books still stacked on my table. They were my only defense, my protection against the forces that had drawn me here. I knew the facts about the 1862 war well enough to dream them at night. I also had a car out in the parking lot with a full tank of gas, ready for flight in case the event proved unwelcoming, or worse, disorganized and a waste of time.

I reached for the fanny pack that I would wear while I walked. From the zippered pouch on the back, I pulled out a photo of my mother that was taken before she started chemotherapy. Smoothing a crease in the corner, I studied her smiling face and thought about our conversation the day before. She was curious about our presence at the March.

"I don't know why you kids are so interested in all that stuff," she said. In the background, I could hear my dad muttering, *Why don't they schedule this thing in warmer weather?* He couldn't imagine why anyone would willingly walk 150 miles in cold November weather for something that had happened so long ago. At the same time, he wanted to help even if he didn't understand. *Do you kids* (I was forty-seven, my brother forty-five) *need any money? Don't hesitate to call if you have trouble. May the good Lord* (Lutheran) *be with you.*

I could not explain to my mother why I was here, except that I had to come. Years earlier, I thought that understanding why she was left at boarding school was all that I needed. Somewhere in the desolate plains of South Dakota I had realized that wasn't enough; images had begun to fill my head, together with scraps of words.

I discovered a new truth: I was searching for the stories that had been lost from our family. In traditional Dakota culture, stories are handed down from one generation to the next. The loss of that oral tradition and the breakdown of communication between generations had set my family adrift, floating aimlessly without history and all its accumulated experience to guide us. As human beings we need our stories surrounding us. We need context, we need myths, we need family legends in order to see the invisible legacy that follows us, that tells us who we are.

Scott Hightower

Conjuring War

Imagine (if possible) a woman dressed in an
endless garment, one that is woven of everything
the magazine of Fashion says, for this garment...
—ROLAND BARTHES, *THE FASHION SYSTEM*

Beyond rough magic, failure of the social
imagination, and freedom charmed
by vigor uneven; the military solution
raptures slavery, class, and prostitution:

sole resort to systematic
haunting, human will to will,
the privilege of hunting,
and the pose of liquidating doubt

(access driving out sacrifice,
feast, excess and its trembling):

status, possession,
and material advantage;

an eye trapped in a perspective
from an artificial green,
a turquoise pool; a tongue
curling in a reservoir. Perhaps
once it was a baroque carriage,
a grotto, a dance step,
or an ammunition sleigh.

Now, in power grids
of structural paradigms
and conflations of language,
is there any right or left left;
or just a vertigo, a trajectory
of devalorized seductions,
a wicked glow of abstract
pleasure and—faux pas—
real humiliation and torture?

Rather than reveling in
ghostly metaphors,
we are better off rapt
in a sacred plume of praise.

Falling Man

Sink then! Or I could also say: arise!
        —GOETHE, *FAUST II*

Forget about the burning towers.
The verticality of the valley
between the two of them.
Who hasn't been hurling into existence?

There are people in boats
in a distance on blue water.
And birds float through blue air.

The falling man floats,
too, artfully cartwheels
like a parachutist spiraling
into the slipstream's inner depth.
This is a threshold. It is spring.

A firm stance in the world
is illusive. "Condemned
to earth—with all
its terrors and beauties—
and to live there,
ejected from the dream-ship
in which the angels
continue on their way."

But at the Church

I didn't mind that someone
had seen fit to drape his coffin
at the funeral home or graveside
service. Who can deny "Taps"
its force? I understood

there were many grieving
who saw him as a patriot
who had survived
and returned to thrive
in peace for another sixty years.
And I—oddly sharpened by grief—
appreciated their veteran
loyalty and desire to bid him
a fraternal farewell. But

we were not a military family.
Hadn't he really just been a kid
trying to stay alive; and much
of that time probably not very sober?

The "war years" had preceded us...
me. And I had my misgivings
about any cohort,
possessing a force
some of us feel best left
only in the hands of God.

Ed Bok Lee
_____

Polygutteral

Dear speaker in a future age,
when only a handful of tongues
remain   I write this to you
as a song, even as I know
it won't do
            Even as I know
the very tongue I speak
is killing

I don't expect you to understand

But I want you to know
there is another language
in which I dream   And sometimes I think it's Korean
And other nights just my halmoni sewing
a broken room
                        Or my neighbors, a family of Ojibwas
welding their mini-van   Summer evenings
the Hmong girl and boy echo hide and seek
with cousins down the street   Or, this spring,
Juan, the Mexican kid next door,
now in his 14th year, shuffling steps
on the corner, baggies stuffed in his shorts,
truant every afternoon—

I see him some days through my window, rapping in a back alley
alone in broken English to his ITunes

As I've seen him since he was ten, youngest of four undocumented
brothers in a boarding room basement I watch
through their window well like an evening TV show whose writers are all
angry drunks

And I wonder what will happen to this slightly dumpy boy's
heart, out of sync with his
tongue—the only two muscles you really have
to move with wings through this world

A shiny black SUV pulls up each Friday,
he climbs in, and I wonder
if I did the right thing three years back by urging my other neighbor,
an old white woman,
not to call the cops on him

Dear speaker in a future age,
when only a handful of tongues
in a basket remain

I write this to you as a magical dictionary
floating somewhere through my mind
A universal plea
Some strange and beautiful repository of human history
Even as I know it's too late for you to bind
and open me

Even as I know yet another world language will become extinct this
week, forever gone, like Atlantis or Montezuma's Kingdom: Sumerian,
Gothic, Goguryeo, Tasmanian, Scots Gaelic, Mowhawk, Iriquois—like a
global hurricane of power and indifference, veering toward Flemmish
and Basque, Ainu, Anishanabe and, yes, one day, if turnabout is fair play,
maybe even this very language I tease
apart for inconsistencies
to house me

I wish I could tattoo this prayer on my palm,
even as I know it's way too long,
longer than my body, my whole life—this eviscerated
pink and black spilling
through the forest of my sleep

And sometimes I think it's the colonial Japanese
screwed into a schoolboy, my Korean father, who later
forced Russian on me—Otyets, wakarimaska?

Or the only three ideograms I remember of all
those my mother sat me down, hand on hand,
ink brush weeping: *e sng one*

Though yesterday just another passionate Somali debate
waking me on the 21A
A mismatched couple whispering
over borscht and piroshkis at Karmarczek's Deli on Hennepin
Or some Greek harangue over the baklava's freshness at Bill's Imported

Ah yes, and the pho tai every Sunday I supersize
whose boney broth brings tears to my eyes in Frogtown

And sometimes I know I'm just another ghost
passing through this century
One of a long line of hungry souls before me
Each a spiritual refugee

Dear Father who art in heaven,
who fled your homeland, war-torn, in flames,
I write this to you, Abonim, from the end of the world
to inform I forgive you for your rage,
even as you emptied its fear
into your own family's tears....
                    To report: the view of Manhattan from the
Williamsburg Bridge this summer is beautiful—at night, an entire island
lit up, scintillating like a Christmas tree asleep so peacefully on its side

Like the one Omoni crowned each December in our living room, a
        newborn king
I relinquish you from the history I learned too late
Spiritual RNA erased by missionaries and sunglassed generals handing out
candy, crosses, and European names

Dear Future, I write you from the Past,
in a secret code I've had to reinvent myself with
to be visible and whole

Associations and inflections
Rawest of imaginations

A Disciple of Time in a patched-together language adrift

Migrant afloat with no motor, canvas, or oars

Only these few city stars in the night for words

In truth, only two:

Dear *Time*, how I envy the cleanliness of your hands

Dear *Love*, why do I need your shadow so deeply inside mine?

I don't know where any of us is going,
but I'm sure on the other side of the world, there is a language I have
        never heard
It is beautiful, and in this dying tongue, there are words for Love and God
that resemble Bread and Wing

Or another forest language in which Mother and Knife
equal Drawer and Sing

and Island Wood is somewhere Desert Milk

and Berry, elsewhere is a Door

and if you added up all these dying words, and the people who speak them
All their memories, histories and lessons
All their Gods, jokes, rituals and recipes

And if you learned and repeated them, over and again, until each was a
        part of your own richer soul,
                wouldn't the marrow of civilization actually levitate?

And yet, what do we say?
Not: Welcome, but
Go back to where you came from if you don't like it this way

And yet, if you really listen, what you hear in these voices is not hate,
or even fear,
                but grief

These closing doors and shrinking portals to history

Dear speaker in a future age
when not 6,000 or 3,000 or even a dozen....

But only one language remains

I write this to you as an elegy

In the beginning, there was a word,
but it got lonely

and so it prayed for brothers, sisters, and neighbors, and yes,
love was born, but along with it came shame, passion, greed, more
love, benevolence, and need

and soon some of the words became flowers and trees

and others animals, and eventually
some were human beings:

Queens and Workers,
Kings and

Thieves

Note: Every week, the last surviving speaker of world language passes away. Over the past 500 years, one half of the world's languages have disappeared, along with their histories, myths, spiritual beliefs, biological, agricultural and medicinal knowledge systems, etc. At present, roughly 6,000 world languages remain. Due largely to industrialization and market migration, at the current rate, linguists estimate that over the next few generations, all but a half-dozen dominant, colonial world languages will become extinct. Latin, a "dead" language, evolved into French, English, etc. "Extinct" languages, with rare exception, are expunged as if they had never been.

Burnt Offering: Mid-November

All these Great Plains towns mid-day
on Main Street like faded breaths
full of frost, alcohol & train wrecks.
An old lady pulls up in a pristine, 20-year-old Cadillac.
This guzzling vessel she shores at the Eagle Diner—
ancestor of another
engine spewing black
flies over bison blinking in grass
a century & a half ago—Could she
& her kin ever dance beside any
non-white dream?

> *Howsitgoing*, I say.

Her vermilion frown cuts me,
then looks away. She, the bad
lover never tickled face-to-face
with a world so sweetly in flames—
Old white Swedish mother of grain, in a sky
blue tractor of history. Her pork-bellied farmer
husband hobbling over a cane eyes me
as they enter for coffee & raisin cream pie.
Got a buck man? I say,
but they're already inside
the warm oven of their lives—

> In the street

I light a torn cigarette
& rise
to new heights.

Frozen in the Sky

It's so cold I'm dying, says the old man.
His walking cane knobbed in one cracked hand,
the other comforts a *Good News Bible*.

We stand in line at the Sunrise Doughnut Shop,
this mumbling U.S. Army veteran
and I. Dark-skinned, unshaven

gray for days, his one good eye black
as polished onyx. This winter
he's wrapped himself in a blue plastic tarp

pinned with a Purple Heart. This old
Indian, Puerto Rican, Mulatto, Mestizo,
whatever he is to me, I don't know. He smells

like the story of my grandfather, who survived two wars
but couldn't stop talking
of the sour urine that plagued the refugee camps

no matter how many times you washed
your belongings in the rain. You know the smell,
that evil homeless stench

alive in a flattened length of cardboard
left on the street; impressed with the paler shape
of a soul whose body's been long

cleared away by the wind and leaves.
Hey, whispers the old man. I saved your people.
A toothless wad of day-old sugartwist

on his tongue. Curdled body
of the second coming, or muffled
lament of a dozen gook legs and bellies

choking the rice paddies
in Saigon. No Gun Ri.
Iwo Jima. Bataan.

Bullet against bone ash,
butane flame to gangrene,
tank tracks on the back scarring mountains—

When my mother describes the corpse
of her baby brother, slung to the crooked spine
of their grandmother, she has no tears.

They are long frozen on the road down to Seoul
she and millions more walked
when the Communists declared victory in the North.

1950. The icy earth was too hard to bury
the little boy's dehydrated shape. It was so cold
I couldn't feel a thing, my mother explains with amazement.

Sometimes the soldiers would throw us
matches from their jeeps. Once Haesuni
got a Hershey bar for just talking

to a young GI. And then the Soviet air bombers arrived.
One blonde soldier wrapped in a head bandage
rifled us into a pig-pen.

Don't move! he screamed. Who are you!
Both eyes landmine craters. Gone.
So we ran, all five of us, your aunt fell down;

I tried to carry her, seven years old, mid-winter,
but it was so cold, my hands were stone, my bare feet
like wooden pegs, and I was on stilts

balancing a mile above that frozen road
toward a gray horizon. At night I thought
I might turn into a dying bird

and fall asleep in the wind, drifting
high above the choppy ocean.
Because birds, you know, the noble ones at least,

before they die, they fly out over a great body of water.
Greater than their own visions can see across.
They keep flapping and hurling

their bodies at the wind
until they can't move their ancient wings anymore;
until they've journeyed so far

pure exhaustion finally frees
their battered destinies
over to the breeze

and waves
and traffic
on Franklin Avenue

yesterday, when I saw that old man on the street corner.
His white breath obscuring whether he
was speaking the truth or just amusing himself.

Some intoxicated archangel
explaining the ways of the world to passing cars,
or just another casualty

of a forgotten war.
A living monument, or blundered memory.
A muttering prophecy

or echo from the past
coming straight at me.
Whether he also sees

dead frozen soldiers,
women
and children

chewing ice,
shrapnel,
feathers

and kidneys on the road to heaven
in his dreams...
Or just another face

on the sidewalk staring
into the paper cup
he jangles to be free.

The Secret to Life in America

My brother sits me down and tells me
the secret to life in America.
I'm twelve years old when this happens.
He grabs my shoulders and says:
No one likes an immigrant.
It reminds them of when they fell down
and no one was around to help them.
When they couldn't talk.
As children when they got lost in public.
Cold and wet, everyone hates an immigrant.

So don't trust nobody.
The whites, they'll teach you
to hate yourself for being silent.
They'll punish you for fighting back.
They'll love the taste of your food and culture, and sister...
and yet spit you out.

The Blacks, at first you'd think they understand loss.
But to them you're just another cracker with a bad case of
jaundice.
Don't expect shit from them,
they can't afford to be generous.
Latins laugh at you behind your back.
Do you know this? I'm trying to tell you
how it is in the city,
he says.

I ask my brother if I can go outside now.

No!, he screams. Our father is dead
and now I have to teach you
how to survive
in America.

Fags are everywhere.
And they want you. 'Cause
to them you're exotic and cute
and will do all the dirty work.
The Chinese look down on you
for using their alphabet. The Japanese have raped

your women through the centuries
and will do it again. In fact, never
do business with other Asians,
'cause they're the greediest people alive.
Next to Jews.

Now I'm crying, because my brother
has pulled off his work shirt.

Open your eyes!
This is where that black boy pulled the trigger
over twenty dollars and a candy bar! Here
is where the whites punctured my kidney in a parking lot outside of
    Denny's...
And the Mexicans just kept drinking their beers.
This is the bruise on my soul
where every American girl ever looked at me
like I was still the enemy.
This is where agent orange first set in.
This is where the DMZ line is still drawn!
Taste the barbed wire on my tongue!
See where that fat white teacher called me a freak
for getting a B in math! Feel
my broken immigrant's throat
that couldn't tell him to Fuck Off!!!
These are my yellow hands!
This is my cock!
These are my eyes wide open!
This is my heart filled with cigarette smoke!
This my aching back
which brought you here
and buried our father!
This is the cheek mother slapped
for the way that I called her
ignorant.

This is the *GQ* subscription sister gave me for Christmas.

Here is my blood, which tastes just like tears.
These are my dreams for the future
dead and shriveled in the corner.
This is my broom. This the face
I couldn't save from myself.

Are you listening to any of this?

       Yes, I tell him. I'm listening.

You're lucky, he says. You'll go to college
when you grow up.

       I don't know, I tell him.

Work your ass off and move away from this shit hole
out to the suburbs. Maybe marry
a white girl.

       I don't know, I tell him.

Go off and write.... Poetry.

       I won't, I say.

Yes you will. And when you do,
do me this one favor.

       What, I ask.

Lie.
And make our father and me

       the heroes

       you always needed us to be.

The Edge of the World—
The Contemporary Environment

WHAT ARE *HOMO SAPIENS*? Human beings? Some would say we're sentient, self-aware animals, a part of, yet apart from, the natural world. Others would argue that we're beings created by a god or gods, and have been given dominion over the natural world. However any of us defines what makes us distinctly *human*, we still live, in some sense, in relation to the natural, non-human world. It often seems that the harder we work to separate ourselves from what might be called the *natural*, the *wild*, the *animal*, the closer we get to actually understanding ourselves within the context of this "other" world. What and where am I along this continuum between nature and culture? Some of the writers in this section explore this vital question. The tensions between nature and culture are as old as human civilization, and as our ability to control and manipulate the natural world grows in scope and power, so too does our responsibility for preserving and nurturing all that is human and nonhuman, all that comprises life on our planet and even the planet itself. The work in this section explores what it means to be human in a more than human world. As we try to dominate and control our environment, we risk losing an intrinsic part of ourselves, the part that binds us to the earth and makes us whole. Some of work here illustrates how we, individually and collectively, inhabit and impact our planet. There is also writing that offers solutions to our environmental crises, and writing that shows us what we can do to slow down the velocity of our seemingly uncontrolled rush toward extinction. Here too, perhaps, are answers to that most critical of questions: What makes me *human*?

Culture, Biology, and Emergence

Before Henry David Thoreau began his twenty-eight-mile walk along the Cape Cod seashore in October 1849, he stopped to witness a shipwreck at Cohasset. "Death!" read the headlines in Boston, "One Hundred and Forty-Five Lives Lost." Thoreau traveled among the many Irish, hundreds of them going to identify bodies, comfort the survivors, and attend funerals. "Many horses in carriages were fastened to the fences near the shore," he wrote, "and, for a mile or more, up and down, the beach was covered with people looking out for bodies and examining fragments of the wreck." The brig *St. John,* loaded with emigrants from Galway, Ireland, had broken on the rocks that Sunday morning, and the atmosphere was not of grief but of "a sober dispatch of business" as coffins were filled, nailed shut, and carted away. Among the crowd picking through the wreckage were men collecting seaweed the storm had cast up, carrying it above the reach of the tide, after separating out fragments of clothing. The horror of turning up a human body in the wreck did not keep them from gathering the "valuable manure" of seaweed. "This shipwreck," Thoreau observed, "had not produced a visible vibration in the fabric of society."

He was not numb to the loss and misery of the wreck, but he admired the social whole and its ongoing pragmatism. He felt that the seashore acquired "a rarer and sublimer beauty" when framed by this event. He admired the industry of the fishermen, farther along on his journey, counting two hundred mackerel boats working offshore near Truro, another hundred on the horizon floating on this "highway of nations," and overall an astonishing 1,500 fishing rigs working out of Provincetown in the mid-1800s. Today one might see a handful, and those nearly always lashed bow and stern and spring lines to the wharf. Thoreau depicts the place with an eye to history, an ear to local story, and an implicit confidence in human enterprise.

Reading this account of his travels, I don't see him as recluse, Luddite, and misanthrope—the pacifist Unabomber of the nineteenth century—as those who grow cynical about human prospects might come to imagine. He is a man who seeks solitude in order to live deliberately and to pass the lesson on to others, a man who commits civil disobedience to goad injustice and advance moral philosophy, and a man who appreciates human thrift and industry.

Thoreau's *Cape Cod* makes a good complement to *Walden,* which grates on me for some of it stridencies, particularly Thoreau's ridicule of technology as "pretty toys" that "distract our attention from serious things." This strikes me as snobbish intellectualism, as opposed to the work's more dominant note of mindful curiosity. What has been more serious to human beings than technology since the first flint struck sparks? Maybe art. Maybe religion. This is the kind of animal we are: tool-making, art-making, symbol-making, and intensely social, engaged in a mutually reinforcing set of activities that make us speed-learners and obsessive connectors with one another. Technology may be sinking us now, but this need not be the case. The question is not whether we can live without technology, but whether we can live with technology in such a way that we do not destroy ourselves and the planet.

The communication and information technologies, in particular, strike me as markers of an emerging shift in consciousness. What kind of good thing might they be? What might be the adaptive aspects to this cultural movement? A form of collective intelligence that no one controls, it evolves in its own organismic way to egg us on toward greater connection, exposure, accountability, and collaboration. Sure, the Internet is full of trash and hype, but the freedom with which information can move makes censorship, deception, and totalitarianism much harder to inflict.

Scott Russell Sanders' "Simplicity and Sanity" makes an eloquent case for simplicity and the role of individual responsibility in facing the crisis of global climate change. I try to follow the principles he offers, taking pragmatic steps to reduce my weight on the planet. But the problems we face are of such profound scope that they cannot be effectively addressed by individual responses alone. The ultimate responsibility for reducing the effects of global climate change is a collective social responsibility that requires policy, regulation, alliance, and law—instruments our culture has failed to provide. I say "culture," not "government," because democratic government is, in theory, an instrument for realizing the will of the people. We do no good by acting as if we-the-people are virtuous while they-the-government are corrupt. The fabric of human culture is being frayed, stretched, and torn by our predicament. Values rule that none of us really believe in: profit trumps all, every man for himself, wealth is health, and, as author William DeBuys coined at a recent symposium, "yoyo": you're on your own.

Not surprisingly, I am at odds with my culture. So many of us are these days, as we free-fall into ecological doom. Recycling, installing halogen bulbs, and writing letters to Congress seem pallid levels of activism when compared to the severity of our collective malaise. We live in a pathological culture that is sick with violence, greed, waste, contentiousness, and a sense of futility. We live in cities we despise for their ugliness, menace, and lack of community (though it's puritanical, I know, at such moments as this to deny the pleasures of the city). We have poor people whom we ignore, leaving them stranded on their roofs in a flood or cast out on the street. We ask their children to die in senseless wars. We have elected leaders who have no business leading, so lacking are they in wisdom and the capacity for reflective thought and empathy; their disdain for learning and scientific research, and their absurdly simplistic posturing about the state of religion in a pluralistic democracy, would make such leaders laughable if their actions were not causing so much anguish around the world and so much erosion of our sense of purpose at home.

No greater proof of our dissident relationship to our own culture is needed than the terrible moment we parents meet when we send our children to school, camp, movies, or a sleepover at a neighbor's house. We feel them slip from the embrace of family and plunge into the turbulence of society. We realize we cannot control the influences that will enter their minds and hearts. We feel sick with fear.

Raising me in the 1950s, my artistic parents wanted to protect me from the conformity of Connecticut's suburban somnolence. Raising my daughter in the culturally contentious sixties, I wanted to protect her from rednecks and the evangelical neighbors who said that her dreams of a beloved dead grandmother were visits from Satan. My grown daughter and her husband—a visual artist and progressive pastor—struggle to raise their boys without taint of the violence, excess, and greed that surround them. We all come to the horrible awareness that we cannot protect our children from the culture in which they live. We do not trust it; we do not want to feel that we are part of it. Yet our children, too, will become creatures of their culture and their historical moment. They will have to learn for themselves what their values are, but we want desperately to *give* them their values, as surely as we gave them their names.

This alienation from and resistance to culture only serves to reinforce the value of bullish individualism, but no matter how much we do as individuals, the larger organism of culture remains impoverished. The old place-based cultures no longer work. John Donne wrote that no man is an island; now we know that no culture is an island, that to be alive cultures must be permeable. This lesson is one that First Nation peoples of the Americas have had to learn through the hardest of lessons. Today, war based upon conflicting fundamentalisms breaks out when people are unable to acknowledge and live with the permeability of culture. Yet the velocity of change is such that we do not know what verities to rely upon. What ideas about culture can we take up in good faith as part of our tool kit for rebuilding the "commons"—those aspects of nature and culture that cannot be owned—as a countervailing force to the market? What ideas about culture might help us to celebrate rather than bemoan the social whole of which we are a part?

*

I return again and again to Edward Sapir's essay, "Culture, Genuine and Spurious," parts of which appeared in the English *Dial* in 1919, barely beyond the shadow of World War I. Sapir explores his "idea of what kind of a good thing culture is," defining *culture* as "any socially inherited element in the life of man, material or spiritual." It includes art, religion, science, inventions, domestic skills, and consumer goods, as well as such society-shaping ideas as democracy, imperialism, civil liberty, and social justice.

I often ask my graduate students on the first day of a creative writing course to write down their cultural influences. I do this because I find that the biggest problem in the student writing I see, other than poor mechanics, is their self-absorption. Too many of them write about personal wounds: drug and alcohol abuse, car wrecks, anorexia, dysfunctional and failed families, failed love affairs, depression, anxiety, and rage against feelings of powerlessness. I don't mean to suggest that these are not suitable catalysts for making literature, but my students tend not to see these stories within a social matrix or cultural lineage. They feel locked within themselves and think of artistic expression as a key that will let them into the kingdom of emotional freedom, rather than seeing art as a mindful reframing of experience and emotion through a forming intelligence. They write with too much "I" and no sense of "we." They can tell me what has happened to them—but they cannot tell me the significance, the moral and psychological consequences. They cannot step outside of their anguish to see the cultural context that shapes them. They just know that they, who are among the most privileged people who have ever lived on Earth, feel they don't belong anywhere.

So, I start out by asking them to write down what they see as their cultural influences within three frames of reference. First, culture as a shared set of traditions and meanings. They can choose any context they wish: ethnicity, gender, race, nationality, sexual orientation, or faith community. They write about being Mormon, gay, goth, punk, jock, transgendered, Chicano, Navajo, or mixed blood. They display an impressive array of political and activist affiliations, holding passionate convictions about social, economic, and environmental justice. The interesting thing is that while some speak of nationality—those whose families have come in recent generations from Italy or Korea or Somalia—not one student has spoken about being American as a significant cultural influence. This just doesn't seem to occur to them—as if, once you get here, you can be anything you want to be, but you can't see yourself as part of the whole.

Second, I ask them to consider culture as artistic expression, and they offer up movies, video games, jazz, performance art, and photography. They seem surprised at how their stories open up when told within such a texture. I, too, can be surprised. A Navajo student who had been silent all semester, listening respectfully each week as other students made presentations on dance therapy, installation sculpture, and finger painting, became eloquent when her time to present arrived.

"I don't really know what you mean when you say 'art,' because in my culture it's not separate from life," she said, holding up in her hands her ceremonial dress and silver squash blossom necklace, and passing "kneel-down bread" to everyone in the room. She was very much a contemporary woman, a jeans and T-shirt fashionista, with a foot in each of two worlds. She described the history and use of the traditional items: Yes, she said, the workmanship of the dress and necklace was artful, and the technique she described in her grandmother's kneeling down to press flour into tortilla-like rounds was artful. But these were simply the way things were done on certain occasions in her culture. No one on the rez thought of them as art.

A woman from New Jersey had worked as a teenage prostitute. She left home in the morning wearing the pleated plaid skirt and tailored white shirt that were the uniform of her Catholic high school. She carried in her backpack a different outfit for her after-school job. This was not an Eliot Spitzer class of prostitution, but a lowlife massage parlor where she did hand jobs on lonely and powerless men. Do you prefer oil or lotion, she would ask. She'd been sexually abused by her father. This work was the first time she'd felt in control of men. Reading her essays was difficult and painful, in part because she felt so affirmed by having been a sex worker; her fellow students could not get past the feeling that she had been degraded. Then she wrote an essay that lifted off the page, framing her experience in the context of prostitutes in cinema. *Pretty Woman*, starring an effervescent Julia Roberts, was the whore-with-a-heart-of-gold du jour, an innocent and redemptive depiction that everyone loved. The student's essay brought reel after reel of such fictions to light, and suddenly I felt complicit in the cultural hypocrisy surrounding sex workers. I did not feel accused, I felt called to understand how a woman might choose such a path.

Third, I ask students to consider culture as a relationship between people and nature or people and a place. This yields stories about places that are lost—the family store run by Chinese-American grandparents on a street corner in Phoenix now devoured by a mall. Or the places people go to get away—the hike in the backcountry, the family cottage at the lake, the study-abroad trip to Malta. I have read no student essay that draws on the depth of experience on the land and in place that writers such as Scott Sanders, William DeBuys, Simon Ortiz, and Wendell Berry so richly portray. Perhaps it is unreasonable to expect such work from the new generation. Culture as it has traditionally been shaped by the terms of nature and place is itself a permeable idea and is giving way to velocity, hybridity, and Google-ality.

Sapir describes culture as "the spiritual possessions of the group rather than of the individual." It is "a spiritual heirloom that must, at all cost, be preserved intact." Which heirlooms, the skeptic may ask. Few people would wish to preserve all aspects of their culture—assuming they could even define who they are as cultural creatures. Cultural identity is becoming a matter of individual choice. Cultural relativism does not have to mean that all cultural traditions are equal. It can mean that a person becomes more deliberate about which aspects of her tradition she wishes to take up and pass on. Vernita Herdman, an Inupiaq community advocate in Alaska, offers the apt metaphor of cabins circling a lake. We each bring our individual histories and cultural legacies to our sojourn in such a place, but at the center is the still and open water. We can look across the lake and see how others do things differently than we do. And we can choose. Herdman describes the tribal woman who walked several feet behind her husband, in deference to his authority and according to cultural tradition, until she saw that in other cultures a man and woman could walk side by side.

A genuine culture, says Sapir, is one in which nothing is spiritually meaningless. By this standard the Aztecs' culture was genuine, even though they were imperialists who continually waged war to capture victims for sacrifice. This practice was meaningful to them. They believed blood offerings completed a circle of reciprocal exchange—that life must be given in order to earn life. By Sapir's standard, the baiting and barking that passes for deliberation and decision making in Washington, D.C., is spurious because it is empty of meaning. It reflects only jockeying for position and power, not any of the ethical principles upon which our government was historically based. The Bill of Rights, the Civil Rights Act, and the Wilderness Act were genuine; the 2002 Authorization for Use of Military Force Against Iraq Resolution was spurious, based upon poor intelligence and false claims.

"It is imperative," Sapir asserts, "if the individual is to preserve his value as a cultured being, that he compensate himself out of the non-economic, the non-utilitarian spheres—social, religious, scientific, aesthetic." The spurious culture is one in which people expect to be compensated financially for all wounds and losses.

Though my father was never a litigious man, he comes to mind here. He was charming and sociable, a man who loved people and entertained them as a radio and television personality. He took the measure of himself in the pleasure of human company and in his handiwork on gardens, stone walls, and brush piles. Yet at the end of his life, after his heart began to fail in his eighties, his days narrowed down to a card table where he sat filling out Publishers Clearinghouse Sweepstakes entries in hopes of an easy million. He still felt the world owed him something, and he did not know where else to look for compensation. By contrast my mother, who lies at the far edge of her life as I write this, suffers enough skeletal disintegration to make her days a torment, yet she has found non-utilitarian compensations that make the prospect of death something she meets with equanimity. She has spent her late nineties completing a sharply written memoir; at ninety-nine she is intrigued by the images that come in dreams, often columns of people dressed in ceremonial robes of shiny pastel colors, which we discuss in our visits as one of many marvels of the inner world, the imaginative process that seems to be guiding her on this most difficult of passages.

"Nature is God," she told me one day. "I don't need religion. I tried it when I was younger. There was nothing there for me. Just think about a seed—all that's packed into that little miracle and the beauty that will unfold."

I picture her examining the stamens and pollen hoards of wildflowers with a magnifying glass, as has been her habit, her eyes growing glassy in love.

"That's all the religion I need," she tells me with the conviction of one shaping final thoughts. She is making a private peace with the terms of her existence, though she too is at odds with her culture.

"The self," Edward Sapir writes, "must learn to reconcile its own strivings, its own imperious necessities, with the general spiritual life of the community."

I know this is necessary for us to do. I don't know how we do it.

*

Culture is an emergent property of our biology. We are social creatures—the worst punishment we can inflict, short of the death penalty, is solitary confinement—and we are successful creatures, compared to many less fortunate species, because culture has made us speed-learners. The problem lies in the speed at which these two mechanisms—culture and biology—work. Culture is fast, biology slow.

Plastics offer a good example here. They are hydrocarbons, and we've made a lot of them. Plastic particles float in the ocean as vast islands of waste. No organism can metabolize this form of hydrocarbon; yet scientists suggest that, given enough time, microbes will evolve that can break the plastics back down into their chemical building blocks, and they will enter again into the molecular flow. This will be a long time coming, too long for the human species to sit back and wait for. But in Earth's time, a biological solution will come for at least some of our cultural excess.

With our increasing awareness of the crisis of global climate change, the science thrust to the forefront of attention is, as J. Baird Callicott pegs it, "biogeochemistry, which reveals a Gaian Earth that is certainly systemic, holistic, internally related, and indeed self-organizing and self-regulating." This shift in awareness is forcing us to pose old questions about our own nature with increasing urgency: What kind of creature are we? What kind of creature might we become? What is given and what is learned? Must we operate on the principle of survival of the fittest or can we shift to survival of the most cooperative? What stories can biology give us that help us revise the story of who we can be?

*

Nothing on this trip to San Diego was as I had expected. Why is it that my fantasies are so often stuck in the past? When I made the hotel reservations on the California coast, I pictured the place as it might have been a century ago. That small black dot on the edge of the map showed ocean blue on one side and forest green on the other, not the grid of freeways so entangled that places overlap and nothing has definition or limit. I pictured the classic stucco-and-mission-tile retreat, a place where the only shows in town are the sun-struck surf and forever-blond sand, plus the bird-of-paradise flowers blooming with orange and blue plumage in December.

What I found was no small black dot, but a panic attack of intersecting velocities. Each town sold shirts wearing its name, and the shirts wore pictures of the classic stucco- and-mission-tile hotel. I found a flier advertising the Blessing of the Pets scheduled at St. Anne's Congregational Church, "all species welcome," with cut-and-paste computer art showing turtle, parrot, cat, iguana, and dog lining up for sanctification. I found sidewalks busy with pedigreed dogs boasting perfect hairdos as they walked with their owners in the glamour of California sunlight—canine celebrities like the beauty queen Irish setter with her gleaming mahogany coat feathering off belly and legs like the chiffons of a veil dancer, and the attentive little Corgi sitting upright in the driver's seat of a parked Range Rover as if he were ready to pull out into the flow.

I had come to California to observe the bonobos (*Pan paniscus*) at the San Diego Zoo. These seductive little apes, along with their cousins the chimpanzees (*Pan troglodytes*), are our closest primate relatives. We three species are descended from an alleged common ancestor, a woodland ape whose fossil remains have yet to be found, an animal dubbed *Pan prior* that lived about 6 million years ago. Traits carried by *Pan prior* come into the modern world—shape-shifted by time—in the bodies and minds of human beings, chimps, and bonobos. To see (more likely than not on TV) a chimp displaying and slapping his way into the social group, or a bonobo gossiping, hugging, and humping her way in, is like finding an old family photo album, the faces and behavior of strangers closely resembling living relatives.

Physical violence is common among chimpanzees. Primatologist Frans de Waal writes in *Our Inner Ape* that the chimpanzee "resolves sexual issues with power." Bonobos, however, almost never show violence. The bonobo "resolves power issues with sex." Want a taste of your neighbor's food? If you're a bonobo, you don't steal it—you offer your rump, or hump your neighbor's thigh, or simply throw a reassuring arm around his shoulder. When groups meet in the forest they exchange constant chatter as if catching up on gossip. In captivity bonobos spend so much time grooming one another they may become temporarily bald. They laugh when tickled, they squeal in sexual pleasure, they have sex face-to-face—and in every other position imaginable—and they enjoy the solo delight of masturbation. Few bonobos are kept in captivity because they are rare and endangered. One can imagine the challenging staff meetings as zookeepers and handlers discuss the appropriate language for interpretive materials. What will we tell the children? That sex is fun and helps these creatures maintain a peaceful and egalitarian society? Perhaps this approach would play in Belgium, but with the abstinence-only regime ruling sex education in the United States, one imagines a somewhat stiffer word choice.

Although the fate of bonobos in the wild is grim, what might the story of their traits lend to our thinking about ourselves? True, we seem to have followed the pathway of the chimp with chest thumping, ground drumming, bullying, assault, and mutilation as very old habits in the primate line. That doesn't mean this is the only path we can follow through the genetic undergrowth. Our species is apparently the only one in evolutionary history to develop refined skills for language, self-awareness, and awe. Symbolic systems that embody these capacities may have developed on other worlds—worlds on which creatures have made it through the bottleneck of learning technological prowess without destroying themselves—but we are unlikely ever to know them. We're stuck with the wonder and challenge of ourselves.

De Waal, studying social intelligence, has spent thousands of hours watching bonobos and other primates. He has been dissolving the distinctions between instinct and intelligence in our distant relations, finding that they, like us, are adept at taking cues from the social prompts surrounding them. Primatologists increasingly speak of "cultural" variability among primates, and this does not apply just to learned tool use and eating habits, "such as chimpanzees cracking nuts with stones or Japanese monkeys washing potatoes in the ocean."

De Waal's most intriguing account is the experiment in which he put juveniles of two different macaque species together for five months; "the typically quarrelsome rhesus monkeys were housed with the far more tolerant and easygoing stumptail monkeys." The monkeys he expected to be aggressive clung fearfully to the ceiling of their cage, making a few threatening grunts. The stumptails weren't impressed, ignoring the challenge. De Waal's writes, "For the rhesus monkeys, this must have been their first experience with dominant companions who felt no need to assert their position."

The rhesus learned the lesson "a thousand times over and also engaged in frequent reconciliations with their gentle oppressors." After five months the two species played, groomed, and slept together "in large mixed huddles." Most impressive was the fact that when the species were separated, the rhesus showed "three times more friendly reunions and grooming after fights than was typical of their kind." Peacemaking was shown to be a social skill rather than an instinct in these primates. Is there something in us then, older than our conflicts, that can bring us peace?

How it stands today:

Bonobos	10,000 (No reliable estimates; may be as few as 5,000 and as many as 60,000; declining rapidly. *World Wildlife Fund.*)
Chimpanzees	200,000 (Mid-range of estimated 172,000–299,700; once inhabited 25 African countries; now extinct in 3 or 4; nearing extinction in many others. *World Wildlife Fund.*)
Human Beings	6,700,000,000 (And ticking. *World Population Clock.*)
Pan prior	0

*

The female beewolf, a European species of wasp, hunts honeybees. After paralyzing them with her stinger, she carries them to a chamber she has built in sandy soil. She paints the walls with white goo she has cultured in her antennae glands, a substance produced by streptomyces bacteria that live in these glands, finding there a warm and moist habitat wherein they thrive. The beewolf lays her eggs in the nursery, where the goo prevents fungus from growing. When the young hatch, they eat the honeybees. They apply the antifungal goo to the threads of their larval cocoons, protecting themselves from the parasitic fungus that might find the warm and humid nest a welcome home. Solitary and commensal, attacking and harboring, learned and brainless, the beewolf is a study in contrasts. The beewolf is its relationships. It does not require thought, but it does require millions of attempts and failures at community among insects, fungi, and bacteria.

Is there sentience involved in this process? We cannot possibly know what the labor of the beewolf feels like. I can imagine the physical intensity of the hunt, the weighty work of flying the prey back to the nest, the fevered robotic housekeeping before the eggs are deposited. But I cannot imagine my way inside the beewolf's experience. Every creature, even a plant, has some degree of sentience, the capacity to read its surroundings and identify signs—"honeybee," "sandy soil," "strep goo"—that trigger what it has to do to survive. Even an amoeba can switch genes on and off in response to changes in its environment: slime your way over here for food; slime away from toxins. This is an elaborate enzyme activity based in chemistry and biomechanics. No consciousness. No decision-making. No reflection. But I can't stop thinking how weird and marvelous it is that mere matter can conjure up such processes.

The simplest life form seems symphonic when I contemplate the unlikelihood of the complexity each creature embodies. If the amoeba is a symphony, then the human being ought to be a cacophony with its 10 trillion cells, 100 trillion synapses, each neuron averaging 1,000 inputs. To really hear the noise of a single person, add to these human cells the 100 trillion live-in bacterial cells (10 trillion individual bacteria of 1,000 different species in the gut alone!), mostly friendly, collaborating in our bellies, hair follicles, tear ducts, and skin, each of them ecstatic in the fecundity of our bodies, each of them welcomed by our bodies, though our minds may find them disgusting, for the contribution they make to our well-being. Hookworms in the human gut, for example, appear to reduce the incidence of allergies. When I think about the complexity of my body, the biological community of my body, my idea of myself begins to wobble. I am essentially two creatures in one: the thinking, feeling, sensing creature I know as me, and the bundle of involuntary processes—electrical, chemical, cellular, rhythmic, and inter-organismic—that go smoothly along beneath my recognition.

This mess of collaboration feels to me like a musical masterwork, though I do not believe any master is involved in its creation. I believe that life is a self-generating, self-complicating, self-correcting, and often self-deceiving process. What are the boundaries between my animality and the microbes that collaborate with my existence, between my voluntary and involuntary actions? There *are* no boundaries—only conflicts and resolutions, an endless process of mutual capitulation that keeps a person coasting along as if she were one discrete organism. Why call it musical? I think of the jazz chords I've been learning for the past couple of years, the sevenths and ninths and thirteenths that add a crunchy dissonance to melody by rendering it more bittersweet and beautiful because they complicate the song, creating the tension that longs for resolution, complexity that longs to know the simplicity of a major chord with nothing funky to challenge the ear. I find oddly comforting the fact that all my desires and sorrows and aspirations are nothing more than 10 trillion cells interacting with each other and with what they—in the guise of an "I"—encounter. My animal heart keeps the beat without anyone counting.

Biologist Ursula Goodenough writes:

> Life can be explained by its underlying chemistry, just as chemistry can be explained by its underlying physics. But the life that emerges

from the underlying chemistry of biomolecules is something more than the collection of molecules. . . . Once these molecules came to reside inside cells, they began to interact with one another to generate new processes, like motility and metabolism and perception, processes that are unique to living creatures, processes that have no counterpart at simpler levels. These new, life-specific functions are referred to as emergent functions.

Emergent functions, Goodenough says, are "something more from nothing but." Emergence is nature's mode of creativity. Atoms made in stars possess emergent properties. Planets and seas are emergent in star ash. Emergent properties abound in nonlife and life. When water turns to ice, it expresses the emergent property of buoyancy. Emergent outcomes in biology, such as motility or awareness, are called "traits." They mean that the organism has a purpose. Fly in tandem with the handful of starlings closest to your side, and the emergent property of flocking is expressed. Paralyze a honeybee and plant it with your young, and the emergent property of nurture is expressed. Write a book, symphony, sermon, prescription, or equation, and the emergent property of culture is expressed. Life insists upon purpose through a continual process of emergence.

Brain-based awareness in human beings emerges to become language. Language-based brains lead to an "I." The self does not feel like matter, but that is all it is. "I" is an emergent property of language-based brains, "something more from nothing but." Maybe it's just an accident that we have self-consciousness. Maybe the feeling we have that some people call "soul" or "spirit" is simply an intuition for the emergent, "the search for the adjacent possible," in Goodenough's words. Where are we heading in this big symphony of emergent chords? With any luck, and given enough time to develop enough collaborative relationships, we are trying to get from "I" to "we" on a global scale: from self to culture, nation to planet, history to biology.

Stuart Kauffman's most recent book, *Reinventing the Sacred: A New View of Science, Reason, and Religion* (2008), explores the significance of the idea of emergence. Kauffman offers a comprehensive theory of emergence and self-organization that he says "breaks no laws of physics" and yet cannot be explained by them. "God," he writes, "is our chosen name for the ceaseless creativity of the natural universe, biosphere, and human cultures."

*

On a 2008 visit to the Cape Cod National Seashore I heard a young naturalist speak about the condition of the piping plover, a species that nests on the beaches in May and June. I'd become interested after walking there and finding areas roped off for "bird use," where plovers had scratched out tiny basins in the sand in which to lay eggs perfectly camouflaged by the sand grains. The parent plovers worked the tidal wash for prey; a pair of turkey vultures scanned the shore for a shot at cleaning up. On Cape Cod this nesting behavior stirs up controversy akin to the trouble roused in the Pacific Northwest by the northern spotted owl. Select bumper stickers boast "Piping Plover: You Can't Eat Just One" and "Piping Plover Tastes Like Chicken."

Cape Cod fishermen pay dearly for off-road permits to drive their Jeep Cherokees and Dodge Rams along the beach and surf-cast for bluefish and stripped bass. Their beach roads coincide with the nesting ground. So the fight is on—birds versus men—though in truth the fight is between one group of citizens and another. I don't see why moderation cannot be a guide here. That appears to have been the course taken by the U.S. National Park Service with its gracefully worded sign, "Bird Use Area," that prods the visitor to consider the motto "Land of Many Uses" as incorporating the interests of species other than our own in our policies.

The lecturer, a young AmeriCorps volunteer doing noble service on behalf of ecological integrity, had been trained to foster audience participation. What I wanted were the facts, the latest research, details about what was at stake for the plovers and how they were doing against the human competition for beach space. But I bowed to the process, with one random half of the audience assigned to the "pro" plover position and the other half to the "con." I was among the pros. No contest in my mind, though I could not get anyone in my group to acknowledge that "all life forms are sacred" was an argument worth holding up to the policy fray. The cons argued "why interfere with the natural process of evolution?" holding forth that since we are the dominant predators and since we have paid good money for our off-road-vehicle permits, it is our right to unseat the nesters.

Our lecturer floated between the two groups. One of our pro colleagues, wanting to find something tangible to hold up against a fishing license, asked her, "Do they have a purpose? I mean, it would be so much easier, if the plovers had a purpose."

Like what, I wondered? Pharmaceutical production, or mosquito control, or the higher purpose that the religious see in life? I know some people see in the science story a life without direction or ethical dimension. Why are their actions what they are? What should their actions be? The facts of life do not answer and the silence looms. I am not among such people. For me, as for my mother, the facts of life are enough of a miracle to induce religious feeling and a sense of purpose.

"No," our guide confided apologetically to the plover pros. "That's the hard part. They really don't."

I wanted to take her by the shoulders and shake her loose from this capitulation to the forces of doom, but I understood that my role here was not to be the hard-hat but to understand how very far my sympathies lay from the general drift of public sentiment.

"Of course they have a purpose," I shouted into my inner megaphone. "Their purpose is to be piping plovers and to make more piping plovers! That's a sacred calling. Life is its own purpose." I remained silent, considering how terribly well my own species had followed the dictates of this imperative to make more of itself. And I sat in the sadness that the argument was not at all a simple one for this random gathering of tourists assembled at the National Seashore on a May afternoon in the first decade of the twenty-first century. If everything is sacred, then how do we know which interests to protect? Our moral philosophy is not yet sufficient to give us clear guidelines.

*

I cannot get out of my head the little Lucy-like hominids whose bones turned up early in the new millennium on the Indonesian island of Flores. Standing a meter tall, with a chimp-sized brain, the remains were similar to *Australopithecus afarensis*, the erect walking hominid that lived in Africa 3.5 million years ago. The team that had discovered the skeleton in Ethiopia celebrated their find while sitting around a campfire listening to "Lucy in the Sky With Diamonds" on a portable tape player. That's how this relic of our deep ancestry got her nickname. But the new find suggested that a similar creature lived on a Indonesian island as recently as 18,000 years ago. An artist's rendering of *Homo flores* depicted him walking home for dinner with a golden retriever-sized rat slung over his shoulder. How many millennia had passed since his ancestors migrated away from Africa and Asia? Three or four or five species of old world hominids were living at the same time. *Homo erectus* was the first colonizer, making it to Java around 1.8 million years ago, according to evolutionary biologist Francisco Ayala. Modern humans are not descendants of those early migrants. The diaspora of *Homo sapiens* from Africa to Asia came much later, starting about 100,000 years ago. The earlier migrants appear to have had a long and relatively peaceful tenure on Flores, and they represent a different branch on the tree of life than do our ancestors. They make us contemplate the possibility that rather than a tree of hominid life, there was a thicket—many starts, many entanglements, many failures—and only we survived. Unless, of course, you believe in Bigfoot. Somehow this time-deep story grows more fascinating as the fear increases that our story may be growing short and that our species' resume may show us to have been terrible animals, heedless devourers of the beautiful Mother that gave all Earth's beings their lives.

But thinking backward in such a time frame also calls up the question of a symmetrically long future. What if we make it? What if this sensitivity to brokenness is tweaking our intelligence to make the next leap in our evolutionary history, a leap that turns the runaway force of human culture toward restraint and mutual aid, toward the acquisition of knowledge rather than junk, toward a ten-thousand-year project to restore Earth to a state as close to Eden as we could come, and to grow an outlying garden on Mars? Is that not an artful technological dream that we could love? I want this to be as possible as our doom. Ten thousand years from now, I want someone to say of us, What amazing courage they had, what spirit, how smart they were, how inventive—and how profoundly they must have loved Earth.

Bill McKibben

Designer Genes

I grew up in a household where we were very suspicious of dented cans. Dented cans were, according to my mother, a well-established gateway to botulism, and botulism was a bad thing, worse than swimming immediately after lunch. It was one of those bad things measured in extinctions, as in "three tablespoons of botulism toxin could theoretically kill every human on Earth." Or something like that.

So I refused to believe the early reports, a few years back, that socialites had begun injecting dilute strains of the toxin into their brows in an effort to temporarily remove the vertical furrow that appears between one's eyes as one ages. It sounded like a Monty Python routine, some clinic where they daubed your soles with plague germs to combat athlete's foot. But I was wrong to doubt. As the world now knows, Botox has become, in a few short years, a staple weapon in the cosmetic arsenal—so prevalent that, in the words of one writer, "it is now rare in certain social enclaves to see a woman over the age of thirty-five with the ability to look angry." With their facial muscles essentially paralyzed, actresses are having trouble acting; since the treatment requires periodic booster shots, doctors warn that "you could marry a woman (or a man) with a flawlessly even face and wind up with someone who four months later looks like a Shar-Pei." But never mind—now you can get Botoxed in strip mall storefronts and at cocktail parties.

People, in other words, will do fairly far-out things for less-than-pressing causes. And more so all the time: public approval of "aesthetic surgery" has grown fifty percent in the United States in the last decade. But why stop there? Once you accept the idea that our bodies are essentially plastic, and that it's okay to manipulate that plastic, there's no reason to think that consumers would balk because "genes" were involved instead of, say, "toxins." Especially since genetic engineering would not promote your own vanity, but instead be sold as a boon to your child.

The vision of genetic engineers is to do to humans what we have already done to salmon and wheat, pine trees and tomatoes. That is, to make them better in some way; to delete, modify, or add genes in developing embryos so that the cells of the resulting person will produce proteins that make them taller and more muscular, or smarter and less aggressive, maybe handsome and possibly straight. Even happy. As early as 1993, a March of Dimes poll found that forty-three percent of Americans would engage in genetic engineering "simply to enhance their children's looks or intelligence."

Ethical guidelines promulgated by the scientific oversight boards so far prohibit actual attempts at human genetic engineering, but researchers have walked right to the line, maybe even stuck their toes a trifle over. In the spring of 2001, for instance, a fertility clinic in New Jersey impregnated fifteen women with embryos fashioned from their own eggs, their partner's sperm, and a small portion of an egg donated by a second woman. The procedure was designed to work around defects in the would-be mother's egg—but in at least two of the cases, tests showed the resulting babies carried genetic material from all three "parents."

And so the genetic modification of humans is not only possible, it's coming fast; a mix of technical progress and shifting mood means it could easily happen in the next few years. Consider what happened with plants. A decade ago, university research farms were growing small plots of genetically modified grain and vegetables. Sometimes activists who didn't like what they were doing would come and rip the plants up, one by one. Then, all of a sudden in the mid-1990s, before anyone had paid any real attention, farmers had planted half the corn and soybean fields in America with transgenic seed.

Every time you turn your back this technology creeps a little closer. Gallops, actually, growing and spreading as fast as the internet. One moment you've sort of heard of it; the next moment it's everywhere. But we haven't done it yet. For the moment we remain, if barely, a fully human species. And so we have time yet to consider, to decide, to act. This is arguably the biggest decision humans will ever make.

Right up until this decade, the genes that humans carried in their bodies were exclusively the result of chance—of how the genes of the sperm and the egg, the father and the mother, combined. The only way you could intervene in the process was by choosing who you would mate with—and that was as much wishful thinking as anything else, as generation upon generation of surprised parents have discovered.

But that is changing. We now know two different methods to change human genes. The first, and less controversial, is called somatic gene therapy. Somatic gene therapy begins with an existing individual—someone with, say, cystic fibrosis. Researchers try to deliver new, modified genes to some of her cells, usually by putting the genes aboard viruses they inject into the patient, hoping that the viruses will infect the cells and thereby transmit the genes. Somatic gene therapy is, in other words, much like medicine. You take an existing patient with an existing condition, and you in essence try and convince her cells to manufacture the medicine she needs.

Germline genetic engineering on the other hand is something very novel indeed. "Germ" here refers not to microbes, but to the egg and sperm cells, the germ cells of the human being. Scientists intent on genetic engineering would probably start with a fertilized embryo a week or so old.

They would tease apart the cells of that embryo, and then, selecting one, they would add to, delete, or modify some of its genes. They could also insert artificial chromosomes containing predesigned genes. They would then take the cell, place it inside an egg whose nucleus had been removed, and implant the resulting new embryo inside a woman. The embryo would, if all went according to plan, grow into a genetically engineered child. His genes would be pushing out proteins to meet the particular choices made by his parents, and by the companies and clinicians they were buying the genes from. Instead of coming solely from the combination of his parents, and thus the combination of their parents, and so on back through time, those genes could come from any other person, or any other plant or animal, or out of the thin blue sky. And once implanted they will pass to his children, and on into time.

But all this work will require one large change in our current way of doing business. Instead of making babies by making love, we will have to move conception to the laboratory. You need to have the embryo out there where you can work on it—to make the necessary copies, try to add or delete genes, and then implant the one that seems likely to turn out best. Gregory Stock, a researcher at the University of California and an apostle of the new genetic technologies, says that "the union of egg and sperm from two individuals...would be too unpredictable with intercourse." And once you've got the embryo out on the lab bench, gravity disappears altogether. "Ultimately," says Michael West, CEO of Advanced Cell Technology, the firm furthest out on the cutting edge of these technologies, "the dream of biologists is to have the sequence of DNA, the programming code of life, and to be able to edit it the way you can a document on a word processor."

Does it sound far-fetched? We began doing it with animals (mice) in 1978, and we've managed the trick with most of the obvious mammals, except one. Some of the first germline interventions might be semi-medical. You might, say some advocates, start by improving "visual and auditory acuity," first to eliminate nearsightedness or prevent deafness, then to "improve artistic potential." But why stop there? "If something has evolved elsewhere, then it is possible for us to determine its genetic basis and transfer it into the human genome," says Princeton geneticist Lee Silver—just as we have stuck flounder genes into strawberries to keep them from freezing, and jellyfish genes into rabbits and monkeys to make them glow in the dark.

But would we actually do this? Is there any real need to raise these questions as more than curiosities, or will the schemes simply fade away on their own, ignored by the parents who are their necessary consumers?

Anyone who has entered a baby supply store in the last few years knows that even the soberest parents can be counted on to spend virtually unlimited sums in pursuit of successful offspring. What if the "Baby Einstein" video series, which immerses "learning enabled" babies in English, Spanish, Japanese, Hebrew, German, Russian, and French, could be bolstered with a little gene-tweaking to improve memory? What if the Wombsongs prenatal music system, piping in Brahms to your waiting fetus, could be supplemented with an auditory upgrade? One sociologist told The New York Times we'd crossed the line from parenting to "product development," and even if that remark is truer in Manhattan than elsewhere, it's not hard to imagine what such attitudes will mean across the affluent world.

Here's one small example. In the 1980s, two drug companies were awarded patents to market human growth hormone to the few thousand American children suffering from dwarfism. The FDA thought the market would be very small, so HGH was given "orphan drug status," a series of special market advantages designed to reward the manufacturers for taking on such an unattractive business. But within a few years, HGH had become one of the largest-selling drugs in the country, with half a billion dollars in sales. This was not because there'd been a sharp increase in the number of dwarves, but because there'd been a sharp increase in the number of parents who wanted to make their slightly short children taller. Before long the drug companies were arguing that the children in the bottom five percent of their normal height range were in fact in need of three to five shots a week of HGH. Take eleven-year-old Marco Oriti. At four foot one, he was about four inches shorter than average, and projected to eventually top out at five foot four. This was enough to convince his parents to start on a six-day-a-week HGH regimen, which will cost them $150,000 over the next four years. "You want to give your child the edge no matter what," said his mother.

A few of the would-be parents out on the current cutting edge of the reproduction revolution—those who need to obtain sperm or eggs for in vitro fertilization—exhibit similar zeal. Ads started appearing in Ivy League college newspapers a few years ago: couples were willing to pay $50,000 for an egg, provided the donor was at least five feet, ten inches tall, white, and had scored 1400 on her SATs. There is, in other words, a market just waiting for the first clinic with a catalogue of germline modifications, a market that two California artists proved when they opened a small boutique, Gene Genies Worldwide, in a trendy part of Pasadena. Tran Kim-Trang and Karl Mihail wanted to get people thinking more deeply about these emerging technologies, so they outfitted their store with petri dishes and models of the double helix, and printed up brochures highlighting traits with genetic links: creativity, extroversion, thrill-seeking criminality. When they opened the doors, they found people ready to shell out for designer families (one man insisted he wanted the survival ability of a cockroach). The "store" was meant to be ironic, but the irony was lost on a culture so deeply consumer that this kind of manipulation seems like the obvious next step. "Generally, people refused to believe this store was an art project," says Tran. And why not? The next store in the mall could easily have been a Botox salon.

But say you're not ready. Say you're perfectly happy with the prospect of a child who shares the unmodified genes of you and your partner. Say you think that manipulating the DNA of your child might be dangerous, or presumptuous, or icky? How long will you be able to hold that line if the procedure begins to spread among your neighbors? Maybe not so long as you think: if germline manipulation actually does begin, it seems likely to set off a kind of biological arms race. "Suppose parents could add thirty points to their child's IQ," asks MIT economist Lester Thurow. "Wouldn't you want to do it? And if you don't, your child will be the stupidest in the neighborhood." That's precisely what it might feel like to be the parent facing the choice. Individual competition more or less defines the society we've built, and in that context love can almost be defined as giving your kids what they need to make their way in the world. Deciding not to soup them up...well, it could come to seem like child abuse.

Of course, the problem about arms races is that you never really get anywhere. If everyone's adding thirty IQ points, then having an IQ of one hundred fifty won't get you any closer to Stanford than you were at the outset. The very first athlete engineered to use twice as much oxygen as the next guy will be unbeatable in the Tour de France—but in no time he'll merely be the new standard. You'll have to do what he did to be in the race, but your upgrades won't put you ahead, merely back on a level playing field. You might be able to argue that society as a whole was helped, because there was more total brainpower at work, but your kid won't be any closer to the top of the pack. All you'll be able to do is guarantee she won't be left hopelessly far behind.

In fact, the arms-race problem has an extra ironic twist when it comes to genetic manipulation. The United States and the Soviet Union could, and did, keep adding new weapons to their arsenals over the decades. But with germline manipulation, you get only one shot; the extra chromosome you stick in your kid when he's born is the one he carries throughout his life. So let's say baby Sophie has a state-of-the-art gene job: her parents paid for the proteins discovered by, say, 2005 that, on average, yielded ten extra IQ points. By the time Sophie is five, though, scientists will doubtless have discovered ten more genes linked to intelligence. Now anyone with a platinum card can get twenty IQ points, not to mention a memory boost and a permanent wrinkle-free brow. So by the time Sophie is twenty-five and in the job market, she's already more or less obsolete—the kids coming out of college just plain have better hardware.

"For all his billions, Bill Gates could not have purchased a single genetic enhancement for his son Rory John," writes Gregory Stock, at the University of California. "And you can bet that any enhancements a billion dollars can buy Rory's child in 2030 will seem crude alongside those available for modest sums in 2060." It's not, he adds, "so different from upgraded software. You'll want the new release."

The vision of one's child as a nearly useless copy of Windows 95 should make parents fight like hell to make sure we never get started down this path. But the vision gets lost easily in the gushing excitement about "improving" the opportunities for our kids.

Beginning the hour my daughter came home from the hospital, I spent part of every day with her in the woods out back, showing her trees and ferns and chipmunks and frogs. One of her very first words was "birch," and you couldn't have asked for a prouder papa. She got her middle name from the mountain we see out the window; for her fifth birthday she got her own child-sized canoe; her school wardrobe may not be relentlessly up-to-date but she's never lacked for hiking boots. As I write these words, she's spending her first summer at sleep-away camp, one we chose because the kids sleep in tents and spend days in the mountains. All of which is to say that I have done everything in my power to try and mold her into a lover of the natural world. That is where my deepest satisfactions lie, and I want the same for her. It seems benign enough, but it has its drawbacks; it means less time and money and energy for trips to the city and music lessons and so forth. As time goes on and she develops stronger opinions of her own, I yield more and more, but I keep trying to stack the deck, to nudge her in the direction that's meant something to me. On a Saturday morning, when the question comes up of what to do, the very first words out of my mouth always involve yet another hike. I can't help myself.

In other words, we already "engineer" our offspring in some sense of the word: we do our best, and often our worst, to steer them in particular directions. And our worst can be pretty bad. We all know people whose lives were blighted trying to meet the expectations of their parents. We've all seen the crazed devotion to getting kids into the right schools, the right professions, the right income brackets. Parents try and pass down their prejudices, their politics, their attitude toward the world ("we've got to toughen that kid up—he's going to get walked all over"). There are fathers who start teaching the curveball at the age of four, and sons made to feel worthless if they don't make the Little League traveling team. People move house so that their kids can grow up with the right kind of schoolmates. They threaten to disown them for marrying African Americans, or for not marrying African Americans. No dictator anywhere has ever tried to rule his subjects with as much attention to detail as the average modern parent.

Why not take this just one small step further? Why not engineer children to up the odds that all that nudging will stick? In the words of Lee

Silver, the Princeton geneticist, "Why not seize this power? Why not control what has been left to chance in the past? Indeed, we control all other aspects of our children's lives and identities through powerful social and environmental influences.... On what basis can we reject positive genetic influences on a person's essence when we accept the rights of parents to benefit their children in every other way?" If you can buy your kid three years at Deerfield, four at Harvard, and three more at Harvard Law, why shouldn't you be able to turbo-charge his IQ a bit?

But most likely the answer has already occurred to you as well. Because you know plenty of people who managed to rebel successfully against whatever agenda their parents laid out for them, or who took that agenda and bent it to fit their own particular personality. In our society that's often what growing up is all about—the sometimes excruciatingly difficult, frequently liberating break with the expectations of your parents. The decision to join the Peace Corps (or, the decision to leave the commune where you grew up and go to business school). The discovery that you were happiest davening in an Orthodox shul three hours a day, much to the consternation of your good suburban parents who almost always made it to Yom Kippur services; the decision that, much as you respected the Southern Baptist piety of your parents, the Bible won't be your watchword.

Without the grounding offered by tradition, the search for the "authentic you" can be hard; our generations contain the first people who routinely shop religions, for instance. But the sometimes poignant difficulty of finding yourself merely underscores how essential it is. Silver says the costs of germline engineering and a college education might be roughly comparable; in both cases, he goes on, the point is to "increase the chances the child will become wiser in some way, and better able to achieve success and happiness." But that's half the story, at best. College is where you go to be exposed to a thousand new influences, ideas that should be able to take you in almost any direction. It's where you go to get out from under your parents' thumb, to find out that you actually don't have to go to law school if you don't want to. As often as not, the harder parents try and wrench their kids in one direction, the harder those kids eventually fight to determine their own destiny. I am as prepared as I can be for the possibility—the probability—that Sophie will decide she wants to live her life in the concrete heart of Manhattan. It's her life (and perhaps her kids will have a secret desire to come wander in the woods with me).

We try and shape the lives of our kids—to "improve" their lives, as we would measure improvement—but our gravity is usually weak enough that kids can break out of it if and when they need to. (When it isn't, when parents manage to bend their children to the point of breaking, we think of them as monstrous.) "Many of the most creative and valuable human lives are the result of particularly diffcult struggles" against expectation and influence, writes the legal scholar Martha Nussbaum.

That's not how a genetic engineer thinks of his product. He works to ensure absolute success. Last spring an Israeli researcher announced that he had managed to produce a featherless chicken. This constituted an improvement, to his mind, because "it will be cheaper to produce since its lack of feathers means there is no need to pluck it before it hits the shelves." Also, poultry farmers would no longer have to ventilate their vast barns to keep their birds from overheating. "Feathers are a waste," the scientist explained. "The chickens are using feed to produce something that has to be dumped, and the farmers have to waste electricity to overcome that fact." Now, that engineer was not trying to influence his chickens to shed their feathers because they'd be happier and the farmer would be happier and everyone would be happier. He was inserting a gene that created a protein that made good and certain they would not be producing feathers. Just substitute, say, an even temperament for feathers, and you'll know what the human engineers envision.

"With reprogenetics," writes Lee Silver, "parents can gain complete control [emphasis mine] over their destiny, with the ability to guide and enhance the characteristics of their children, and their children's children as well." Such parents would not be calling their children on the phone at annoyingly frequent intervals to suggest that it's time to get a real job; instead, just like the chicken guy, they would be inserting genes that produced proteins that would make their child behave in certain ways throughout his life. You cannot rebel against the production of that protein. Perhaps you can still do everything in your power to defeat the wishes of your parents, but that protein will nonetheless be pumped out relentlessly into your system, defining who you are. You won't grow feathers, no matter how much you want them. And maybe they can engineer your mood enough that your lack of plumage won't even cross your mind.

Such children will, in effect, be assigned a goal by their programmers: "intelligence," "even temper," "athleticism." (As with chickens, the market will doubtless lean in the direction of efficiency. It may be hard to find genes for, say, dreaminess.) Now two possibilities arise. Perhaps the programming doesn't work very well, and your kid spells poorly, or turns moody, or can't hit the inside fastball. In the present world, you just tell yourself that that's who he is. But in the coming world, he'll be, in essence, a defective product. Do you still accept him unconditionally? Why? If your new Jetta got thirty miles to the gallon instead of the forty it was designed to get, you'd take it back. You'd call it a lemon. If necessary, you'd sue.

Or what if the engineering worked pretty well, but you decided, too late, that you'd picked the wrong package, hadn't gotten the best features? Would you feel buyer's remorse if the kid next door had a better ear, a stronger arm?

Say the gene work went a little awry and left you with a kid who had some serious problems; what kind of guilt would that leave you with? Remember, this is not a child created by the random interaction of your genes with those of your partner, this is a child created with specific intent. Does Consumer Reports start rating the various biotech offerings?

What if you had a second child five years after the first, and by that time the upgrades were undeniably improved: how would you feel about the first kid? How would he feel about his new brother, the latest model?

The other outcome—that the genetic engineering works just as you had hoped—seems at least as bad. Now your child is a product. You can take precisely as much pride in her achievements as you take in the achievements of your dishwashing detergent. It was designed to produce streak-free glassware, and she was designed to be sweet-tempered, social, and smart. And what can she take pride in? Her good grades? She may have worked hard, but she'll always know that she was spec'ed for good grades. Her kindness to others? Well, yes, it's good to be kind—but perhaps it's not much of an accomplishment once the various genes with some link to sociability have been catalogued and manipulated. I have no doubt that these qualms would be one of the powerful psychological afflictions of the future—at least until someone figures out a fix that keeps the next generations from having such bad thoughts.

Britain's chief rabbi, Jonathan Sacks, was asked, a few years ago, about the announcement that Italian doctors were trying to clone humans. "If there is a mystery at the heart of human condition, it is otherness: the otherness of man and woman, parent and child. It is the space we make for otherness that makes love something other than narcissism." I remember so well the feeling of walking into the maternity ward with Sue, and walking out with Sue and Sophie: where there had been two there were now, somehow, three, each of us our own person, but now commanded to make a family, a place where we all could thrive. She was so mysterious, that Sophie, and in many ways she still is. There are times when, like every parent, I see myself reflected in her, and times when I wonder if she's even related. She's ours to nurture and protect, but she is who she is. That's the mystery and the glory of any child.

Mystery, however, is not one of the words that thrills engineers. They try and deliver solid bridges, unyielding dams, reliable cars. We wouldn't want it any other way. The only question is if their product line should be expanded to include children.

Right now both the genes, and the limits that they set on us, connect us with every human that came before. Human beings can look at rock art carved into African cliffs and French caves thirty thousand years ago and feel an electric, immediate kinship. We've gone from digging sticks to combines, and from drum circles to symphony orchestras (and back again to drum circles), but we still hear in the same range and see in the same spectrum, still produce adrenaline and dopamine in the same ways, still think in many of the same patterns. We are, by and large, the same people, more closely genetically related to one another than we may be to our engineered grandchildren.

These new technologies show us that human meaning dangles by a far thinner thread than we had thought. If germline genetic engineering ever starts, it will accelerate endlessly and unstoppably into the future, as individuals make the calculation that they have no choice but to equip their kids for the world that's being made. The first child whose genes come in part from some corporate lab, the first child who has been "enhanced" from what came before—that's the first child who will glance back over his shoulder and see a gap between himself and human history.

These would be mere consumer decisions—but that also means that they would benefit the rich far more than the poor. They would take the gap in power, wealth, and education that currently divides both our society and the world at large, and write that division into our very biology. A sixth of the American population lacks health insurance of any kind—they can't afford to go to the doctor for a checkup. And much of the rest of the world is far worse off. If we can't afford the fifty cents a person it would take to buy bed nets to protect most of Africa from malaria, it is unlikely we will extend to anyone but the top tax bracket these latest forms of genetic technology. The injustice is so obvious that even the strongest proponents of genetic engineering make little attempt to deny it. "Anyone who accepts the right of affluent parents to provide their children with an expensive private school education cannot use "unfairness" as a reason for rejecting the use of reprogenetic technologies," says Lee Silver.

These new technologies, however, are not yet inevitable. Unlike global warming, this genie is not yet out of the bottle. But if germline genetic engineering is going to be stopped, it will have to happen now, before it's quite begun. It will have to be a political choice, that is—one we make not as parents but as citizens, not as individuals but as a whole, thinking not only about our own offspring but about everyone.

So far the discussion has been confined to a few scientists, a few philosophers, a few ideologues. It needs to spread widely, and quickly, and loudly. The stakes are absurdly high, nothing less than the meaning of being human. And given the seductions that we've seen—the intuitively and culturally delicious prospect of a better child—the arguments against must be not only powerful but also deep. They'll need to resonate on the same intuitive and cultural level. We'll need to feel in our gut the reasons why, this time, we should tell Prometheus thanks, but no thanks.

Deborah Keenan

So Much Like a Beach After All

Turn the alley sideways, running north to south.
Remove the houses on the south side of the alley.
Remove the years of cobblestones, tar, small stones.
See for quite a distance, knowing the water
Is just out of sight. Take a chair to the alley
Which is no longer an alley but a strip
Of ancient beach which your beautiful imagination
Has made. Sit in your chair and listen
For the waves.

It Is Fair to Be Crossing

Fair to choose the other side
And cross towards it.

Fair to cross over.

Fair to spend one hour
Of one's life considering
The meaning.

Fair to be humble
Yet take the chance.

Now you're on it
And you wonder:

What holds it in place
What if the wind
Picks up
Will the beloved
Be waiting
Will anyone else
Think it fair

That you have crossed
Will what you imagined
From steel and air
Be true
When you arrive
And go no further?

Not Getting Tired of the Earth

He can go to the moon. And Mars, too.
Take his patronizing face, vicious voice,
His appalling definitions of loyalty,
He can go.

The rest of us, we need to not get tired
Of the earth. Need to care for parrots,
Even if we don't, revere sand, and buffalo,
Butterfly weed and dunes. We need to not
Get tired of the shattering beauty we live with,
Need to not get tired of wacky little city
Gardens, need to not be bored with
Starlings circling, the holy crows
Calling, the prairie grass replanted,
Blade by blade. No sleep! No sleep!

Or, at the very least, no sleeping
All at the same time. The ones who
Want to leave for Mars seem never
To sleep, yet seem unable to hear wrens
Arrive in spring, the last lion roaring
Out his furious, golden protest.

I won't get tired of the earth. Will
Love the moon from here, will
Rejoice when those who do not
Love the earth can only imagine
It from their new permanent homes
In the sky.

Between Now and Then

Art and nature...that's what lights it up.
—JEAN VALENTINE

The cottonwood tree was what mattered first to me.
Cottonwoods meant water close by, I could follow
The trees which led to the creek which led to the river.
And I did.

The prairie was what mattered first to me. How the wind
Moved the fields, how the wheat and prairie grasses
Lay down to let the wind pass by, rose up to hide
The wild turkeys, the frantic, focused field mice,
And me, not frantic, not focused, just a girl in the middle
Of the country.

The sun was what mattered first to me. We would drive
North to find my Swedish relatives, stop near open fields,
Throw down a blanket, eat our lunch and watch red-winged
Blackbirds race and spin in the ditches, the sun burning
Away the smell of my dad's cigarette some, my mom's
Low voice.

Summer was what mattered first to me. Freed from proving
My goodness each school day I would walk in the bed
Of the creek as farmland gave way to wildness. On lucky
Days the cotton would be floating and flying, turning
The ground white, or landing on the water, and the water
Would rush the cotton away. Better than snow, in that heat
The cotton would cover the world as I knew it, and no voice
Could reach me in that little valley.

Between then and now matters to me. This northern star
State where I have abided, my ancestors arriving in
New York harbor, making their way to Moorhead,
Living by the Red River, farming, running newspapers,
Building little cabins and tiny saunas,

Stealing away from their endless labor to linger
In summer sun for just a few days. And we would
Drive towards them, through hours and hours of
Silver gold fields, and it mattered to me.

But the first thing that mattered to me was the cottonwood
Tree, anchor and glory, shade and beauty, sign
Of water nearby, tree I could follow, then and now.

Donald Morrill

Lone Tree, 1986

All over Iowa it stands on the fence line between two fields—
a cottonwood, or an oak, or maybe an elm. It might have been
part of a grove once. Who would know? Natural history here
resides mostly in the museum and the agronomist's lab, like
the high-grass prairie ploughed under by pilgrims delivered
in Conestogas. And family history is of questionable longevity.
Anything beyond the stories of great-grandparents is the work
of genealogists selling their research through bulk-mail solicitations.
My father bought one of their offers, and we found
that our line is related to "Uncle" Ike Morrill, once famous as
the oldest postmaster in the United States. And, more distantly,
perhaps, to Justin Smith Morrill, a Vermonter and senator, who
wrote the Morrill Land Grant Act, 1862, which gave each state
a tract on which to build a university. The balance of family
memory is arrowheads, curled photographs, and the vanished
privacies of the dead. As for public memory, there are street
names and statues—and the Centurlon, the "spire of time"
on the state fairgrounds, which contains messages to Iowans
of 2054, yearbooks and annual reports of dozens of groups,
letters from the heads of foreign nations, two works by Karl
King, composer of marches, and "every common seed and fertilizer
in use in 1954 in Iowa."

That tree. The fields surrounding it are what one French
writer whom I otherwise admire called "a giant food factory."
Corn, soybeans, sorghum. I'm city raised—Des Moines, "A
Surprising Place," as the town slogan asserts hopefully—so I
grew up feeling superior to the bumpkins baling hay, deepening
their "farmer tans." I smiled indulgently at the plumpish
girls, graduated in classes of forty from consolidated high
schools, who moved to my capital to type in the insurance
offices on Grand Avenue. But I could not abide such an observation
about the land. City boys with soft hands can afford
a sweeter pastoral than sons stuck hosing down hogs prostrated
by a scorched August. No debts await the city boys at
harvest. They gaze across the ripeness in good years. They

drive on and regard the new spring rows flipping past like
spokes in a Chinese fan. And one day, of course, they step
into the high corn and discover that its undulating blades
are rough like a shark's hide, and sharp. Insects there, in
abundant numbers, bite.

But this only complicates the attachment to the landscape,
if not the land. Fifty years after my grandfather left the farm of
his boyhood for a job on the railroad and then at a cereal mill
in Omaha, he still tuned in to the morning market reports on
the radio. He was hard of hearing, so my siblings and I awoke
to the brisk drone of the oracles declaiming the fates of winter
wheat, feeder pigs, August corn. They still connote for me an
ethos of early rising—to which I can only aspire—as well as
a mid-morning "lunch" of a Denver sandwich and pie at the
town cafe. In middle age, I have stood on the edges of hybrid
test plots with one of my childhood friends, now an executive
marketing those magically calibrated beans. The wind over
their leaves ripples no less like invisible fingers across velvet.
Every suburbanite with a television knows a litany of herbicides
and fertilizers, almighty figures in the fertility cults of ad campaigns.
We drink the runoff in our lemonade and iced tea.
We also mourn a little—though there is the myth that farmers
are rich—when fields are too wet for planting, when early frost
smites green hope.

People not from the Midwest often assume that I am one
of the bumpkins, and I am, though not of the sort they imagine.
I'm not from the farm but from among the farms. I stand
between them, overlooking them like that lone tree, somehow
not in the way of the work yet springing from that same
earth, some of that surrounding green investing my fiber. This
betweenness is a metaphysical condition of the Midwest. Iowa
can feel like the center of the country, perhaps the cliché heart
of the country, and yet it's rarely a destination. Its horizons
declare that it's on the way to elsewhere. One can learn here,
however, that one is both the center of all and just another
center among the innumerable centers of all.

That tree stays. According to the last census, Iowa, of all
the states, has the largest proportion of native-born population.
But lightning can lay hands one hot night on the outstretched
limbs, and that tree strides off for good, seeking a mountainside

or seashore, some white-watery sublimity or
sheer plummet to oppose the minute variations in the pitch of
the glacial table. There's much to leave. The Arctic winter boring
with a sorrowful moan, like a dull drill bit, through each
keyhole. The homely small-town beauty shops. The roads and
their right angles. And the greenness in which one has taken
so much undue pride.

The further it lay behind me, the more I gloried in my
association with it. Of course, I sought by this to protect the
green within me. Still later, I hoped to eradicate it, abhorring
my regionalism, the great quiet of Iowa that seemed, to my agitated
pith, a quiescence of mind.

One feels alone in this opposition until one meets another
who has also walked away. A Minnesotan I know who now lives
in San Francisco and Italy speaks derisively of his birthplace as
"chipped-beef-on-toast culture." Every time he goes back, he
remains astonished that the people of his origins live as they
do. His fury for the accurately damning phrase suggests how
much he is possessed by the need to live differently than they—
more stylishly, less decently. Seemingly, he hopes to subdue his
native wholesomeness with suave garments from Milan, the
irony of the Mission District, and the ambered vistas of Renaissance
despots.

I laud his passion. Wholesome leads the parade of Midwestern
stereotypes, followed, in no particular order, by neighborly,
comfortingly normal, modest, well adjusted, taciturn, easygoing,
uncomplicated, colorless, placid, dumpy. There is truth in this vague
and sentimental pageant, but hardly more than in claiming that
Southerners are born tale-spinners or New Yorkers swift and
cynical. My Minnesotan is, by nature, a changeling, as am I. We
have gone off to live as we must. Yet this notion of Midwestern
salubriousness wearies. Look at our writers—our Fitzgeralds
and Twains and Cathers. And at that special Midwestern repression
featuring, for instance, the closeted lesbian rising in
the local company, good with figures, smart and tough, acquiring
stock options and a house on the lake, smoking too much,
perhaps, because there is nowhere to go and nothing to do.
But is there ever? All around: no hungering after ultimate
meanings. And red-checked tablecloths, fourth-graders filling
in the bubbles on their basic skills tests, Swedish towns

rivaling their Norwegian counterparts just down the road, the
automatic one-finger wave from the steering wheel of passing
pickup trucks. Mix these with the glue sniffer next door, the
hunter shotgunning the NO TRESPASSING sign, the boy seated in
the burlesque show tent at the state fair as the tattered, seamy
comic opens his hands folded in a mock prayer for sex and
announces "no sooner spread than done." Punch line, followed
by the girl with the Band-Aid on the back of her thigh,
the one who earlier crouched among the carnival trailers with
her head down, now one of the dancers.

My Minnesotan and I carry our gratitude for this gift of
place (and it is a gift) like initials carved into a tree trunk,
marks that ascend with age and expand and crack open, dubiously
skin deep. And we cast our own shadows as well.

My family remains in Iowa and Nebraska predominantly.
I go back. According to that same census, Iowa is second only
to Texas in the number of towns with fewer than one hundred
residents, and second only to Florida in the proportion of its
population over sixty-five. Thus, the old have held out on their
porches—though in recent years something of a boom has
pushed Des Moines, for instance, far west of its long-standing
borders. Mostly treeless, the developments there abound in
"executive homes," with square footage exceeding those at
twice the price in Connecticut or New Jersey. My relations
shake their heads at the burgeoning: "I don't know who can
afford them." Perhaps Des Moines is a new grooming ground
for ascending management, a little Charlotte, some would like
to think. No doubt, the reputation of reduced commutes and
increased safety lure this younger blood, though the national
social damages still come as well, albeit like late-arriving fashions.
"A good place to raise kids," we hear it said repeatedly. I
say it myself. Kids and corn: good soil for them. Certainly this
is—and was—a place in need of land for a university, for at least
a different kind of quiet than that which fills up the green days,
acreage where one might stumble onto Suetonius or Tolstoy, or
a different vision of self than the general offer. I can thank my
remote relative in his cool, stony Vermont homestead for that
grant, as can those new Iowans in their kitchens edging across
what were soybean fields toward the grain elevator in Waukee,
fields once traversed by tribes doomed to slaughter—fields

that were, long before that, the floor of an ocean teeming with primordial monsters swimming through ordinary lives.

One old Iowa woman I know says she likes a tree most of all in winter, when its leaves have fallen away and she can see its character in full. I want to disagree with her, to argue that leaves are no ruse of obfuscation and no decoration. But she, too, longs to penetrate the greenness, to witness bones and essences. Something of the soul stands alone against the luminous, overcast January night, perhaps scarred its full length by lightning and thus vulnerable to infestation, but clear and singular, hardly a windbreak, a stark perch. She looks to winter, as I look to a cold word, for the truth about our state and the existence we sometimes share in kind.

D.A. Powell

continental divide

had no direction to go but up: and this, the shattery road
its surface graining, trickle in late thaw—is nothing amiss?
—this melt, the sign assures us, *natural cycle*
                        and *whoosh*, the water a dream of forgotten white

past aspens colored in sulfur, they trembled, would
—poor sinners in redemption song-shed their tainted leaves

I tell you what boy I was, writing lyrics to reflect my passions:
the smell of a bare neck in summer
a thin trail of hairs disappearing below the top button of cut-offs
the lean, arched back of a cyclist straining to ascend a hill

in the starlight I wandered: streets no better than fields
the cul-de-sacs of suburbia just as treacherous, just as empty

if wood doves sang in the branches of the acacias, I could not hear them
anyone lost in that same night was lost in another tract

the air pulsed and dandelion pollen blew from green stalks
                        —that was all

and yes, someone took me in his car.   and another against the low fence
in the park at the end of our block.   under the willow branches
where gnats made a furious cloud at dawn and chased us away

I knew how it felt to lie in a patch of marigolds: golden stains
the way morning swarmed a hidden rooftop, the catbirds singing
the feel of ruin upon lips rubbed raw throughout the night

granite peaks: here, the earth has asserted itself. and the ice asserted
and human intimacies conspired to keep us low and apart

for an ice age I knew you only as an idea of longing:
a voice in the next yard, whispering through the chink
a vagabond outlined against the sky, among the drying grass

we journey this day to darkness: the chasm walls lift us on their scaly backs
the glaciers relinquish their secrets: that sound is the ice bowing
and the sound underneath, the trickle: the past released, disappearing

you pinnacle of my life, stand with me on this brink
half-clouded basin caked in flat grays, the very demise of green

you have surmounted the craggy boundary between us

you open the earth for me, receiving these amber last leaves

cancer inside a little sea

for the rivers, draining toward the coast, carry such silt
and the red mangrove, entwining root with excrescent root
prospers its mighty nation—bubbleshell, jingleshell, rotting chips

the flecks of understory leaves, crud and algae, scum—
like a submerged derrick, its network of cables impenetrable
and profuse, the trees knot and twist, trap the water's swill

a ratsnake in the branches, girding the lowest bough
and the strangler fig constricting trunk to trunk, arterial mass
wrapped over, in the insidious embrace of virginia creeper

what has been garnered of this wetland except the twigs
organic and inorganic mud, quartz-rich and mercury-laden
the accumulation of contaminants, cadmium, diquat, toxaphene

and always, the sandbars eroding at the periphery
where freshwater meets saltwater, and sawgrass swamp
drains into estuaries and bay.   and always the balance

upset, as herbicides eradicate cat's claw vine
which has choked out carrotwood, which has displaced cypress
and the sea absorbs the toxins and eliminated matter

what does it matter now, what is self, what is I, who gets to speak
or who does not speak, whether the poems get written
whether the reader receives them whole, in part or not at all

child to come, what will you make of this scratched paradise
this receptacle of soil, water, seed, bee, floating scat and spore
brutal wind and brutal tide.   the insignificance of fortunes

Anthony Doerr

Cloudy Is the Stuff of Stones

Whenever I'm outdoors for more than ten minutes I start picking up rocks. In Patagonia, in Phoenix, in a Home Depot parking lot—my gaze is invariably sucked downward into the gravel. I weigh the merits of pebbles by some fickle and mutable aesthetic and either pitch them back or pocket them and stack them among hundreds of their brethren on the counter behind our kitchen sink like fortifications against an army of tiny invaders.

Pebbles from Canada, pebbles from Cleveland, pebbles from carriageways in Caledonia. Maybe the echoes of miners reverberate in my genes; maybe I share a That's-Pretty-and-I-Want-It covetousness with thieves and princesses and bowerbirds. Maybe I hope someday I'll finally overcome the fundamental truth of pebbles and find one that looks prettier dry than wet. Or maybe I'm just an introvert, a down-gazer, a bad conversationalist.

But every night as I wash another dish or fill another mug with water, my little hoard stares up at me with its thousand imperturbable faces.

Oh, him, the stones seem to whisper. He'll be gone soon enough.

Take this nugget of quartz: milky, egg-shaped, the size of a breath mint. Quartz is *hard,* harder than all the common minerals, and on its journey from mountain to dust this pebble has reached the way station of my kitchen counter by passing through an almost unfathomable series of gauntlets. This little thing is a master of endurance: survivor, abider, traveler; inside it is folded a story of creation and time so large it threatens the imagination.

Born as a crystalline vein inside some huge extrusion of granite, it probably rode a thrust fault into the light a few hundred million years ago, helped bulldoze up a mountain range, got pulverized by a glacier. Over a few millennia ice, weight and lichen weathered the vein into boulders, the boulders into stones. Maybe this pebble was driven by a cloudburst into a great fan of other pebbles; maybe it was—after another ten thousand rainstorms—sucked back underground where it was compressed into conglomerate by heat and pressure, until it rose again, smaller and rounder, to be polished for a few more centuries in a creek bed before the creek disappeared and the sand swallowed it, incubated it, and hatched it years later into the gulch below my house.

Until last Tuesday, when it traveled into the whimsy of my frail attention. Into my pocket, onto the pile behind the sink. It sits there now and dares me to outlast it.

The lesson of rocks, of course, is not a lesson in permanence but rather the opposite. Change, that's the only music a pebble (or person) can count on, and in the lifetimes of stones change comes in relentless concatenation on scales so large our brains aren't quite evolved to understand them.

Over time the landscapes beyond our kitchen windows rise and fall as surely as ocean waves. The green and blue maps tacked to the walls of our children's classrooms are merely snapshots, out-of-date the moment they were printed. Tomorrow Australia will have an observably different shape, North America will be farther away from Europe, and the Pacific Ocean will be deeper. Mount Everest is getting taller, Polynesia is sinking, and any day now California might calve off from the rest of the United States and slide smoking into the ocean.

What's California to a nugget of quartz? What's a Tuesday; what are a few hours in a damp pocket; what are a couple of decades on a kitchen counter? Pompeii, Krakatoa, Paricutin; the vast basaltic plates on which our continents drift and our lives play out move at roughly the same speed as our fingernails grow, and that may not seem like much until one remembers 2004, Boxing Day, the event scientists now call the Great Sumatra-Andaman earthquake, ten minutes in which the whole planet vibrated like a thumped watermelon and 230,000 people died. Civilization is a blink in the eye of a pebble, and pebbles are but heartbeats in the trillion-day lifetime of the earth.

At three in the morning I creep to the kitchen sink. I fill my mug with trembling hands. The eyeless faces of my stones stare up me. They say: Enjoy your drink, little man. They say: We stared up through rushing streams at the stars a thousand years before you were born.

Sometimes I wonder: If four-and-half billion years ago an Archean God suspended a time-lapse movie camera over the latitude and longitude at which I now stand, and could run the reel back to me at high speed, what would I see? Floods of molten basalt would cross the screen, cooling and hardening. Spasms of airborne ash would blot the view now and then. Oceans would seethe and evaporate. Galaxies of clams might appear, flapping their shells at the sun, then vanishing beneath successive sheets of mud. A cubic mile of ice would show up several times. Puddles would fill and drain away in a breath. Soils would build and be scraped away; stands of prehistoric trees would surge up toward the viewer and fall and rise again in succession. And all the while swarms of pebbles would dart to and fro like bees. In this movie everything around me right now, water in my mouth, crickets shrieking in the yard—stones, refrigerator, house, heartache—would not stay put long enough to register in a single frame.

If these kitchen-counter pebbles had memories, if they could unpack their lithic histories and unroll them across the floor like scrolls, they'd show us flashes of heat in the crucible of the earth, epochs of darkness, the heavens spitting snow, then rain, then light. On those scrolls would be wildernesses of silence so vast that to dwell within them for a fraction of their length would be to make us insane with terror and loneliness.

After I'm dead, someone will have to decide what to do with all the stones I've stockpiled. Pitch them over the backyard fence or dump them into a box or wall my carcass in with them. Eventually everything I know— my children, my friends, this language, these hills—will be something else.

Not much longer now, the pebbles whisper. Just a few more years. While electricity twinkles between the dendrites of my mind, insufficient against whatever erosions lay ahead.

Linda Hogan

Humble

Where the road ends,
where the land ends,
where layers of earth history
are revealed by the constant taking
of the sea,
a solitary house stands in ocean spray.
Once filled with life, no one lives here.
All is abandoned, yet it still makes a stand
in the place where people of the whale lived.
You'd think whatever forces there are
would at least have taken this into their arms,
embraced in love,
but even stars come apart
in the play of universal wind.
I love this house of unrest,
the handiwork ever to be outdone
by the carpenter of wind,
the craftsman of waves.
As for me, loving the lone house
perhaps because it is so like the body,
that other amazing architecture waiting,
also believing the world should open its arms
and hold it in a great kindness,
not merely to be salt and skin, dissolving
day by day.
I am still a beginner in this world
without a hold, without money or love or tools.
I am down on my knees.
Maybe now I can begin to learn something.

Rapture

Who knows the mysteries of the poppies
when you look across the red fields,
or hear the sound of long thunder,
then the saving rain.
Everything beautiful,
the solitude of the single body
or sometimes, too, when the body is kissed
on the lips or hands or eyelids tender.
Oh for the pleasure of living in a body.
It may be, it may one day be
this is a world haunted by happiness,
where people finally are loved
in the light of leaves,
the feel of bird wings passing by.
Here it might be that no one wants power.
They don't want more.
And so they are in the forest,
old trees,
or those small but grand.
And when you sleep, rapture, beauty,
may seek you out.
Listen. There is
secret joy,
sweet dreams you may never forget.
How worthy the being
in the human body. If,
when you are there, you see women
wading on the water
and clouds in the valley,
the smell of rain,
or a lotus blossom rises out of round green leaves,
remember there is always something
besides our own misery.

The Radiant

In night,
at the dark limits of earth
where land ends and water begins,
at the elemental border
where you can go no further
without one entering the other,
the green light goes on.
It's not the man who fishes here,
not a light of human making
because we are the ones who measure light
and because light was created before us
from blood of flesh and sea
like this animal light of the manta ray
traveling the latitudes of night
and longitudes of darkness
knowing the blue unfathomable shifts
and dark ranges of the world beneath water.

It travels a rich sea away from us,
its light falling on plankton,
bringing food and fish toward it,
as if it is moonlight
opening across water,
it passes over the fished-out places
beyond the reef where coral is dying,
out past the point where the British captain was killed
by those who first thought he was a shining god.

It moves steadily out into the darkness
to where the colder darkness begins to well up
from the sea depths that have no bottom,
the place where I have feared the pale face of a shark
with its deadly touch
against my naked legs.

The ray travels over the many
other lives that have light
and below them is the blindness
of fish who need no sight,
and out toward the place where sun left the sky,

to where the largest creatures live,
where fishermen once found their boat cast in shadow
and looking up, saw what kind of cloud it was,
the manta ray risen out of water, a leap
so large it darkened the sky.
The men returned haunted by
everything that was larger than they were,
more beautiful and bearing its own light.

Tonight on this dark shore,
watching the animal light go over the horizon,
I long to be in water heading for open sea,
for no other power,
no other light.

The Night Constant

At night, outside the house,
I feel the lion
near the black pine trees.
Sometimes walking on the road
before the eyeshine in darkness
I can tell it is
walking just before me,
cutting across the field
toward the dog and the goat.
I feel it with the naked eye of skin,
the fine hair, the animal trappings of my body
begin to rise, a beast remaining,
and there is a feeling, too, of awe and respect,
and, yes, remorse
for our kind who have tried to reach heaven,
learn a universe
and found the stars that swallow light,
that bounded darkness is a matter
between light and broken light,
and we don't even know
the animals that walk outside our sleep
yet we have traveled there so often
there are not so many of them now

where light falls across the hunting grounds
we call a world that's small
because we've matched it to ourselves
and with all the lies we tell ourselves
so we won't see the world collapse
but when it does
it is not from what is known
but from what is never seen.

Barrie Jean Borich

Waterfront Property

Water pulls the body forward. Water hems the body in. Nothing feeds longing like uncertainty and nothing is more uncertain than a horizon line where the long haze of water swallows the hard border of sky.

Triptik New Orleans—Look, I shouted to my father. I was the one who spotted her, my role, as my father's inquisitive daughter, to be the one who points things out. She was the White Lady of the New World, the statue inviting wanderers to her shore, standing there at the gateway like an imperious guardian angel, like the rich lady who owned the joint.

The monument to the immigrants, on the New Orleans waterfront where the Mississippi rolls past the French Quarter, was another version of Columbia Gem of the Ocean, hers an amalgam of all kinds of American body beautifuls—breasts and belly sheathed in white drapery, toes grazing the river, long hair blowing back toward the land, right hand raised to the portside sky the way a TV evangelist choir mistress holds the palms of her hands out to receive.

The sultry river wind drowned out my voice as my parents and my spouse Linnea rambled by. Hey, I shouted. Linnea stopped first, then my white-haired father turned. My little frowning mom, who can't hear too well, especially outside, ears stoppered by the bluster of port breeze and the tourist hubbub and the whap of paddleboat wheels, didn't slow her gym-teacher trot until she noticed she'd walked a good block ahead on her own.

Drago and Klara Cvitanovich, names inscribed into the front of the statue, were what stopped me. We'd met that actual guy, Drago, a grumpy octogenarian in a tropical-print shirt, just the night before, at his oyster joint in a disheveled suburb on high ground at the other end of the city. *Look* at *that*, my father said. Once my mother trotted back she said it too. *Look*. They bent over the name. Drago. We all stared, as if the statue were speaking Drago's name out loud.

Linnea walked around the back of the statue, her polo shirt rippling in the river wind as she bent over to read. Her hair was still long enough to be curly then, rumbling up over her forehead, making her appear a couple inches taller than her actual measure.

I moved in behind her to see where the sculptor had inscribed his name, Franco Allessandrini. One of your people, I said to Linnea. The family laugh breaks across Dad's craggy face. It's an old joke in our family, the Croats vs. the Italians. Whatever we might have thought of each other back in the old country, here we were all the children and grandchildren of those long dead Mediterraneans who'd been born with just a sliver of Adriatic between them. My Italian-American spouse and I are the last generation likely to keep the joke going.

When I asked Linnea if she'd noticed all the Italian names engraved on the base of the sculpture, she said, you gotta be kidding. There's nobody *but* Italians here. I looked to where she pointed, saw all the names ending in either *i* or *ich*. A roster of Croats and Italians ran around the circumference of the monument's base. Except for all those Croats, I said.

The stone roll call left out most of the New Orleans immigrant polyglot. Typical of European Americans to think they are the only ones with an immigration story worth remembering. But sins of omission aside, this was the first I'd heard of Croats coming in not from the Atlantic or Pacific waterfronts but instead from the bottom up, the first of them, it turns out, making landfall before the American Civil War, entering down here through the basement door when the French were still in charge. Some of the Croats who came here in the 19th century—to this waterfront, not so different from Croatia's Dalmatian coast—were sailors who bailed off boats docked in the Port of New Orleans and became the Delta's oyster harvesters, calling their new waterfront property Dalmatia on the Mississippi.

On the other side of the waterfront monument, at the angel's rear, hovering just above Franco's name, looking back into the city, were statues of the prototype European immigrant figures—the bewildered mother, father, son and infant daughter, the boy just old enough to carry a sling over one shoulder, like the boys in any of hundreds of Lewis Hines' photos. Was this Ellis Island, or the bayou? The stone bodies were the standard bundle and babushka types, bearers of old stories that have hardened into myths as unyielding as this statue, un-budged even by Hurricane Katrina. Here was an imprecise portrait of our Grandmother Kata, her husband Big Petar and their little boy Petey, not out East but here, in the Mississippi Delta, just a half day's drive along the Gulf from my parents' retirement home.

Allesandrini's stone immigrants, their backs to the water, look bewildered, as if New Orleans were a blinding light. The too easily floodable southern city stretches out before them, the curlicued French balconies and trees dripping magnolia blossoms below sea level, not any home these newcomers recognize. It's too late to choose another route. They've already crossed over.

Overlook: Anniversary View

I wasn't sure I wanted to make this trip to New Orleans. It was my parents' fiftieth wedding anniversary and for months the family had been arguing. Should we all travel back to Chicago? Book rooms in a resort town or try for discount cruise ship tickets? Gather at Mom and Dad's golf course? No one could agree. Who would have to travel further and which sibling owed which other sibling a visit and who had more kids to cart around or dogs to board and which one of us would get stuck with the work if the party happened on our part of the map? If we'd turned out to be one of these families who'd stayed put we would have just rented a Chicago south side Knights of Columbus hall, or set up tables in someone's south suburban garage and rented a keg. Now, instead, everyone was scattered to the four points, and everyone was mad. If you want to find me on my anniversary, my mother said to me when the fighting was at its worst, look in the Biloxi casinos.

Then Katrina hit. The last I heard of my mom's favorite casino it was sitting in the center of Highway 10.

Point of Departure: Anatomical Geography

My friend El and I are sitting in the front seat of her red, step-up-to-ride truck, on the way to a lesbian wedding, when I tell her about Drago. This was before I'd met the guy. My dad had just emailed me to tell me he'd read about Drago's oysters on the Internet. El and I are both dolled up for the festivities, although dolled up is not the right word to describe El, she in one of her fancy-man suits looking a bit like Humphrey Bogart. I'm wearing a leopard-print dress and fat-heeled pumps, my ankle and shoulder tattoos showing. El is filling in, at Linnea's request, as my wedding date because Linnea's working the party, best man for her old college buddy Peg, one of the brides. Of the two women getting hitched, Peg seems, to her friends, notably un-bride-like, thus her need for not a matron of honor but a best man. Linnea is in charge of event logistics, in-law schmoozing, and stocking the bar. I won't be seeing much of my husband at this shindig.

So I ride to the wedding with El, my stand-in date, who is a transplant from Macon, Georgia. On the way we chat about Linnea and my upcoming trip and my family's plans to eat at a Louisiana Croatian oyster house. El doesn't get what I'm saying. What kind of oyster? I'm wondering if El thinks that a lifelong Midwestern girl like me doesn't know how to pronounce Creole.

Croatian, I tell her. My father is Croatian American. I know this doesn't mean much to her. It used to be—before the messy Balkan wars and the crackup of former Yugoslavia—people outside our family neighborhoods had never even heard of Croatia. Is that some part of Germany? Is it Poland? One of those little provinces obscured by the USSR? Once even I had to work at knowing where Croatia was located on the map, hours spent, when I was in my twenties, staring at atlases, tracing my fingers up around the outline of the blue Adriatic from southern Italy, through Venice and around the bend into the rocky Dalmatian mountains.

Chicago's East Side and Slag Valley are little post-immigrant countries strange even to lifer Chicagoans, unless they're Croatian or Serbian or Polish or Mexican and their people are from there. Unless they know those wood houses swaying in the wind of Lake Michigan, those steel bridges rising into the mill fog, that rotten-egg stink from the mills. Unless they remember those Croatian taverns like the Golden Shell, with its cevapici, breaded shrimp and beer, the velvet wallpaper, smoke-smudged mirrors, and big-haired waitresses, the cluttered stage where the tamburitza bands played their skinny-necked Yugoslavian guitars and button-box accordions and where their dads, smiling after a few beers, sing along to some embarrassing polka.

When I say to El, *Croatian Oyster*, I mean to convey both memory and dissonance. Like steel-city people and Mississippi Delta seafood. Like Lesbian Best Man. Like Peg and Bride. El tries, but she doesn't get it.

Triptik New Orleans—Here's the thing about fiftieth wedding anniversaries. Everyone I talk to from my generation tells me their family turned it into some kind of fracas, an old tradition that used to be fun but somewhere along the way cracked up on a New World shore. The New Orleans trip came about after Linnea and I opted out of the big anniversary argument. No more fighting for us. For Barrie and Linnea's fiftieth anniversary anti-bash we offered to meet my parents anywhere, whenever they wanted, as long as we didn't have to get anyone else in the family to agree.

My folks chose New Orleans because it was where they went every May, just six hours' drive west along the broken Gulf Coast. At first I balked. According to the news, nine months since the post-Katrina floods, the French Quarter was open for business. Still, I wasn't sure about taking my parents out to dinner in a ruined city that was home to none of us. Would we gawk at all that waterfront property that had been so recently under water? Would we bother those people down there?

When we got to this city where most of the famous restaurants were open and most of the not-so-famous homes were uninhabitable, the locals said thank you thank you for coming, and it seemed like they meant it.

Point of Departure: Matrimonial Crossings

The theme of the lesbian wedding is Etta James's version of the song *At Last*. At long last home for two women in their forties. During the testimonials one of Peg's brothers shouts *it's about time*, and everyone laughs.

It's hot, unseasonably so for May in Minneapolis. My dress is sleeveless, so I'm coping. El is handsome in her neat crew cut and mystery date wedding clothes, but her face is a little too red. I ask, are you hot?

I'm dying, she admits, which makes me laugh, only because El, wearing Georgia on her sleeve, usually complains she can never get warm enough in cold Minneapolis. So I poke her and ask, have you finally assimilated?

No, she says, and I flinch at her edge. I ought to know better than to badger people about their geography. Now El will never take off her hot jacket and get comfortable in this airless church basement where both brides are sweating in white satin and hose.

A lesbian wedding is a vortex of both geographical and anatomical crossings. Families cross state lines, cross gender lines. The wedding guests dress every which way. Peg is Linnea and El's butch/Bubba/football buddy, the type who joins them on motorcycle trips, the sort they'd always assumed would be a groom before she'd be a bride. A week before the wedding the Bubbas held a bachelor party. The wives, such as myself, were not invited. There was a cake, I heard later, decorated with a naked Barbie doll, and screenings of 1950s-era burlesque films, from the days, as Linnea described the show, when women weren't afraid to have hips.

When is a bachelor party not really a bachelor party? When the bachelors are neither bachelors nor bachelorettes? When the rituals are pantomimes of the actual rituals of actual bachelors, gestures toward a realm these technical females can't enter, and what's more have no wish to enter? At this bachelor party, the plasticized image of the American girlfriend emerged from waves of chocolate frosting, Columbia of the nipple-less breasts and crotch as smooth as the bridge of a nose, while a stripper—who was young when she made this movie, but must by now be old enough to be any of these Bubbas' grandmother—bumps and grinds on the home DVD screen, her moves chaste compared to what runs these days on network TV any day of the week. All this and good steaks, and martinis, and the endless toasts ribbing Peg about her agreement to do as her bride has asked. She would wear what? A dress?

Every kindergartner knows brides wear dresses. Two brides equal two dresses. But Bubbas like Linnea, a woman who owns more cufflinks than most people's grandfathers, are women to whom clothing is a transcontinental map. I have a picture of Linnea as a baby wearing a lace-hemmed dress, and even then, age two, with her boyish smile and wide-legged gait, she looked like a tourist in the country of girls. Peg, a short wide woman, normally wears jeans, wears slacks, wears motorcycle boots. The Bubbas feared Peg would end up a stranger at her own wedding.

Yet on her steamy wedding day, Peg seems nearly at home in her dress, floor-length, white, a satin sheath billowing from her shoulders to the tips of her shoes, a more tailored version of Columbia's white angel sheath; and what's more, her face flush with a sappy grin, she looks happier than I've ever seen her. I don't understand the dress, El says to me. You would never ask Linnea to wear a dress, she says. You take pride in Linnea's dress jacket and cufflinks and wingtip shoes, she says. I agree. I love Linnea's Italian gangster dress-up clothes.

No one I know would dare ask Linnea or El to wear a dress, but El tells me stories about her family, who love her but refuse to understand why she won't grow out her hair. They once even barred her from a family funeral because she wouldn't put on a skirt. I cringe at the thought of Linnea in a skirt. Early in the planning Peg told Linnea that everyone in the wedding party, according to the wishes of Peg's bride, would wear some kind of skirt. Linnea laughed and said, so you think so?

But citizenship can be a funny proposition. Should traditions cross over to meet the irregular body or should the irregular body cross over to meet the tradition? Peg's bride sees it one way. Peg's friends see it another. Peg is at home in the middle. The thing about the unconventional woman is even her unconventionality may vary. Sometimes she faces out toward the water, a few shreds of a dress clinging to her breasts. Sometimes she is the one wearing the pants, looking hard into the land.

Overlook: Water View

The thing about waterfront property is, in the real estate ads, the city port view is what makes a property pricey. It used to be the urban waterfront was the back door where the ships came in and the sewage flowed out, but now, instead, it's where to find the condos, lofts, and houses with wraparound decks facing out toward some shore. In Chicago the riverfront, once a grave-yard of abandoned warehouses, is now the location of upscale apartments with iron balconies overlooking the river, the same river where 19th-century engineers reversed the current to keep the raw sewage from emptying out onto the shores of Lake Michigan.

The thing about cleaned-up views of the water is the way water pulls like longing, like craving, like sex. There must be some who stand before the glass, look out at the shore, toward the frothy surf or the clip of the current, shuddering before they turn away. People, for instance, who come from the wars in Croatia or Rwanda, or the floods in New Orleans, where floating bodies lead them to believe the water takes more than it gives. But for the rest of us the shore can be the picture of crossing over, where it all, at last, begins to get better.

The thing about New Orleans is that TV news can't begin to show what happened there. When Linnea and I asked people working in the French Quarter how they were holding on since the storm, they said barely. Their houses were gone. Some got FEMA to give them a trailer, but then they had to wait a month before anyone remembered to hand over a key. The land-lords of what was left of livable shelter were kicking people out.

Everyone needs shelter, a place to dry off, to make dinner, a safe bit of somewhere to sleep. In that old song from *West Side Story*, when Tony and

Maria dream of a place, they are longing not just for a room for the night but also landfall, a shoreline.

Triptik New Orleans—IT'S ALL DEMOLISHED NOW, Mom said, practically the first thing out of her mouth when my parents picked up Linnea and me at the airport. All gone. A big flat nothing. Both Mom and Dad shook their heads as they spoke. They couldn't stop talking about the devastation all along the Gulf Coast. My dad's white hair tufted up a bit in the hot wind of the airport parking lot. I noticed my mother was wearing shorts. How hard must it be to try to fix a moldy mess of a house in this climate where it was already in the nineties in May?

Dad drove us around to look at post-Katrina New Orleans. We were no longer worried about gawking because no one was home to see us stare. What we saw caused me to hold my hand over my heart. The French Quarter, the Garden District, all the guidebook locations were on high ground, relatively unscathed, but the neighborhoods on all sides looked like what's left after a war. If the houses were upright they were knocked off their foundations, missing window glass, holes in the roof where rescue workers cut their way in or people trapped in the attic punched their way out. Frayed patches of curtains trembled in the muggy breeze. Dead gray magnolia trees lined the center of boulevards. Cars killed by the water sat in shattered driveways as if the people were still at home, making dinner for the kids, petting the dogs. The people who used to live here had shipped out to Texas, Florida, Minnesota. Some left messages spray-painted on the outside of their houses. *TONY + MARIA R SAFE—GONE 2 FLA*. Nobody was home there, not for miles.

Can you imagine, my mother kept repeating, losing a home like that? Home for my mother is what she's spent her whole life making, in order to leave her southeast side Chicago projects, and her uneasy sense of homelessness, behind.

Overlook: Population View

Who's at home in New Orleans? All those names engraved into the base of Drago's statue, all those Croats, all those Italians—they seem to turn their backs on too many others who make up the city. The African slaves, bought and sold, free or not. The waitresses and cooks in the French Quarter restaurants. The Creoles who used to own the famous brothels. The girls, some of them who used to be boys, circling the late-night streets, smiling slyly at the passing cars. The French military personnel who came to town and never left. The aging gay men with one pierced ear and short shorts who walk the same route every morning for their coffee and news, who'd hunkered down in some pre-Stonewall bar to wait out the storm. The lawyers and the realtors, the city workers and the cops. The carriage drivers and the bartenders. The ones who stayed. The ones who fled. The ones descended from those taken from some other place before they ended up here. The ones who'd never felt at home anyplace else.

Day Trip: A Far Better Place

Kata and Petar arrived at some new port, not this one. Their ride was shorter and more direct than the voyages of the Croats who came here a hundred years before, those Dalmatian sailors who traveled around the tip of Africa on their way to New Orleans or Louisiana, island people, seeking cities that shone like the sea.

When my brother and uncle traveled to old Yugoslavia in the 1980s they found a whole island of people who bore our family name. But my great grandfather was born in a mountain shack, up a scrubby hillside too rocky to farm. Big Petar was just fifteen, and those were the years young men like him, born to the provinces, were doomed to end up as ammunition in the Austro-Hungarian empire's army. The army may be why Petar and his seventeen-year-old bride hopped the boat. Or maybe he heard the stories, a neighbor or cousin just back from the New World with postcards in their pockets. They wouldn't have known what was in store, blast furnaces spitting out enough soot to blot out the sun, mineshafts like gullets.

When Big Petar, Kata, and little Petey made landfall in the harbor of Baltimore, Petar's grimy hat in his hands, his dirty blond hair lifting and falling in the harbor wind, Kata's hands, already rough from field work, squeezing the hand of her second-born and only living son, they must have thought, where is it? Squinting and leaning. Tasting the salt air as the squat houses of Baltimore slid into view. Kata may have spotted no more than a smoky tendril rising from a box of red brick. At last.

Triptik New Orleans—At first Linnea and I didn't notice the bathtub ring around New Orleans, or rather we noticed it, but it didn't occur to us what it could be, that sludge-colored line that was in some spots knee-high off the ground, in other spots just below the cracked eave of the roof. The line was the color of rust, the color of slag, what I think of as an old Chicago color because so much of the waterfront property of my childhood bordered the detritus of the steel mills, rusted, abandoned, boarded up. The broken parts of one city look a lot like the broken parts of any other—piles of bent things, wrecked warehouses, shattered glass, splintered wood, waterlogged cars, a junked-up harbor, unmeltable, unburnable debris. Human, natural, and industrial disaster look spookily the same. Except, in New Orleans, there was more of it than I'd ever seen in one place before.

The New Orleans bathtub line wasn't exactly a line, not a sharp edge so much as a wide, rusty smear, an impression stained into the body of the house, as indelible as a tattoo.

The thing about the people of New Orleans, the lucky ones who were back, is it wasn't hard to get them to tell us their story. This became what Linnea and I did on our vacation; we talked to anyone who met our eyes, asked how they'd weathered the storm.

The woman in the praline shop said she was fine, but business was bad and the woman who worked for her hadn't been right since her home came apart in the flood. The hotel bartender was OK for the moment, but customers were few, her landlord was tripling the rent, and no place cheaper wanted to deal with her dogs. The hotel desk clerk wouldn't be able to fix his house until the electricity in his neighborhood finally came back on, but even now, nine months after the floods, no one from the city could tell him when. The guy who sold me the used book, Italo Calvino's diary of American cities, said his French Quarter store and apartment were fine but his friends' houses were wrecked and the clean-up work, tearing out the mold-infested walls and floors, was no good for anyone's health. The waitress at the restaurant near the courthouse lived on high ground, but the others cleaning up the lunch shift with her—and here she stopped, pointing them out one by one. She lost her house. He lost his. That one's on high ground so she's OK, but this one here lost hers and she did also, and her—how about you honey, are you OK? But him over there, he lost his house too.

Overlook: Flood View

Imagine what it would be like if your city flooded. First your carpet is damp, then your shoes. Imagine huddling upstairs with your lover or your kids or your dogs and what little drinkable water you thought to carry up with you. Imagine they tell you the dogs have to stay behind, once the rescue workers pull you through the hole in your roof. Imagine spray-painting these words on your siding—*Maria + Tony OK. Plz save 2 dogs in bathroom.* Imagine later your house is branded with a red X, like the markings of a marauding army, the date search and rescue crews boated by, leaving numbers and code. *1 body. 2 dogs. DOA.* Imagine all your furniture and clothes and family photos vomited out onto the street, your walls furry with mold, and imagine you develop asthma from air turgid with water rot, with garbage no one is paid to pick up, with dead bodies the volunteer workers still haven't found. Imagine your home has such an excellent waterfront view that the water lines stain a rusty measure just below your bedroom windows.

Point of Departure: Geographical Crossings

Minneapolis is a city that's hard to see because it doesn't wear history on its sleeve. All but one of the glass skyscrapers were built in the last two decades. The city's most noticeable waterfront, aside from its lakes strung together like a blue glass necklace, is the shore of the same Mississippi that runs all the way down to New Orleans, but the river is narrower up here, lined not with riverboats but with the shells of flour mills on their way to becoming lofts with waterfront views.

Linnea and I own a house in Minneapolis, as does El. Like us, she bought hers when city real estate was cheap. El rebuilt the inside of her house herself, and the deck too, around which she planted honeysuckle, lilies, strawberries. If I were to describe El as a woman, I'd say she's of medium height, medium build—but she's not quite female. As a guy she's on the short side. Her hair, cropped to a curt bristle, is surprisingly soft to the touch, a fact I will discover later on, when Linnea's hair grows back after a head-shaving and El lets me run my fingertips over her noggin, to compare.

Although she's not the talkative sort, El's the definitive host. Her perfect portrait would portray her framed in an open doorway. Most lesbian artists I know in Minneapolis have attended parties on El's deck, grabbed a beer out of El's fridge, or if they're AA members, like me, made tea on her kitchen stove. I was among a few dozen women who took off their shirts in El's kitchen the night she turned thirty, accepting a dare to compare brassieres. (We all realized en masse that the early days of lesbian feminism had passed when we saw that most of us were actually wearing brassieres.) It was in El's kitchen, in front of Linnea, during the same session of Truth or Dare, that I kissed a hunky lesbian firefighter on the lips, only to be embarrassed later that summer when the firefighter became one of our neighbors. Since then we've eaten Christmas dinner in El's dining room, told stories in El's living room, shared popsicles on El's deck with a swarm of children and their lesbian moms. When El turned forty we attended a party where El's then-girlfriend performed a 1940s-style pin-up girl striptease under the backyard honeysuckle. Sometimes I'll be introduced to a woman at another party or art event who seems familiar, and we'll look hard into each other's faces, then laugh and say right, I've seen you at El's.

At the time of Peg's wedding El and her lover, the one who'd honored her birthday with such excellent burlesque, had just broken up again. El's on-and-off lover was a traveling theater artist, a woman in love with El but not in love with the way most of us define home. Linnea and I became accustomed to this friend's visits, but no matter how many times you visit a city, visiting is not living. The visiting body grazes, takes off her clothes without ever getting bare. The body who lives here becomes more than naked, opened up and healed over, part of the grit and greenery, whether she comes to love the city or not. That's finally the difference between the tourist and the resident.

At Peg's wedding El tells me her ex-again lover finds home in people, not places. I both understand and don't. Perhaps some of what El fell in love with was her lover's beautiful fleetingness, a body never static, painted toes grazing the water but never falling in.

Who would I be without the skin of a constant city? I have imagined leaving my house with the screened-in porch and brick back patio and my books and collections and two grinning blond dogs and Linnea, who still laughs at my wisecracks. I've imagined myself as a girl in a 19th-century novel, stepping off a train, a new metropolis inhabiting my hips and thighs like bordello jazz, city lights heaving up around me, the lit-up spires projecting across my chest, like those old films of dancers in jazz clubs, knees and elbows crazy, careening, palms open, faces askew with frenzied smiles.

And then what? A touch? Another marriage? A new home? A glass coffee pot and a checked apron? Sitting alone in a chair drugged up by a daydream of myself as another body, stepping out of another train, another city, another music inhabiting my hips?

I worry about leaving home. I worry about losing home. El's itinerant lover won't have to worry about her ground washing away. I'm not sure which one of us has it worse, or better.

Triptik New Orleans—New Orleans is not my home but what I've learned about the city shimmies its hips in me. Both rock-and-roll and jazz are pervasive here, and loud, even with so many musicians in exile since Katrina, opposite sounds competing at the cacophonous crossroads of the club district. Palpable on the tongue, in the nostrils, are the smoky gumbos, the blistering jambalayas, Drago's charbroiled oysters. The divides of class and race are unmistakable, in the ways I remember from my youth in Chicago, particularly on the streets surrounding the French Quarter, tourists circling in air-conditioned cars and service workers hovering in the muggy haze waiting for broken streetcars that never seem to show.

The famous voodoo vibe has become, on the surface, a commodefied artifact, reformatted to fit the racks of tourist-trap storefronts—T-shirt shops, their doors wide open to the street, witchy rock music overwhelming the sidewalks, but the old spells might still reside in the relaxed postures of the locals, black-and- white-and-mixed, driving tour buggies or playing horns on street corners for tips, dependent on, oblivious to, the gaze of tourists like my family and me.

Beyond the Quarter are neighborhoods that could have been the bombed out blocks of south central L.A. or south Chicago or any disheveled city avenue—these apocalyptic blocks somebody's mortgage, someone's broken box of a life, a street where all these months later no army has arrived to clean up, where stinking, post-Katrina refrigerators still sit on the curbs, FREE GUMBO and SMELLS LIKE FEMA spray-painted across the doors.

The absent bodies on these streets are some of the same bodies absent from Drago's waterfront monument, and their absence, in both standing evidence and in the inscriptions of history, is some of what keeps this post-Katrina New Orleans numb. Where is the waterfront statue remembering the sold and liberated slaves? The Creole business owner? The crisscross Indians who became black and the Africans who became some kind of Indian? The Korean immigrants serving coffee and beignets at Café du Monde? The flood victims? The tranny girl Linnea and I saw from our Dauphine Street balcony, sashaying and swishing until she catches the eye of a man driving a blue pick-up and points him to a quiet spot around the corner?

But what keeps this city more awake than most is the way this Southern stew collects shadows of all the rendezvous that have transpired here. It was even possible to glide past the Bourbon Street girlie shows in the company of my parents without flinching. My dad was so relaxed in New Orleans he invited Linnea and me out to see the go-go dancers at Harrah's, the emergency police headquarters during the storm now back to its roots as a jittering casino that might be the corporate future of New Orleans.

My dad stood in Harrah's next to his daughter's lesbian spouse, the city humidity crimping Linnea's salt-and-pepper curls, the loose cut of her jeans obscuring, from behind, the technicalities of her gender. My clingy black dress may have been a mistake in all that air conditioning, the chill a little too noticeable across my chest, as I walked past all those slurry-eyed men slumped over their slots. We three didn't so much gawk at the gyrating college girls dancing bare-thighed on the raised pedestals as notice they were working hard enough to perspire, burly security guards pacing below, staring down any guy who wandered in too close.

I wondered if Dad had invited us to the casino because in a city like New Orleans he could finally see Linnea as the son-in-law he always imagined for me, a smarty-pants buddy who'd banter about good books, bad Republicans, jazz history, the cultural significance of go-go girls and bars like this one, drink glasses set down in a fog of dry ice, the drinks themselves appearing to be voodoo offerings; while outside, at the waterfront, Miss Columbia stared out over the shore, hair streaming back, breasts welcoming all comers. Her back side sheltered either a promised land or a broken promise. Is this home? At last?

Day Trip: Waterfront Property

When Big Petar and Kata made landfall they stepped right off the boat and onto the train. The B & O Railroad in Baltimore Harbor had special cars for the immigrant workers. Herded in, jerked forward, they headed west.

Once, while traveling for work, I went to the old immigration port of Baltimore to look for the island pier where Kata and Big Petar had landed. I had a few hours' reprieve from a conference. A harried Visitor's Center clerk pointed across the water. I smiled and said please to the skipper of a water taxi, and he varied his usual slow-season route between the new Marriott and the chain restaurants, all built on landfill that used to be a grimy industrial port remade into visitor's-only space, unnatural gatherings delineated by profession—this week creative writing teachers, next week industrial marketers. At the dock of the Locust Point piers I high-stepped over un-shoveled snowdrifts, a choreography for which I had not packed adequate shoes. I was looking for my family's back story. I found a new office park. Train tracks. Old-time taverns. Drago had built no statue here. There wasn't even a plaque.

I walked further into a neighborhood of brick row houses where no one seemed to be home. A ceramic Madonna shrine shone from one picture window, Our Lady surrounded by plastic roses, evidence of the family life of an old-time company town. But which company? The docks were abandoned. The orange-lit Domino Sugar sign, wide and tall as a semi truck, shone its blood orange beacon over the harbor, but the water-taxi driver told me that sugar was no longer processed there.

A massive grain elevator shadowed the tight blocks where I walked, in the middle of the street to avoid the snow. I kept walking until the mill was at my back, and only then did I begin to understand why the streets of this neighborhood were so deserted. Parked along the curbs were shiny late-model SUVs, Volvos, and a Lexus or two, in between first one building site then another, with billboards that read NEW MULTI-USE PROPERTIES—UNITS START AT $300,000.

Still, a bit of a leftover world was visible here and there. An old white woman with high hair and a yellow babushka slipped down her front steps and stepped into a twenty-year-old white sedan. And some of the taverns had their original signs. *Down the Hatch. Bloomers.* At *Fran and Bill's* the sign taped to the window demanded NO LOITERING. Who was around to loiter?

I noticed the ad for a historical calendar published by the local Chamber of Commerce. BUY IT HERE. I walked into *Fran and Bill's*, a narrow neighborhood joint. The beefy guy behind the clean bar was settled into his seat and looked half asleep. He reminded me of my Polish uncles from my mother's side. Another guy who could be my uncle slouched at the end of the bar in the comfortable pose of a regular. An older dame with ratted hair and wearing a blue windbreaker was working the pinball machine. The bartender was startled when I asked to buy a calendar. Well sure, he said, you can buy all of them. It was late February. He had a few left over.

The bartender told me the looming grain mill had closed just that past January. No one knew what would happen to the site. Getting so fancy I can't afford to live around here anymore, the bartender said, which caused him to chortle, along with the regular. Even the broad who pumped quarters into the pinball machine let out a few snorts. Probably make it into waterfront property, the regular at the end of the bar slurred, and they all cracked up.

Before leaving Baltimore I bought a ticket to the "Top of the World" observation deck of the Baltimore World Trade Center, which the sign in the elevator told me was the tallest five-sided building in the world. Five-sided was the key phrase here, because as far as buildings go it was not so tall, just the tallest thing in sight, aside from the Domino Sugar sign.

The music piped in through the speakers was an endless loop of Anne Murray singing "Top of the World." From the observation windows looking out over Baltimore Harbor, I could imagine the German steamer, carrying Big Petar and Kata and Little Petey, riding in toward the docks. There would have been no beacon advertising Domino Sugar in 1908. No twenty-story hotels or fenced-off patches of gravel marked on the map as sites of future development.

The printed guide said that this waterfront was a no-man's-land before the developers saved it, but I thought it must have been *some* man's land. I could make out the finger of ground reaching into the harbor—Locust Point —and the pier pilings where my relations would have stepped off the boat, dizzy, hungry, elated after the nauseating voyage. Most of the immigrants, I'd read, who disembarked here had contracts with the Midwestern mills and mines, and so stepped right off the boat and onto a train, ushered by anxious mine agents, counting heads. From the "Top of the World" I could see the train tracks I'd walked across the day before, and from that vantage point I walked along the hexagon of windows, tracking the route the train would have taken, away from that waterfront property, deep, deep into the land.

Overlook: Memorial View

Looking at New Orleans after the floods, it's not hard to remember that all the glorious old cities in history did eventually die. Ur, Eridu, Babylon, all once the site of functioning governments and religions, once places people lived, are now just archeology sites, as well as the locations of end- less war. Post-Katrina New Orleans might be the start of such a crumbling, although, granted, the dissolve might take centuries.

I find I expect the cities to dissolve. Most of the apartments I've lived in since moving to Minneapolis have been torn down. Most of the cars I've driven on the streets of my little city were junked after the last time I drove them. Half of the industrial suburb where I lived during grade school, once a booming company town, is boarded up, abandoned, unsaved. I perpetually expect to turn around and see the geography of my past crumbling like what's left of a tissue-paper city after it catches fire.

But in calmer moments I don't expect the cities to burn or drown, and I long to live on high ground, in a loft with big windows, one of the new ones overlooking the old flourmill ruins in downtown Minneapolis, with views of the Mississippi curving through the University, then disappearing south toward New Orleans.

But what if all the levees break and the rivers overflow? What if the cities of America are replaced by conference cities, museum cities, Waterfront Property Inc., precious replicas under glass?

Triptik New Orleans—After dinner at Drago's Oyster Bar my dad asked a stranger to take our picture with old Drago himself. Drago nodded without cracking a smile, his bald head bobbing lazily, his bushy eyebrows reminding me of Croat uncles on my father's side. Sure, sure, glad you're here, Drago's posture told us, but if you weren't then some other customer would be sucking up the same air, so please don't take up too much of my time. I stand next to Drago in the snapshot, his arm on my shoulder, my arm on Linnea's shoulder, my dad and mom completing the chain, Dad and Linnea echoing each other's open stance, Dad and Drago wearing similar summer Hawaiian-print shirts, our bodies together a statue in themselves, of several crossings.

When I tried to talk to Drago he wasn't too interested in my questions. Your oysters, I asked, is this the way they're prepared back on the Dalmatian islands? Sure, sure, he said, but what did he care about what they did over there? Drago was part of New Orleans now, and had been for something like fifty years. Any wars he'd lived through were here. But his restaurant, safe on suburban high ground, didn't flood too bad this time, and business was good.

Point of Destination: High Ground

The un-bride-like bride flushes red, happy all the way through her wedding, even as her pantyhose shreds from her thighs to her ankles, some crossings only temporary. When I look up from my reception table huddle, Linnea is standing behind me with a box of water bottles, her face ruddy with the heat, her short hair curling tighter in this muggy underground. She kisses me on the neck and I lean back into her belt.

When Linnea moves on to deliver more water to the masses I notice, across the table, a woman with a puff of gray-blond hair—she'd come with one of Linnea's motorcycle buddies—watching me. In her silver-blue blouse she looks cooler, and less at home, than the rest of us.

She used to know Linnea, the woman volunteers. They'd worked together, once. Some committee at the University. Turns out she'd been listening to my conversation with El, about whether open marriage ever works, about losing love, about what it might take to start over, to date again. The woman must have heard something in my voice, the restless part of me, twenty years married, musing, too loudly. Maybe she thinks I'm flirting with El. Maybe she doesn't get that I'd no more flirt with any of the butch and Bubba relatives than with Nea's Harley-guy brother. Maybe she finds it indefensible that I can't seem to love my home without imagining it gone.

I see now that this woman, despite her ice-blue aura, has anxious eyes, the ungrounded look of someone recently flooded out. By her hard squint I see that she doesn't think much of me. When she said *I know Linnea*, did she mean she thinks she's caught me doing something I shouldn't? And had she? Now she asks, but it's not a question—Why do you wonder about the problems of dating? You're the one who won the lottery.

She's sure I don't deserve my prize. And maybe I don't, but still, I bristle. Yet all I can do is gaze back through her bright blue ice. Say yes, I know, I've been lucky so far, all these years on love's high ground.

Triptik New Orleans—In New Orleans the difference between high and low ground was striking. As Dad drove us past the shells of smallish houses I noticed how similar they were to the brown brick bungalow we lived in when I was in grade school, the first home my parents owned. You work your whole life for a home, Mom said, and then what do you do when it's all of a sudden ruined?

I sidled up to Linnea, pressed my arm into hers. We didn't come here to celebrate fifty years of family squabbles. My parents' marriage was their business, but home was another thing.

As Dad drove us into the city, down Canal Street and through the sodden and demolished neighborhoods, I kept one hand on my heart, as if I meant to keep it from spilling out. We are safe among the survivors, celebrating fifty years of some kind of high ground. We are driving by the museum of the end of the world, hands on our hearts, wondering how to celebrate the longevity of refuge in a place where nobody's left at home.

Alice & Emily, Diana & Dunes

In winter, the Indiana Dunes are cold, gusty, deserted. The Northwest Wind blows across Lake Michigan and lifts the dunes' grainy surface so that the hills seem to smoke with swirling sand. The beach is a blank slate, tamped-down, and everything is so still I think I can *see* the dunes moving, mountains retreating, grain by grain, from the vast, encroaching flatness of this Great Lake. The windblown sand rushes down the slopes and I hear the dull, hollow moan that makes geophysicists call these "singing sands." As a girl, I was fascinated by haunting tales of the region; fifteen years later, I still feel the landscape evokes a certain calm and eerie despair. Tourist season has ended and this visit is a solitary one, a Midwestern pilgrimage to seek out writer and naturalist Alice Gray, the so-called "Diana" of these Dunes, and to reconcile ghost story, legend, and truth.

For decades, it's been said that on a cloudy night on the shore between Lake Michigan and the Indiana Dunes you can see a ghostly figure—all vapor and mist—walking the cold damp sands, slipping into the water. They say Diana of the Dunes still haunts the sand hills she once roamed, still bathes in the icy gray lake. In 1915, she left Chicago society to nurse a broken heart, retiring to a simpler life, a lonely sabbatical on the then-desolate shore. Twice daily she stripped off a threadbare shift and swam. When she emerged, dripping like a naiad, she ran across the sands until her bare skin was dry. Years later, she shared her driftwood cottage with a giant of a man, a drifter, enchanted by her charms. They say one night her dog howled and cried so loud and mournful, that villagers set off down the beach to see what was the matter. Her giant was gone, her broken limbs scattered up and down the shore; some claim to see her face floating, almost as if walking, where the water washes over the sand.

As a girl, my summer mornings were devoted to daily swimming lessons in an aqua-colored public pool. Two hours later, I climbed the hill to my neighborhood branch of the Indianapolis library, where I, still dripping, shivered in the sudden air-conditioning. I perused books about girls living alone in the wilderness—*A Girl of the Limberlost* and *Island of the Blue Dolphins*—and tallied my points for the summer reading program. In the afternoons, my mom left me at the city's children's museum. Even though the main floors offered hands-on dinosaur digs and recreated Egyptian temples, I was a daily patron of the Ruth Lilly Children's Theater in the basement, a rapt audience for dramatized readings and professional storytellers. When

I went home, I typed up my own stories about brave girls—princesses, twin sisters separated at birth, pirate's daughters, and plucky orphans—who lived alone and fended for themselves in the woods or by the sea. One autumn night, my mom took me to the Hoosier Storytelling Festival on the banks of the White River. I lay on a scratchy blanket under the stars listening to quietly chilling Indiana ghost stories set against a spooky backdrop of lapping water and rustling trees. A melancholy daydreamer even then, I fell in love with the eerie tales of Diana of the Dunes.

My belief in these ghost stories found support in the still-popular northern Indiana legend—romanticized accounts of the South Shore's historic hermit Alice Gray. In 1915, the young woman—a writer—left nearby Chicago and took up residence in an abandoned shack on the Indiana shore of Lake Michigan. She called her new home Driftwood and furnished it with whatever she could scavenge from the beach, selling berries and souvenirs of the Dunes and living in relative solitude—a bohemian figure who scandalized locals with her stark lifestyle and nude swims. It's said the general store sold out of binoculars for weeks on end—area fishermen were eager to catch a glimpse of the beach goddess. Chicago newspapers caught wind of the story and the girl became a media sensation, christened "Diana of the Dunes." One wrote, "If you were lucky one night when the moon was up and bathing the dune crests in its soft greenish glow, you could see Diana. She would stand there, beautiful in the moonlight, arms outstretched…breasts firm, thighs gently curving, like a statue of Galatea." Newspapers around the world picked up the modern-day myth, writing of her idyllic life and styling her as a champion for the Dunes' preservation. A Texas rattlesnake hunter heard tales of her ethereal beauty and wild exploits and set off to make her his own. She accepted him into her solitary life, but ultimately their love soured and Diana died of uremic poisoning (complicated, it's said, by repeated blows to her small frame). Her lover vanished, but today the region's residents give rise to the ghost story, claiming to see her still—a slender young woman darting across the sand and into the water.

When I was a little girl, my family often came here to the Indiana Dunes. Even in summer, the water was too cold to really swim: I remember pacing up and down the beach. The waves packed the sand down at the shore and I liked the way I could walk all the way to the pier without leaving a footprint. Today is the first time I've been here in winter; the beach is empty and the picnic shelter abandoned. The dunes are young and bare by the water; close to the shore, the sands move and even hardy marram grass can only take hold farther away from the waves. In front of me, the blue-gray of Lake Michigan, cold but not yet icing up; behind me, the slowly shifting landmass of the Indiana Dunes; above, the sky a flat, cloudless gray, clear but not sunny. On a lonely November day, this feels like the end of the world, and indeed, it is the end of Indiana, the lake cutting a crescent from the perfect right angle of my home state's northwest border.

Lake Michigan carries the sand to the South Shore, and the constant Northwest Wind pushes little rises of sand into new dunes. Over the years they drift away from the water, until their movement slows, the smooth slopes broken by marram grass, then jack pine and black oak, until they are no longer even recognizable as sand dunes. Today, I follow the trail around Cowles Bog; it winds inland, by the South Shore Line railroad and takes me around the marsh and fen, all the way back to the lake. These wetland dunes are in a state of transition—they are not bare and shifting, singing like those close to the water, but they are not quite still. The trees' grip is tenuous and smaller plants and groundcover are rare. Even between the trees, the trail is sandy and steep, and my boots sink back, pulling me down half a step for every labored uphill stride. I walk along the peak, the slipface, this fine ridgeline where the slowly sloping sand no longer resists the wind, but collapses over the ridge.

When I was young, my geologist father spent summers and much of the rest of the year working here; a hundred years ago, he would have been a consummate woodsman, and he tried to entice his bookish daughter with camping, hikes, and impromptu science lessons. On road trips, he only let me sit in the front seat if I would put away my novel and watch the landscape go by, listening to his narration of the region's geologic history. My mom, little sister, and I drove up I-65 from Indianapolis on summer weekends to stay in his motel room and spend our days at the Dunes. On Sunday mornings, it was our ritual to climb the highest "living" dune, Mount Baldy, and breakfast on gritty milk and sandy doughnuts on top. Called a living dune for its wandering tendencies, I liked to think I could *feel* its annual four-foot drift, could tell how much farther it crept from the water's edge each year.

I didn't make sand castles, but instead collected driftwood for my own tiny cottages. I scoured the beach for soft pieces of sea glass, broken bottles worn dull and smooth by sand and the tide. They became green, white, and brown paths that led up to diminutive fences—upright mussel shells wedged into the sand. Our favorite beach was unpopulated, and I pictured myself as a winsome wilderness maiden—fair-haired and freckled and alone. Walking far enough down the beach that our station wagon was out of sight, I half hoped my mom would forget me one day. I imagined myself finding shelter under the boardwalk stairs and weaving skirts out of bent grass. I would have a pet gull or maybe a sandpiper. I would find spare change in the sand and subsist on candy bars from the nearby Nature Center. I would write my stories on peeling white bark from the birches that surrounded Cowles Bog, leaving them for park rangers to find.

Lately, I've been thinking of Alice Gray again. At eleven, I was attracted to the ghost story—a howling dog, a giant, a water spirit, scattered limbs—but as I grew older, I became more attached to the legend, less grisly, but more mystery and romance. I pictured a young, misunderstood writer and idealized what must have been a harsh and lonely life. I liked to imagine her spirit pacing the shore, remembering the area as it was when she first retreated there in 1915. Once a near wilderness celebrated by Chicago artists and activists, and later eroded by the rapidly growing steel town of Gary, the Indiana Dunes are now segmented and claimed by state and national parks, preserved for hikers, naturalists, and beach vacationers, and I wonder what she would think of it all.

I need to find my own Diana, and so I've driven north, through small-town Indiana, to revisit the Dunes of my youth and hers. I've come in winter, partly because I can't wait for spring, and partly because when I picture Alice Gray's Dunes, the beach is cold and unpopulated. I haven't climbed the dunes in almost twenty years and I feel a bit like a wilderness pioneer with my bottle of hand-pressed apple cider and a cellophane-wrapped loaf of pumpkin bread, both purchased this morning from a roadside stand in Crown Point.

No longer satisfied with ghosts and legends, I want to know the real woman, Alice Gray. I've sifted through the fact and fiction of newspaper clippings, myth, and personal account but the few consistencies only suggest a bare-bones truth. Alice Gray was a recluse whom no one knew well, and she remains elusive; understanding her story lies just beyond my reach. I thought if only I could experience her solitude, walk through her woods and on her beach, see what she saw in this place, I might uncover some intuition of what brought her to this desolate shore.

Alice Gray was the educated daughter of a prominent Chicago couple and thirty-five (positively middle-aged in 1915) when she left the Second City for the Indiana Dunes. Nothing about her suggested a youthful naiad; her frame was short, stout, her skin, browned from exposure, and her hair, hacked-off—she cropped it herself, looking at the shadow it cast on the sand. Newspaper illustrations of a beautiful, sylph-like maiden are belied by the few remaining black and white photographs that prove her to have been quite plain, a decidedly unromantic figure.

The legends of her naked swims seem to have been based on fact; word of a comely and immodest beachcomber lured fishermen seeking a peek and raised the ire of one errant man's confrontational wife. She found this imagined Bathsheba to be far from an ethereal temptress; Gray brandished a gun and chased her from the beach. The wife informed the *Chicago Examiner* and from her angry account, area journalists fabricated a legend that would cast a ripple to newspapers around the world, a beautiful beachcomber, a "water nymph." For several years, the tale of this "Diana of the Dunes" would resurface as public interest in the Dunes waxed and waned and as Alice Gray became a permanent fixture on the shore. Later, the same publications would denounce her as "brown as a berry and tolerably husky," speaking almost as if it were Alice Gray's intent to deceive, as if she too had a romanticized view of herself and her odd, reclusive life on the harsh shore of Lake Michigan.

As a girl, my vision of Diana of the Dunes was idealized; I wanted the legend to be real, a life within my reach, but now I crave the prosaic facts of my heroine's life. Perhaps the reality seems far more admirable, attainable. Rather than a wisp of a girl in love with the drama of crashing waves, singing sands, and shifting dunes, the real Alice Gray was decisive, strong, and very intelligent, resolute in her decision to forge an independent life.

After her 1903 graduation from the University of Chicago, the twenty-two year-old Alice Gray worked for the U.S. Naval Observatory, where she is remembered as a noteworthy researcher; later, she moved to Germany to study astronomy and tidal patterns at Göttingen University, and there she was introduced to the *Wandervogel* movement. Its young followers made plans to abandon society and pursue a more natural existence in the wild. Though she wouldn't act on it for years, the idea of a free hermitage alone on the lakeshore she'd loved as a child must have haunted her.

After extensive education and travel, Alice Gray returned to work—some say as an assistant editor and some say as a stenographer—for the University of Chicago's *Astro-Physical Journal*. It frustrated and enraged her that male colleagues were paid more than she, and that there were scant opportunities for a woman writer. At thirty-five, she retired to a reclusive life on the South Shore—she would later explain to reporters that a city-bound life as a wage-earner was "slavery," and that she longed for Byron's ideal: *In solitude, when we are least alone.*

I imagine her stepping off the South Shore Line and feeling, after ten years in Chicago, as though she could finally release a pent-up breath. I've been walking all morning, and every time I pause, to look around, to reassess, I almost shudder at how different, how relaxed and unburdened, I feel here. In winter, this place is quiet, still, almost dead, but more than any other wilderness I've seen, it makes me want to write, and more than that, to simply be still, to watch and to listen.

On my childhood summer vacations, my golden little sister only loved the beach on days when it was so fair and clear we imagined we could see Chicago, and when the water was finally almost warm enough to swim. But even on sunny days, the palette of the Great Lakes seems a little grayer, more Midwestern and real, than coastal beaches. I liked the overcast days—they made me think of gloom and mystery, ideas that offered more scope for my quiet imagination. I didn't mind the clammy water, standing with my bare feet in the cold, dull sand. Looking out at the muted expanse of Lake Michigan, I felt very small, but alone and free.

In winter the shore bears only the mark of the Northwest Wind, writing cursive ripples into a beach unmarred by footprints and tire treads. When it's very cold, the crashing waves build an ice shelf: delicate mounds of dingy white filled with airy pockets, the shelf a rough blanket that can extend hundreds of feet from the shore. But it's November yet, and not so cold I can't imagine spending the night here, curling up under the boardwalk, scribbling in my notebook by moonlight.

In solitude, when we are least alone: it sounds contradictory but I too find my favorite company to be my own and am only lonely when surrounded. Most days, I want what she had at the Dunes. Here, with a life uncluttered by engagements, obligations, restrictions, and deadlines, Alice Gray could finally feel free to pursue her research and writing. In her own words, she moved to the Dunes with nothing but "a jelly glass, a knife, a spoon, a blanket and two guns." Her last paycheck funded nearly a year on the lakeshore—she bought only bread and salt. Her life sounds difficult—the Northwest Wind is harsh and cold—but even so, I think for her, staying in Chicago, ambition and temperament stifled, settling for a meager life editing and typing the work of others, was unbearable. Little of her prolific writing remains, but what survives is researched and poetic prose that reflects an education grounded in universities and the wild, and a wholehearted devotion to the natural landscape of the South Shore. She must have felt caged in the city, and despite her academic achievements and scientific studies, she would have been branded a spinster.

As I stand in the woods and look down at the beach, at the dunes and Lake Michigan, I wonder what I am really looking for today, why Alice Gray and Diana of the Dunes weigh so heavily on my mind of late. Is it just that I envy her solitude, a quiet sojourn on a very lonely and poetic lakeshore? Or am I awed by the mental, emotional, and perhaps spiritual fortitude that she must have summoned to come out here in the first place? As much as I want this freedom, this life all my own, I make my own distractions, always finding new projects and endeavors and relationships that tie me more securely to my cluttered life. Even Alice Gray chose a stretch of shore that was secluded and *almost* wilderness, but the small town of Ogden Dunes was near—just seven miles—and she walked there each week for supplies and library books.

Ever the geologist's daughter, I stop to read every sign and placard I encounter on my hike. There is nothing to indicate that these trails have been disturbed for days, and I like the way park tourism is implied but presently absent. From my father, I know that glaciers once moved across the Midwest, carving out great hollows and peeling back the land, leaving behind the vast, flat, once wooded landscape of my home in Indiana. As the Laurentide ice sheet receded north, melting, it filled these five basins with Lakes Huron, Ontario, Erie, Superior, and Michigan, the largest lake group on Earth.

The Dunes were an overlooked wilderness until ecologist and botanist Henry Cowles brought them international attention in 1899. The two-billion-year-old collision of tectonic plates left the area with a unique collage of an ecosystem: prairies and bogs, marshes and forests, savannah and sand hills—at the Dunes, arctic bearberry grows next to desert cactus. I've always understood the writer Alice Gray's wish for solitude but it is only today, really looking at the landscape, accompanied by my brand new *Hiker's Guide to the Indiana Dunes*, that I really understand the scope the Dunes offered her as a scientist.

When the Industrial Revolution transformed Northwestern Indiana into Steeltown, USA, stabilization of an ever-shifting landscape effectively killed most of the "living" dunes. The largest—Hoosier Slide—was hauled away, boxcar by boxcar, to Muncie, Indiana, to be made into Ball Glass jars—it's likely Alice Gray's single jelly jar had the Ball script raised on its front.

Today, for the most part, these great sand hills remain where we think they should—only a few wandering dunes still creep toward great beach houses, threatening to smother their lakeside porches in sand. As the dirty steel industry of Gary, Indiana, encroached on and eroded the shore, a concerned Cowles founded the Prairie Club, a preservation movement devoted to saving the Dunes. He was completing his doctoral work at the University of Chicago just as Alice Gray was beginning her study of astronomy, mathematics, and tides.

Sixteen years later, surely inspired in part by Cowles' efforts, she became the Dunes' most dedicated researcher, writing of its natural history, its flora and fauna. Though it's said Alice Gray gave nature tours to area children, she only wanted the Dunes preserved for herself and other true naturalists—not for the curiosity seekers attracted by her legend and the newspapers' descriptions of the scenic shore. Even so, she agreed to speak at the "Great Dunes Pageant of 1917," a publicity stunt she must have found ridiculous, with its actors and dancers costumed as American Indians and soldiers, satyrs and naiads, gulls and mosquitoes. Her scientific description of the Dunes' geologic history was lyric and persuasive; parts of the essay she read that night were published in the *Prairie Club Bulletin* and she is often quoted for the poetic characterization of the Indiana Dunes as the "child of Lake Michigan and the Northwest Wind." She implored the audience to preserve the South Shore: "Besides its nearness to Chicago and its beauty, its spiritual power, there is between the Dune country and the city a more than sentimental bond—a family tie. To see the Dunes destroyed would be for Chicago the sacrilegious sin which is not forgiven."

But residents of the largely industrial region resented the interference of city-dwelling progressives, and the local paper, the *Chesterton Tribune*, attacked her. From the beginning, she hated her celebrity and begged journalists to understand her wish for solitude; it must have stung to be accused of wanting attention, especially when one paper even cast doubt on the originality of her writing, deriding her talent as a false facet of the fabricated Diana mythology. They suggested that she was naïve to let herself be used as a tool—a pretty figurehead—by the men from the National Dunes Park Association, and they reprimanded her for not leading a life more purposeful. Perhaps, they suggested, she should consider the Red Cross. She was belittled as a lovesick spinster not worthy of attention.

As much as I might want her solitude, as good as it feels to be alone, it also feels a little vulnerable to love only books and walks and writing. I've grown so attached to having the quiet life I always wanted, that few people ever seem worth a shift—from giving up my Saturday evening to sharing a dresser drawer, I am reluctant to sacrifice even a small piece of my time and space. It is necessary ties to work, school, and family that make me want a companion with whom to navigate the life beyond my peaceful home; like Alice Gray, I know what it is to find a partner with a similarly reclusive nature, someone who loves you enough to leave you alone. I can almost understand why, after five years of a solitary life, she joined her fate to Paul Wilson, a brash, violent, and passionately devoted man who was likely responsible for her death.

Alice Gray's entanglement in the push to "Save the Dunes!" tied her once more to the society and conflict she had tried to escape and I think it was then that she needed the companionship of the fiercely protective and possessive Paul Wilson. At six and a half feet, he would come to be known as the "Giant of the Dunes" and she spoke of being initially struck by his "magnificent physique"—an observation that would have sounded baldly sexual in 1920s Indiana. He had a suspicious history with the law and was alleged to have a violent temper; Wilson probably wasn't even his real name, but one he adopted, leaving behind the convict Paul Eisenblatter. His pairing with the local beachcomber seems unlikely, but I picture her, gun in hand, running off an intrusive fishwife, and I think she would have understood the conflicts between a recluse and the world and appreciated the brash and handsome man, a giant who worshipped at her feet. Besides, he was resourceful and strong, content to share a new shack they christened the Wren's Nest. By all accounts, he was jealously devoted, and he defended her from the journalists who hounded and slandered her, drove off meddlesome tourists.

Alice Gray was forty when they met, and a forty-year-old single woman in 1920 was much older than she would be now. Just when the romance had faded from her seclusion, when newspapers were more aggressive than enraptured, and the shore and the marsh and the woods were thoroughly explored, a man presented himself, one who identified with her peculiar and unconventional life and wanted to share it, just as it was. After five years alone, how must it have felt, at a time and place where she could have never expected it, to encounter a rare being who would see in her the myth and the woman at once?

By all accounts, Paul Wilson and Alice Gray were happy for two years— they planned to marry at the long anticipated opening of the Dunes as a national park, but this delayed distinction would not be made for the sand hills until 1966, more than forty years after her death. But in part due to Gray's preservation advocacy and the public's continuing interest in Diana, the Indiana Dunes increasingly brought summer vacationers to the beach. The couple's relationship took a downward spiral soon after it was speculated that they were responsible for several beach house burglaries; when a man's body was found on the shore by the Wren's Nest, Wilson was an immediate suspect. The unscrupulous deputy sheriff was making it his business to lead tourists to the driftwood shack for a glimpse of the still famous beach goddess; linking Wilson to the possible murder case was a convenient way of drawing the violently protective Giant away from his Diana.

The day Wilson's name was cleared, he returned to the Wren's Nest and found the profiteering intruder. The details of the altercation are unclear but the deputy was arrested, and Paul Wilson and Alice Gray hospitalized—he sustained a gunshot wound in his foot and she suffered a cracked skull, a trauma from which she never fully recovered. While Wilson and Gray convalesced, locals raided the Wren's Nest for souvenirs—Gray's writings were lost.

It seemed that Alice Gray could never really have the seclusion and quiet she wanted. The next few years of her life—the last, as it turned out—were marked by turmoil. Her cachet as a local curiosity was dwindling and the couple were unwelcome in the now bourgeoisie summer community. They made plans to transplant to a houseboat and travel to the Gulf of Mexico— perhaps she hoped an escape and new wild landscape could revive the relationship. Their whereabouts were unknown for some time and it was said they may have reached New Orleans, or even Texas. But the journey was unsuccessful and they returned to the Wren's Nest—after that, the papers abandoned the romanticized legend and wrote only of her and Wilson's altercations with the locals.

Alice Gray had resisted the Diana myth for so long; I wonder if she wished she had embraced it and thus received the accepting allowance given a charming eccentric, rather begrudging tolerance. She'd been happy alone and must have realized that Wilson's stormy temperament jeopardized the peaceful, reclusive life she'd sought for so long. Perhaps if they'd had the solitude of castaways, they would have remained, coexisting, in a simple and solitary life on a quiet lakeshore. It surprises me that a woman of such unconventional intelligence and strength would have borne his temper and rumored abuse. But she was still suffering from her head wounds, and troubled about a strained and contentious relationship with locals—perhaps more than ever, she felt dependent on her Paul Wilson.

No one knows for sure what happened on a February night in 1925. A local developer said Wilson came to his house, seeking a doctor for an unconscious Alice Gray—and that later that night she died in her giant's arms. An Indianapolis newspaper wrote that she "scorn[ed] medical treatment, preferring death on the sand." A 1970s researcher revealed that Wilson was in jail that night and could not have seen his lover dying of uremic poisoning, caused and complicated by his beatings.

Her funeral was a Diana-of-the-Dunes tourist frenzy, replete with souvenirs, and only once did her obituary refer to her not as Diana, but as Alice Gray. An enraged and devastated Paul Wilson fired his gun into the crowd, vowed revenge on the journalists, and threatened suicide; though no one was harmed, he was removed by authorities. He stole a car and within a year he was dead, shot in a bungled burglary.

Alice Gray was buried in Gary, Indiana, in a grave that went unmarked until 1997. It seems a restrictive and too conventional end—she wanted to be cremated, her ashes scattered from the peak of Mount Tom. At 192 feet, it is Indiana's highest dune; from the summit, you can see Chicago.

After hours of hiking, I'm finally warm and I stuff my wool hat and gloves in my coat pockets. At low points, the sandy trail gives way to a boardwalk that keeps my boots dry and steers overzealous hikers from traversing the delicate marshland and the floating fen—a sort of peat moss island. I sit for a while, drinking my cider, and though it's against park regulations, I tear off a small twist of cinnamon fern and the brilliant orange-red bittersweet that skirts the trail, and tug it through my jacket buttonhole—a Diana-esque corsage.

I walk slow the last mile to the shore—I'm finally close enough to hear Lake Michigan and Alice Gray seems very near. I wonder why she remained with Paul Wilson, and I imagine her pacing the shore and thinking of her years alone, living in the shack she called Driftwood. In my vision, she no longer runs—she is forty-five—and she won't swim naked anymore. The beaches have new rules and regulations, and though once a local curiosity and even a champion for dune preservation, she is now merely tolerated, her presence here tenuous—perhaps she desires the protection and companionship of even a violent fellow recluse. She let the Northwest Wind carry her from Chicago to the Indiana Dunes, deposited on the shore to gather a legend about her, growing larger and more mythic than any normal woman. Having shifted the pieces of her solitary life to make room for a cause and then a partner, she can't move them back—like the dunes, she can only wander in one direction, moving ever further and further from the lake and the shore, until no longer recognizable.

I finally reach the lakeshore again—gloomy and overcast. I can't see anyone and the fog makes Gary smokestacks and distant Chicago skyscrapers invisible. The blank palette of sand chokes out so much clutter; sea rocket, leathery sand cherries and clumps of bent grass seem planted there by magic and I can't imagine what succor their roots might find. The low moan of the wind on the singing sands is a white noise that strips away the hum of traffic and the industrial surroundings.

As a girl, I always wanted to find a large nautilus shell, imagined holding it to my ear and listening to the ocean, but lake ecology is less exotic than saltwater and I only ever found zebra mussels, an invasive species not even native to the Great Lakes. My logical father showed me that only the concave shape was needed—I could hear the *whoosh* of the waves in my cupped hand. But I still preferred the idea of Diana whispering to me from a chambered shell.

Before scientists wrote of singing sands, I imagine South Shore natives must have thought the soft rumble of the wandering dunes sounded ghostly—the way wind carries sand up to the crest of the dune until there is a tipping point, and all those rough granules slide down—a soft, low roar, a sigh. Despite my father's unromantic explanation for the phenomenon, I like to imagine the free spirit of an independent woman, pacing the packed, wet sand and chasing scraps of her purloined papers across the shore.

As I write this, there are few tangible traces of Alice Gray and Diana of the Dunes—a plain granite slab in Gary, scraps of her prose in journalists' quotes. Chesterton beauty queens no longer compete for Diana's crown in the once annual Diana of the Dunes Festival, and I only hear of her in ghost stories and Hoosier poems. I don't know that I've found my mythic Diana, but today I feel very close to the woman Alice Gray, and almost ready to leave this vast, quiet shore and return to my small and cluttered life. Sunset comes early in late November and park regulations dictate that I must be off the beach by twilight; today, that will mean a little before five. I crouch down in the slack, the valley-like trough between the dunes. Alice Gray's Northwest Wind lifts the sand so that Mount Tom appears to smoke—wisps of sand rise up and sway like spirits and I can't help but think she found her way here after all. Though overcast, the beach is dry and the low, dull moan of the singing sands brings to mind ghost stories, quiet and desolate. Each crescent shaped dune cries like a geodynamic loudspeaker; they seem to project long-ago recordings of Diana, a call that is eerie, sad, and hauntingly real.

Rights and Permissions

Contributors

JONIS AGEE is the author of thirteen books, including the novels *Sweet Eyes; Strange Angels;* and *The River Wife;* and the short fiction collections *A .38 Special and a Broken Heart; Taking the Wall;* and *Acts of Love on Indigo Road.* Three of her books—*Strange Angels, Bend This Heart,* and *Sweet Eyes*—were named Notable Books of the Year by *The New York Times.*

ELIZABETH ALEXANDER is a writer whose poetry collections include *American Sublime; Antebellum Dream Book; The Venus Hottentot;* and *Body of Life.* Her poems, short stories, and critical writing have appeared in *Paris Review, American Poetry Review, The Village Voice,* and *The Washington Post.* She teaches in the English and African American Studies Departments at Yale University.

SHERMAN J. ALEXIE, JR. is a Spokane/Coeur d'Alene Indian whose first collection of short stories, *The Lone Ranger and Tonto Fistfight in Heaven,* (Atlantic Monthly Press, 1993) received a PEN/Hemingway Award for Best First Book of Fiction. Alexie was named one of Granta's Best of Young American Novelists and won the Before Columbus Foundation's American Book Award and the Murray Morgan Prize for his first novel, *Reservation Blues,* (Atlantic Monthly Press, 1995). His second novel, *Indian Killer,* (Atlantic Monthly Press, 1996), was named one of People's Best of Pages and a New York Times Notable Book.

DOROTHY ALLISON describes herself as a feminist, a working-class story teller, a Southern expatriate, a sometime poet and a happily born-again Californian. Allison's short story collection, *Trash* (1988) was published by Firebrand Books. *Trash* won two Lambda Literary Awards and the American Library Association Prize for Lesbian and Gay Writing. Allison's novel *Bastard Out of Carolina,* (1992) was a finalist for the 1992 National Book Award. The novel won the Ferro Grumley prize, and an ALA Award for Lesbian and Gay Writing. *Cavedweller* (1998) was a *New York Times* Notable book of the year, finalist for the Lillian Smith prize, and an ALA prizewinner.

MARVIN BELL is a poet whose first book, *Things We Dreamt We Died For,* was published in 1966. His collection *A Probable Volume of Dreams* (Atheneum, 1969), was a Lamont Poetry Selection of the Academy of American Poets; and *Stars Which See, Stars Which Do Not See* (1977), was a finalist for the National Book Award. Bell has published numerous books of prose and poetry, most recently *Mars Being Red* (Copper Canyon Press, 2007), which was a finalist for the Los Angeles Times Book Award.

BARRIE JEAN BORICH is the author of *Body Geographic*, forthcoming in the American Lives Series of the University of Nebraska Press (2012). *My Lesbian Husband* (Graywolf) was awarded the ALA Stonewall Book Award and she's the recipient of the 2010 *Florida Review* Editor's Prize in the Essay and the 2010 *Crab Orchard Review* Literary Nonfiction Prize. She's an assistant professor in the MFA/BFA programs at Hamline University, where she's the nonfiction editor of *Water~Stone Review.*

NICKOLE BROWN'S books include her debut, *Sister*, a novel-in-poems published by Red Hen Press, and the anthology, *Air Fare,* that she co-edited with Judith Taylor. She was the editorial assistant for the late Hunter S. Thompson, and is the Editor for the Marie Alexander Series in Prose Poetry at White Pine Press. She serves as the National Publicity Consultant for Arktoi Books.

PHILIP BRYANT has published poetry in *The Iowa Review, The Indiana Review, The American Poetry Review*, and *Nimrod*. Crossroads Press published *Blue Island*, a chapbook, in 1997. New Rivers press released *Sermon on a Perfect Spring Day* in 1998. Blueroad Press published his collection of Jazz poems, *Stompin' at the Grand Terrace* along with accompanying CD in 2009.

JAMES CIHLAR is the author of the poetry book *Undoing* (Little Pear Press) and chapbook *Metaphysical Bailout* (Pudding House Press), and his poems have been published in *Prairie Schooner, Painted Bride Quarterly,* and *Verse Daily*. His reviews appear in the *Minneapolis Star Tribune, Western American Literature, Coldfront*, and *Gently Read Literature.*

ALISON HAWTHORNE DEMING is the author of *Science and Other Poems*, winner of the Walt Whitman Award of the Academy of American Poets, and three additional poetry books, *The Monarchs: A Poem Sequence; Genius Loci;* and *Rope*. Deming has published three nonfiction books, *Temporary Homelands; The Edges of the Civilized World*; and *Writing the Sacred Into the Real.* She edited *Poetry of the American West: A Columbia Anthology* and co-edited *The Colors of Nature: Essays on Culture, Identity, and the Natural World.* Her work appears in *The Norton Book of Nature Writing* and *Best American Science and Nature Writing.*

ANTHONY DOERR is the author of four books: *Memory Wall; The Shell Collector; About Grace;* and *Four Seasons in Rome*. His fiction has won three O. Henry Prizes and has been anthologized in *The Best American Short Stories, The Anchor Book of New American Short Stories*, and *The Scribner Anthology of Contemporary Fiction.*

MARK DOTY is an award-winning poet and memoirist. His eight books of poetry include *School of the Arts, Source, Atlantis,* and *My Alexandria*. His *Fire to Fire: New and Selected Poems* won the National Book Award for Poetry in 2008. Doty has published four volumes of nonfiction including the memoirs *Heaven's Coast, Firebird,* and *Dog Years.*

HEID E. ERDRICH writes poetry, non-fiction and drama. She is the author of three books: *Fishing for Myth* (New Rivers Press); *The Mother's Tongue* (Salt Publishing); and *National Monuments* (Michigan State University Press); and co-editor of *Sister Nations: Native American Women on Community* (MHS Press). In 2008 she co-founded, with her sister Louise, Birchbark House, a non-profit clearinghouse for indigenous language publications and Native American literature.

LOUISE ERDRICH is the author of thirteen novels as well as volumes of poetry, short stories, children's books, and a memoir of early motherhood. Her novel *Love Medicine* won the National Book Critics Circle Award. *The Last Report on the Miracles at Little No Horse* was a finalist for the National Book Award. Most recently, *The Plague of Doves* won the Anisfield-Wolf Book Award and was a finalist for the Pulitzer Prize. Erdrich is the owner of Birchbark Books, an independent bookstore.

B. H. FAIRCHILD is the author of several acclaimed poetry collections, including *Usher*; *Early Occult Memory Systems of the Lower Midwest*; *Local Knowledge*; and *The Art of the Lathe*. He has been a finalist for the National Book Award and winner of the William Carlos Williams Award and the National Book Critics Circle Award.

NICK FLYNN has worked as a ship's captain, an electrician, and as a case-worker with homeless adults. He is the author of two collections of poetry: *Some Ether* and *Blind Huber*, and *Another Bullshit Night in Suck City*, a memoir. His most recent book is a memoir: *The Ticking is the Bomb*.

KENNY FRIES is the author of *The History of My Shoes and the Evolution of Darwin's Theory*, which received the Outstanding Book Award from the Gustavus Myers Center for the Study of Bigotry and Human Rights, as well as *Body, Remember: A Memoir*. He is the editor of *Staring Back: The Disability Experience from the Inside Out*. His books of poems include *Anesthesia* and *Desert Walking*. He received a grant in innovative literature from Creative Capital for his new book *Genkan: Entries into Japan*.

ERIC GANSWORTH (Onondaga) is the author of nine books, including the PEN Oakland Award winning *Mending Skins*, and *A Half-Life of Cardio-Pulmonary Function*, (National Book Critics Circle's "Good Reads List," 2008). His work has appeared in *The Kenyon Review*, *Shenandoah*, and *The Boston Review*. *Extra Indians*, a novel, was published in 2010.

RAY GONZALEZ is the author of ten books of poetry including *Faith Run* (Univ. of Arizona Press, 2009), *Cool Auditor: Prose Poems* (BOA Editions, 2009), *The Religion of Hands* (2005), which received the 2006 Latino Heritage Award for Poetry; *Turtle Pictures* (2000), a winner of a 2001 MN Book Award, and *The Heat of Arrivals* (1996), a winner of a 1997 PEN/Josephine Miles Book Award. He is the author of three books of nonfiction and two books of short stories.

J.C. HALLMAN is a writer whose books include *The Hospital for Bad Poets; The Chess Artist; The Devil is a Gentleman;* and *In Utopia: Six Kinds of Eden and the Search for a Better Paradise.*

PATRICIA HAMPL'S most recent book is *The Florist's Daughter,* named a *New York Times* "100 Notable Books of the Year." *Blue Arabesque: A Search for the Sublime,* was published in 2006, and *A Romantic Education* received a Houghton Mifflin Literary Fellowship. Her poetry collections include *Woman before an Aquarium,* and *Resort and Other Poems.* Hampl also published *Spillville* and *Virgin Time. I Could Tell You Stories,* her collection of essays, was a finalist for a 2000 National Book Critics Circle Award. *Tell Me True: Memoir, History and Writing a Life,* co-edited by Ms. Hampl and Elaine Tyler May was published in 2008. Hampl received a MacArthur Fellowship in 1990.

GREG HEWETT is the author of four books of poetry: *darkacre, The Eros Conspiracy,* and *Red Suburb* (all from Coffee House Press) and *To Collect the Flesh* (New Rivers Press).

SCOTT HIGHTOWER is the author of *Part of the Bargain* (Copper Canyon Press, 2005), winner of the Hayden Carruth Award for New and Emerging Poets, as well as *Tin Can Tourist* (2001) and *Natural Trouble* (2003). Hightower's poems have appeared in the *Yale Review, Salmagundi, Ploughshares, AGNI,* and *The Paris Review.*

TONY HOAGLAND is the author of *Unincorporated Personas in the Late Honda Dynasty* (Graywolf Press, 2010), *What Narcissism Means to Me* (2003), a finalist for the National Book Critics Circle Award; *Donkey Gospel* (1998), which received the James Laughlin Award; and *Sweet Ruin* (1992), chosen for the 1992 Brittingham Prize in Poetry.

LINDA HOGAN (Chickasaw) Writer in Residence for The Chickasaw Nation, is an internationally recognized public speaker and writer of poetry, fiction, and essays. Her two new books are *Rounding the Human Corners* (Coffee House Press, April 2008) and *People of the Whale* (Norton, August 2008). Her other books include novels *Mean Spirit,* a finalist for the Pulitzer Prize; *Solar Storms,* a finalist for the International Impact Award, and *Power.* Her nonfiction includes *Dwellings, A Spiritual History of the Land;* and *The Woman Who Watches Over the World: A Native Memoir.*

JAVIER O. HUERTA'S poems have been included in numerous anthologies, including *Red, White, and Blues* (University of Iowa Press, 2004), and journals such as *Punto de Partida* at the Universidad Nacional Autónoma de México. His first book, *Some Clarifications,* won the University of California-Irvine's 2005 Chicano/Latino Literary Prize.

DEBORAH KEENAN is the author of eight collections of poetry. Her newest, *Willow Room, Green Door: New and Selected Poems,* was published by Milkweed Editions Press in 2007, and received a Minnesota Book Award.

TED KOOSER is one of the nation's most highly regarded poets and served as the United States Poet Laureate Consultant in Poetry to the Library of Congress from 2004–2006, and he won the Pulitzer Prize for *Delights & Shadows* (Copper Canyon Press, 2004). He is the author of twelve collections of poetry. His work has appeared in many periodicals including *The Atlantic Monthly, The New Yorker, The Nation,* and *The American Poetry Review.*

YUSEF KOMUNYAKAA'S twelve books of poems include *Taboo, Warhorses, Talking Dirty to the Gods,* and *Neon Vernacular: New and Selected Poems,* for which he received the Pulitzer Prize.

ED BOK LEE is the author of *Real Karaoke People,* winner of a PEN/Beyond Margins Open Book Award. Other awards include an Asian American Literary Award, an Urban Griots Best Book Award, and a McKnight Artists Fellowship. His forthcoming collection will be published by Coffee House Press in 2011.

BOBBIE ANN MASON has won the PEN/Hemingway Award and was a finalist for the National Book Critics Circle Award, the American Book Award, and the PEN/Faulkner Award. Her first collection of short fiction was *Shiloh and Other Stories.* Her novels include *In Country; Midnight Magic; Clear Springs;* and *Feather Crowns.*

BILL MCKIBBEN is an American environmentalist and author. In 2010 the *Boston Globe* called him "probably the nation's leading environmentalist" and *Time* magazine described him as "the world's best green journalist." His first book, *The End of Nature,* was published in 1989. Subsequent books include *The Age of Missing Information; Hope, Human and Wild; Maybe One; Long Distance: A Year of Living Strenuously; Enough;* and *Wandering Home.* In 2007 *Deep Economy: the Wealth of Communities and the Durable Future,* was released, followed in 2008 by *The Bill McKibben Reader.*

DONALD MORRILL has published two collection of poetry: *At the Bottom of the Sky* and *With Your Back to Half the Day;* and four collections of nonfiction: *Impetuous Sleeper, A Stranger's Neighborhood, Sounding for Cool,* and *The Untouched Minutes.*

DAVID MURA is a writer, memoirist, poet and performance artist. A third-generation Japanese-American, he has written intimately about his life as a man of color and the connections between race, sexuality and history. Mura's books include *Famous Suicides of the Japanese Empire; Turning Japanese: Memoirs of a Sansei;* and *Angels for the Burning.*

KRISTIN NACA is the author of *Bird Eating Bird,* selected for the National Poetry Series mtvU Prize (Harper Perennial, 2008). The collection was named finalist for the Audre Lorde Prize and Lambda Literary Award.

MARK NOWAK, a 2010 Guggenheim fellow, is the author of *Coal Mountain Elementary* (Coffee House Press, 2009) and *Shut Up Shut Down* (Coffee House Press, 2004). He designed and facilitated "poetry dialogues" with Ford autoworkers in the US and South Africa (through the UAW and NUMSA), and Muslim/Somali nurses and healthcare workers (through Rufaidah), and others.

D. A. POWELL is the author of a trilogy of books, including *Tea* (Wesleyan, 1998); *Lunch* (2000); and *Cocktails* (Graywolf, 2004), which was nominated for the National Book Critics Circle Award. His most recent book, *Chronic* (Graywolf, 2009) received the Kingsley Tufts Award and was nominated for a National Book Critics Circle Award.

HILDA RAZ recently retired as a professor of English and Women's and Gender Studies at the University of Nebraska—Lincoln, where she was the Glenna Luschei Endowed Editor of *Prairie Schooner*. Her collections of poetry include *All Odd and Splendid, Trans, What is Good, The Bone Dish*, and *Divine Honors*. She is the editor of several anthologies, including *Living in the Margins: Women Writers on Breast Cancer*, and *The Prairie Schooner Anthology of Contemporary Jewish American Writing*.

ADRIENNE RICH'S most recent books of poetry are *Telephone Ringing in the Labyrinth: Poems 2004-2006* and *The School Among the Ruins: 2000-2004*. She edited Muriel Rukeyser's *Selected Poems* for the Library of America. *A Human Eye: Essays on Art in Society*, appeared in April 2009. *Tonight No Poetry Will Serve: Poems 2007–2010*, will appear in 2011 from Norton. She is a recipient of the National Book Foundation's 2006 Medal for Distinguished Contribution to American Letters among other honors. She lives in California.

SCOTT RUSSELL SANDERS is an award-winning author of more than twenty books including novels, collections of stories, and works of personal nonfiction, including *Staying Put, Writing from the Center*, and *Hunting for Hope*. His latest books are *A Private History of Awe*, a coming-of-age memoir, love story, and spiritual testament, which was nominated for the Pulitzer Prize, and *A Conservationist Manifesto*, his vision of a shift from a culture of consumption to a culture of caretaking.

PATRICIA SMITH is the author of five books of poetry, including *Blood Dazzler*, a finalist for the 2008 National Book Award, and *Teahouse of the Almighty*, a National Poetry Series selection. Her work has appeared in many literary journals, including *Poetry, The Paris Review*, and *TriQuarterly*, and she has received a Pushcart Prize.

BRIAN TURNER is a soldier-poet whose debut book of poems, *Here, Bullet*, won the 2005 Beatrice Hawley Award, the New York Times "Editor's Choice" selection, the 2006 Pen Center USA "Best in the West" award, and the 2007 Poets Prize. His second poetry book, *Phantom Noise*, was released by Alice James in 2010.

EMILY C. WATSON earned her MFA at West Virginia University and her essays have been published in *AGNI* and *River Teeth*. She lives in Indianapolis.

DIANE WILSON is a prose writer whose memoir, *Spirit Car: Journey to a Dakota Past* (Borealis Books, 2006) won a 2006 Minnesota Book Award. Her work has been featured in the anthologies, *Fiction on a Stick* (Milkweed Editions) and *Homelands: Women's Journeys Across Race, Place, and Time* (Seal Press).

About the Editor

WILLIAM REICHARD is the author of four collections of poetry: *Sin Eater* (Mid-List Press, 2010), a finalist for the Minnesota Book Award; *This Brightness* (Mid-List Press, 2007); *How To* (Mid-List Press, 2004), a finalist for the James Laughlin Award from the Academy of American Poets; and *An Alchemy in the Bones* (New Rivers Press, 1999), which won a MN Voices Prize. Poems from *This Brightness* and *How To* have been featured on NPR's "Writers Almanac." Reichard has published one chapbook, *To Be Quietly Spoken* (Frith Press, 2001) and is the editor of *The Evening Crowd at Kirmser's: A Gay Life in the 1940s* (University of Minnesota Press, 2001).

Dr. Reichard holds an MA in Creative Writing and a PhD in American Literature from the University of Minnesota, and he is currently Program Director for the Higher Education Consortium for Urban Affairs, a Minnesota-based alliance of 18 liberal arts colleges, universities, and associations dedicated to education for social transformation and community building.

NEW VILLAGE PRESS is a public-benefit publisher and the first to specialize in grassroots community building. Its titles address social justice, community-based arts, urban ecology, and progressive education. Important works by New Village include:

By Heart: Poetry, Prison, and Two Lives by Judith Tannenbaum and Spoon Jackson—A moving, reflective double memoir of two sensitive artists, their very disparate childhoods, and the poetry that unites their humanity.

Acting Together—A two-volume collected work about creative transformation, through performance and ritual, of conflict in regions of violence throughout the world. Edited by Cynthia Cohen, Roberto Gutiérrez Varea, and Polly Walker.

Art and Upheaval: Artists on the World's Frontlines by William Cleveland—The product of an eight-year journey to flash points across the globe documenting the struggles and triumphs of artists working for peace and freedom.

Awakening Creativity by international artist and social pioneer Lily Yeh—A beautiful full-color hardcover, documenting the metamorphosis of a derelict factory into a school for children of migrant workers that is filled with art and joy.

Asphalt to Ecosystems—a comprehensive guide to creating schoolyards that integrate nature into learning and play by Sharon Gamson Danks. Illustrated with over 500 color photographs from exemplary schools around the world.

What We See: Advancing the Observations of Jane Jacobs—Thirty-five fresh and provocative essays by leading thinkers about what enlivens our cities, our culture, and our economies. Edited by Stephen Goldsmith and Lynne Elizabeth.

Undoing the Silence: Six Tools for Social Change Writing—Guidance to help citizens and professionals influence democratic process, by Louise Dunlap.

Works of Heart: Building Village through the Arts—A full-color celebration of citizen artists revitalizing their communities, edited by Lynne Elizabeth and Suzanne Young.

New Creative Community: The Art of Cultural Development—A seminal book that defines the emerging field of community cultural development, by Arlene Goldbard.

Arts for Change—Activist arts educator Beverly Naidus and colleagues reveal the motivation and challenges of engaging students in critical social and environmental issues.

Beginner's Guide to Community-Based Arts—Ten graphic stories about artists, educators and activists across the United States, by Mat Schwarzman and Keith Knight.

Building Commons and Community—The late Karl Linn's masterwork on creating shared neighborhood spaces in grassroots projects over five decades in thirteen cities.

Doing Time in the Garden—Personal and practical guide to the country's most successful in-jail and post-release horticultural training program at Riker's Island, NY, by director James Jiler.

About the Type

The text of this book is set in **ITC STONE SERIF** type, designed by Sumner Stone in 1987. It is a contemporary take on 18th-century Transitional type design, as it transitioned from 16th- and 17th-century Old Style to 19th-century Modern, reflecting improvements in printing technology. Transitional faces are considered to be especially readable because of their regularity and slight contrast between think and thin.

The display types are **MYRIAD PRO** and **MYRIAD PRO CONDENSED**, related sans serif faces classified as Humanistic and designed by Robert Slimbach & Carol Twombly in 1992. The face is characterized by slightly organic bowl shapes and modulated strokes in contrast to other more mechanistic san serif faces, making Myriad Pro especially readable.

The author and designer have made a concerted effort to reproduce each poem's original text spacing and apologize for any inaccuracies.